THE TRIUNE CREATOR

CREATOR

A Historical and Systematic Study

COLIN E. GUNTON

EDINBURGH UNIVERSITY PRESS

For
Michael Banner, Douglas Farrow, Paul Helm, Brian Horne,
Christoph Schwöbel, Graham Stanton, Alan Torrance and
Francis Watson
with gratitude and affection

Edinburgh University Press
22 George Square, Edinburgh

Typeset in Bembo
by Pioneer Associates Ltd, Perthshire
Printed and bound in Great Britain by
Cromwell Press, Trowbridge, Wilts

A CIP record for this book is available
from the British Library

ISBN 0 7486 0792 7

CONTENTS

PREFACE

In his study of *The Religious Origins of Modern Science*, E. M. Klaaren remarks that 'incredible as it may seem, there is no comprehensive scholarly history of the doctrine of creation as a whole'.[1] This book is not designed to be such a history, but, given the situation there characterised, the theological questions are in each case treated within a framework of historical discussion. The history is, however, *theological* history, by which is meant that the dogmatics of creation are erected upon a theological critique, no doubt somewhat one-sided, of the way in which the doctrine has developed. That historical account has something of a Harnackian ring, for it holds that early in the process serious mistakes were made which led to highly problematic outcomes, among them the effective de-christianising of the doctrine and the effective divorce of theology from science. Simply expressed, although the doctrine of creation is a crucial factor in the development of modern science, the opposite often seemed, and indeed still seems, to be the case. It is also the case that in the modern age scientists became to a large extent the theologians of creation, until recent times effectively excluding the theological altogether.

Ideally, this would have been a two-volume work, giving full space to history and dogmatics alike. As it is, the incorporation of much historical material inevitably means that systematic topics are given less attention

1. Eugene M. Klaaren, *Religious Origins of Modern Science. Belief in Creation in Seventeenth Century Thought* (Grand Rapids: Eerdmans, 1977), p. 30.

ix

than they deserve in an already long volume. I would therefore refer the reader to a number of other works, many of them preparatory for this volume, in which other aspects of the topic are treated in more detail. In particular, a discussion of the bearing of the doctrine of creation on the ontology of social relations – in parallel with the various discussions of the theology of nature in this book – is to be found in the latter half of *The One, the Three and the Many: God, Creation and the Culture of Modernity. The 1992 Bampton Lectures* (Cambridge: Cambridge University Press, 1993). Similarly, an extended discussion of christology in relation to the doctrine of creation is to be found in *Christ and Creation. The 1991 Didsbury Lectures* (Carlisle: Paternoster Press and Grand Rapids: Eerdmans, 1992).

Among papers written preparatory to this book, or in parallel with it, are 'Relation and Relativity: The Trinity and the Created World', in *The Promise of Trinitarian Theology* (Edinburgh: T. & T. Clark, second edition, 1997), pp. 137–57; 'The Doctrine of Creation', in *The Cambridge Companion to Christian Doctrine*, edited by Colin E. Gunton (Cambridge: Cambridge University Press, 1997), pp. 141–57; 'Introduction', 'Between Allegory and Myth: The Legacy of the Spiritualising of Genesis', 'The End of Causality? The Reformers and their Predecessors', all in *The Doctrine of Creation*, edited by Colin E. Gunton (Edinburgh: T. & T. Clark, 1997), pp. 1–15, 47–62 and 63–82; and 'Lecture 3. "No other foundation . . ." Revelation and the theology of nature', *A Brief Theology of Revelation. The 1993 Warfield Lectures* (Edinburgh: T. & T. Clark, 1995), pp. 40–63.

The dedication is to signal my debt to some of the many colleagues who have enriched my life theologically and in many other ways at King's College in recent years.

Colin E. Gunton
King's College, London
Epiphany, 1998

1

'MAKER OF HEAVEN AND EARTH':
AN INTRODUCTION TO
SOME ESSENTIAL CONCEPTS

—∿∿∿Я∩⊙Я∩∿∿—

I THE UNIVERSALITY OF BELIEF
IN CREATION

Why is there something rather than nothing? That question, or something like it, is universal in human history. It is the question about creation, at least in the sense that all cultures have their myths or theories of creation, the atheistic end of the spectrum of modern scientific views being no exception. The most anti-religious scientists use the word 'creation', while it is clear that the vehemence with which some of them defend their world-views indicates that they have come to serve for them as substitutes for religion, if not a form of religion themselves.[1] Beneath the wide range of uses of the word, two need to be distinguished, though for the most part in this book the context will indicate which is being used. The first is creation as an action, as when we say that God creates the world or Geoff Hamilton a garden;[2] here, creation refers to

1. See Mary Midgley, *Evolution as a Religion. Strange Hopes and Stranger Fears* (London: Methuen, 1985) and *Science as Salvation* (London: Routledge, 1992).
2. Strictly, of course, as J. R. R. Tolkien once pointed out, we finite agents do not create; the human action is better known as sub-creation. 'On Fairy Stories', *Tree and Leaf* (London: Allen and Unwin, 1982), pp. 11–70 (pp. 43–50).

1

the act of creating. The other use is for the product, that which is created, as in the description of a hat as 'a creation' or the universe as 'the creation'.

Christian theologians have often claimed that belief in creation is universal in the human race, and it is this which will enable us to develop the theme of the chapter. Let us take Irenaeus (fl. c. 180 AD) as an example, for he will serve in many places in this study as a model theologian of creation. He is particularly interesting in view of the fact that much of the space in his great book is devoted to a sustained attack on what he regards as grossly mistaken accounts of creation to be found in the teaching of the Gnostics. So, at the outset, when we read him saying:

> That God is the Creator of the world is accepted even by those very persons who in many ways speak against Him, and yet acknowledge Him, styling Him the Creator . . . all men, in fact, consenting to this truth . . .[3]

we should remember that his is a dialectical position in the sense that it is held in tension with a highly particular account of the Christian understanding of creation, and in that respect is far more satisfactory than those of many of his successors.

What do we mean when we say that belief in creation is universal? At one level, it may simply be a factual claim, that all cultures of which we are informed have, throughout history, held some kind of belief about the origin and nature of the universe. Such a factual claim would be difficult to establish, and possibly of limited value. But theories of what can be called limited universality are interesting, and introduce us to important aspects of our topic. Let us look at two of them. The first is Stephen Hill's *Concordia*, in which the author argues that there is, at the root of Western civilisation and deriving from its Indo-European roots, a common idea of creation, by which is meant, generally, the emergence of a meaningful universe.[4] The biblical texts, insofar as they are treated at all, are in his book used alongside and in some subordination to the Hindu and Greek literature, both Homeric poems and philosophy. A rather more nuanced variation on the theme that the idea of creation is common to a number of the major religious traditions is argued by Keith Ward.[5]

3. Irenaeus, *Against the Heresies*, 2. 9. 1.
4. Stephen R. Hill, *Concordia. The Roots of European Thought* (London: Duckworth, 1992), especially chapters 1–7.
5. Keith Ward, *Religion and Creation* (Oxford: Clarendon Press, 1996).

It is here that we reach the first of the crucial conceptual distinctions which will remain with us until the end. By 'creation', Hill does not mean what many Christian theologians have meant. In the tradition of Greek cosmology, whatever is the case with India, creation always means the creation of this universe out of some already existing material. Even in Plato's *Timaeus*, which is often treated as a kind of parallel to, even a preparation for, the Christian doctrine which later emerged in conversation with the Greeks, something, indeed three kinds of thing, are eternal. Let us pause to look at one of the things that Plato says in this strange and speculative document, leaving further comment on his cosmology until the next chapter. According to this book, there are three eternal realities, eternal form (the 'model'); the 'receptacle' (unformed, shapeless, chaotic matter); and the demiurge, or divinity, who does not create but shapes that which is of equal eternity with him.[6] While Plato does here affirm that the cosmos as we experience it did come into existence, it did not come into existence out of nothing, but as the result of the demiurge's bringing together of two realities eternally ready to hand, form and matter.

In the light of this, a thesis such as Hill's is, I believe, unacceptable, and for two main reasons. The first is that it avoids one central question of the doctrine of creation, that concerning who or what does the creating, and what is the form of the act. There are, probably, ultimately only two possible answers to the question, and they recur at different places in all ages: that the universe is the result of creation by a free personal agency, and that in some way or other it creates itself. The two answers are not finally compatible, and require a choice, either between them or an attitude of agnostic refusal to decide. The second reason is that Hill tends to assume that all theologies of creation are of the same type, and in the following chapters many reasons will be given for questioning that thesis. The Christian doctrine of creation is not to be understood simply as one instance of a single general theory,[7] but is so distinctive in some of its features that it demands to be treated in its own right. This is not to say that there are no links with other theories, and specifically that it has no connection at all with the question of why there is something rather than nothing. It is rather that other questions are more important for it, and that connections with other doctrines are a matter for factual examination, to see whether they have anything in common, and what that is.

6. Plato, *Timaeus*, 52.
7. Nor, for that matter, are Islamic or Buddhist doctrines of creation, if any, to be so treated.

The second theory of the universality of creation belief takes us nearer to an examination of the latter point, and it concerns the history of the interpretation of that document which is the cause of so much speculation and misunderstanding, the opening chapters of the book of Genesis. To understand what is at stake, we need to glance at the history of modern biblical interpretation. During the early history of the historical-critical movement, there was a tendency to give the creation stories in Genesis a kind of universality. They provided, it was often held, simply one example of the species known as ancient creation myth. 'The ancient world is everywhere alike', said one of the critics, and did not mean it in a complimentary sense. The point was rather the disparaging one that these texts were all alike in telling us more about the workings of the primitive mind than about God or the world. They were primitive science, and as such were destined to be replaced by modern science, which said what they had to say differently, better, indeed in the only really satisfactory way. However, the dismissal of the Old Testament accounts of creation has not gone without criticism. In more recent times the higher critical view came to be replaced, in the works of some scholars, with an emphasis on the particularity and distinctiveness of Genesis. Far from being one ancient myth among many, this was unique in saying things that no other ancient text was able to say. We shall examine some of aspects of the uniqueness later in the book, but for our purposes what is important is to see that particularity was at this stage being played off against universality. The Bible is different, and, it might be suggested, the conveyor of a unique message, and so could not be dismissed as simply another instance of ancient myth.

There is much to be said for this claim, but it cannot be made too soon, or without important qualifications. A recent article by H. H. Schmid has propounded a revised version of the universality thesis.[8] His argument is important because it shows that we can appreciate what is in common in the ancient texts without dismissing them on the grounds that they are 'primitive'. He makes the following points. (1) There is no ancient culture without extensive talk of creation, so that in a sense it is right to say that the ancient world is everywhere alike (if not everywhere the same). The ancient accounts are all concerned with the same kind of thing, even if they see it differently. (2) The various texts are not simply concerned with the past establishment of the world,

8. H. H. Schmid, 'Creation, Righteousness and Salvation: "Creation Theology" as the Broad Horizon of Biblical Theology', in B. W. Anderson, ed., *Creation in the Old Testament*, pp. 102–17.

but with the way it provides a framework for the present order of things. This is partly a matter of social order, and there is in the ancient teaching always a relation between the order of creation and the order of society. This leads Schmid to reject what was widely taught by Old Testament scholars of a previous generation, that biblical accounts of creation represent a relatively late development which was a response to the history of salvation. For example, it is sometimes held that it was events like the Exodus that enabled Israel to realise that God was lord of creation also, so that creation is in some way a function of salvation. Against this the Old Testament, in line with the thought of the time, argues Schmid, understands creation as determinative for all aspects of life in the world, so that this aspect of its teaching is not an afterthought. (3) This matter, Schmid argues, is of important contemporary relevance, for it enables us to realise something of the interrelation of justice, politics and nature. 'What creation – that is, orderly and harmonious (*heil*) world – is, or should be, is a general human perception, to which *mutatis mutandis* the Enlightenment also came in a new way centuries later.'[9] When we come to say something of Plato in the next chapter, more of the point of this will be realised.

At this stage, however, we shall examine some different accounts of the claim, made in relation to the doctrine of creation, that it, or something like it, is a general human perception. The biblical basis of such a theory is to be found in particular in the opening chapter of Paul's letter to the Romans. In that chapter, Paul makes a number of affirmations, several of which have to be taken into account if we are to understand the ramifications of the question. (1) The passage with which we are concerned begins with an affirmation of the universality of the Christian gospel – 'the power of salvation' – for everyone who has faith (v. 16). (2) Paul then proceeds to say that this gospel is made known in face of the wrath of God against sin, of which he has a number of definitions, central to which is an understanding of sin as idolatry, or worshipping the creature instead of the creator (v. 25) – that is to say, an offence against the creator. It is this which is at the root of the moral disorder which Paul attacks in much of that chapter. (3) Yet the sinner has no excuse, because God has made himself known *universally*. 'Ever since the creation of the world his invisible nature, namely, his eternal power and deity, has been clearly perceived in the things which have been made' (v. 20). (4) In conclusion, the claim is that God as creator is made evident from his creation, yet this revelation is culpably ignored, the

9. Schmid, 'Creation, Righteousness and Salvation', p. 111.

outcome being the – equally universal – disorder that Paul describes. That is to say, side by side there are a universal knowability of God and a factual refusal to acknowledge his reality, and this is the starting point for Paul's treatment of salvation in the following chapters.

In the history of Christian thought, different things have been made of this passage, depending on the emphases that have been made. If a theologian stresses point (3), 'ever since the creation of the world . . .', there is a move towards what can be called a natural theology of creation, a belief that something like a doctrine of creation is universally discoverable by human thought independently of revelation in Christ. One good example of this is the way in which Thomas Aquinas, by adapting Aristotelian concepts of causality, develops, in his Five Ways, a demonstration of one 'whom all call God.'[10] This procedure presupposes that one can find, by philosophical analysis of known features of the world, universally acceptable conclusions about the relation of creature and creator. The supreme cause of all is the creator, although it is important to note that for Aquinas the idea of a beginning of the creation in time cannot be thus derived, and must come from authoritative revelation.[11] In this respect, the mediaeval theologian recognises that at most only a part of the doctrine – the belief that the world depends upon an infinite being – can be established universally.

The Enlightenment radicalised Aquinas' teaching to the extent that some of its representatives turned the whole of the doctrine into a common human perception. A belief that God made the world as a machine-maker makes a machine – with perhaps an eschatology of rewards and punishments after death – was made into the whole of 'rational religion'. This effectively ruled out those aspects of the doctrine of creation which make it a basis for a continuing involvement of the creator with the world, as is supposed by the doctrines of Christ, the atonement, grace, the church and the sacraments. As we shall see, this was an era, to some extent with us still, when the doctrine of creation tended to be reduced to an item of natural or philosophical theology, and it came to be believed that only or chiefly the sciences were able to tell us anything about the world.

The reason why there is good reason to doubt the wisdom of a strong association of the doctrine of creation with a natural human intuition

10. Aquinas, *Summa Theologiae* 1a. 2. This is not to suggest that there is to be found here Aquinas' doctrine of creation, but that a framework for theology consisting of a kind of account of creation is being developed.
11. Aquinas, *Summa Theologiae*, 1. 46. 2.

about the world becomes clear when we look at the fourth of Paul's statements, the claim that despite the universal visibility of God's glory in the created order, it is also the case that it is everywhere ignored, indeed in such a way that human intellectual faculties are seriously damaged. John Calvin's position, in the fifth chapter of the *Institutes* Book I, is more nearly that of St Paul. First, he affirms the universal presence of the evidence: 'men cannot open their eyes without being compelled to see him'; '[t]here are innumerable evidences both in heaven and on earth . . .'.[12] The human being provides for Calvin the chief evidence, and he is here quite happy to draw on the traditions of the Greek philosophers. 'Certain philosophers long ago . . . not ineptly called man a microcosm because he is a rare example of God's power, goodness and wisdom . . .' (1. 5. 3). There is thus for Calvin external evidence for the existence of God wherever we look. And this is not simply a theoretical matter. God reveals his lordship over creation in all kinds of ways. Calvin gives a long catalogue of ways in which God can be recognised from his world, providence and the government of society prominent among them (5. 7–8). Yet at the same time he emphasises that in point of fact pagan thought totally fails to understand the true nature of things. Its chief mistake is in confusing the creature with the creator (5. 5), but there is also a general human failure to recognise God for what he truly is. '[J]ust as waters boil up from a vast, full spring, so does an immense crowd of gods flow forth from the human mind . . .' (5. 12). This is particularly the case with the history of philosophy, which reveals a 'shameful diversity of gods'. In sum, therefore, despite the universality of evidence, there is in practice a corresponding universality of failure to read it correctly, deriving from the human heart's universal tendency to fabricate idols. Thus Calvin agrees with Paul that the outcome 'shows it not to go farther than to render them inexcusable' (5. 14).

There are other reasons for qualifying Schmid's claim that creation is a general human perception. There may be a universality about it, but the emergence of the Christian doctrine, often in polemical relation to the beliefs of ancient philosophy and science, shows that the word is not always used in the same sense; there is creation and creation. It is for this reason that we cannot ignore the fact that the doctrine of creation is an article of the creed, and is bound up with beliefs about Christ and redemption, as we shall see. We shall also note that in *content*, too, it is distinctively different from anything else. Simply, the Christian account says things that have not been said elsewhere. That is why Paul's teaching

12. John Calvin, *Institutes*, 1. 5. 1–2.

in Romans should be taken in its whole context, with especial attention to the first of the statements to which attention was called, that even the claim for a general perception can only be understood in the light of the gospel. The Christian doctrine of creation has suffered much from being considered simply one instance of a general belief in creation. We shall examine some of the history of this in future chapters.

II SOME IMPORTANT CONCEPTS

'I believe in God the Father, maker of Heaven and Earth.' These familiar words introduce a remarkable and unique intellectual development, and point us to the distinctive form of the Christian intellectual achievement. Not that it is distinctive without further qualification; there is a sense in which the demiurge of Plato's *Timaeus* is also the maker of heaven and earth, as we shall see. The marks of distinctiveness are as follows. First, the credal or confessional form of the words shows that the doctrine of creation is not something self-evident or the discovery of disinterested reason, but part of the fabric of Christian response to revelation. It cannot be stressed too strongly that 'I believe' is not (or not necessarily) the same as saying 'I know intuitively' or 'reason shows me that . . .'. The words form the first article of a creed of a community of worship and belief which continues to say other things without which they cannot be understood.

Second, the word 'maker' is ambiguous. On the one hand, it may refer to one who is like a human maker, a potter for example, who makes an object out of a material that is already to hand. If God is like that, then there is something on which he is at least partially dependent, as the potter is dependent on the qualities of clay. On the other hand, the maker may be one who, so to speak, makes both the material and that which is shaped from it. As we shall see in more detail later, the unique contribution to thought made by Christian theologians of creation is in developing a view that God creates 'out of nothing'. It is not a belief that can be found unambiguously in the Bible, or in the earliest theologians, but emerged as the result of a conflict with a philosophical tradition which held to different versions of the belief that there has always been a universe of some kind. God or the gods may, according to this, have formed *this* particular universe, but were not believed to have been responsible for the matter from which it was formed. In general, Greek thought held that matter was both eternal and inferior to mind or spirit. The intellectual breakthrough of second-century Christian theology came from contending against both of these doctrines, in teaching that matter both had a beginning and, for that reason, was not inferior but intended by a good creator.

Third, the early theologians were able to achieve what they did by virtue of the form of Christian confession. When in the second century Irenaeus of Lyons taught that God the Father created by means of his 'two hands', the Son and the Spirit, he was able to bring to a preliminary completion a process of intellectual development during which the implications of the specifically Christian form of creation belief were drawn out. The achievement of this distinctive theology was possible only because of the trinitarian shape of early theology. We shall understand the distinctiveness of the Christian theology of creation only if we realise that these three themes – creation as an article of the creed; creation out of nothing; and creation as the work of the whole Trinity, Father, Son and Holy Spirit – are in some way bound up with each other, both historically and systematically. But the uniqueness of the development does not mean that it can be understood in abstraction from other more general concerns. It can still be understood as a version, if a revolutionary one, of the universal human interest which we have already reviewed.

What does this revolutionary doctrine of creation distinctively say? The following will be proposed as an outline of some of the essential features. First, as we have seen, creation was 'out of nothing'. This teaching is fundamental and makes the Christian teaching unique. It affirms that God in creating the world relied on nothing outside himself, so that creation is an act of divine sovereignty and freedom, an act of personal willing that there be something other. It further implies that the universe had a beginning in time and is limited in space: it is neither eternal nor infinite. We shall explore the meaning and implications of this unique teaching as we follow later in the book some of the steps through which it was developed.

But, second, it does not follow that this was an arbitrary act upon the part of God. It is purposive in two senses, that it derives from the love of God, not simply his will, and that it exists for a purpose – to go somewhere, we might say. It is here that we can begin to understand something of the place of the doctrine of the Trinity in the development. Because that holds that God is already, 'in advance' of creation, a communion of persons existing in loving relations, it becomes possible to say that he does not need the world, and so is able to will the existence of something else simply for its own sake. Creation is the outcome of God's love indeed, but of his unconstrained love. It is therefore not a necessary outcome of what God is, but is contingent. This is important, because it enables us to say that the world is given value as a realm of being in its own right. It is in the words of Genesis 'very good', not only partly good or as a means to an end, but simply as and for what it is: the created order.

Third, and this is the same point expanded, a trinitarian theology of creation makes it possible to understand that the creation remains in close relation to God, and yet is free to be itself. There are christological and pneumatological dimensions to this notion. According to the New Testament, creation is *through* and *to* Christ, and this means that it is, so to speak, structured by the very one who became incarnate and thus part of the created order of which we are speaking. It is good because God himself, through his Son, remains in intimate and loving relations with it. Similarly, when Basil of Caesarea described the Holy Spirit as the perfecting cause of the creation,[13] he enabled us to say that it is the work of God the Spirit to enable the created order to be truly itself. Together the christological and pneumatological structuring of the doctrine provide a ground for the knowledge of both creator and creation, as they are both in themselves and in relation to one another.

Fourth, because the doctrines of the Son and the Spirit enable us to articulate an understanding of the way in which God works in and towards the world, our understanding of the divine work of creation is not limited to the beginning and the end. In various ways God can be understood to continue to be involved in the world, guiding its movement and enabling anticipations of its final perfection to take place. From christology and pneumatology together flow those further aspects of the doctrine which are indicated by words like 'conservation', 'preservation', 'providence' and 'redemption'. The first two of those expressions refer to God's continuing upholding of and care for his creation. God does not, like the machine-maker deity of some conceptions, simply leave his world to go its own way, but actively maintains it in being. The latter expressions have a more forward-looking orientation, and refer to the forms of action by which God provides for the needs of the creation and enables it to achieve the end that was purposed for it from the beginning. We shall in later chapters fill in the meaning of some of these conceptions as we discuss the way in which they have been developed in the history of theology.

Fifth, the word 'redemption' requires a little more notice here because it introduces a whole range of new questions, and particularly the question of evil. If it is claimed that creation is good, and has a destiny that

13. Basil, *On the Holy Spirit*, 15. 38.

involves some kind of perfecting or completing, we meet the problem of evil in a very serious form. While Greek thought tended to trace the origin of evil to matter, Christian theology came to the view that, because all that God creates is good, evil must be something extraneous to or parasitic upon creation as a whole. If the universe is created good, and with an end in view, evil becomes that which thwarts the divine purpose for it. At the centre of the problem is the doctrine of the fall or fallenness of the human race, according to which human sin in some way involves the whole created order in evil. The human fall is sometimes traced to the fall of angels, or to some other force or agency, but the point for our purpose is that evil is attributed not to a fault in God's creating activity but to something which subverts it and must be overcome. Its existence means that creation's purpose can be achieved only by its redirection from within by the creator himself. Once again, we discover the centrality of christology. Given the all-polluting power of evil and its centre in human sin, redemption can be achieved only by the one through whom the world was created becoming incarnate, dying and rising as the way through which the creation can be redeemed (bought back) from its bondage to destruction.

In the Christian tradition there is a range of views about the relation between creation, the fall and the redemption that undoes the fall. We shall meet leading representatives later, but at this stage we need to sketch some of the possibilities. For example, it is possible to see the creation as so completely finished and perfect in the beginning that a fall can only be away from that perfection, and redemption can only mean a return to the condition of perfection. I shall call the conceptions of salvation consequent upon this redemption as restoration, because they concentrate on a reforming or restoring of that which has been defaced, rather as one might restore a painting slashed by the knife of a vandal. Origen and Augustine tend to take this approach. Such conceptions generate a corresponding eschatology, one of 'return', in which redemption is understood as essentially a return to a perfection which already existed before the fall.

Again, one might suppose a view of the matter according to which the fall is minimised as little more than a brief impediment, or is even celebrated as a step on the way, to the perfecting of that which was in the beginning. On this understanding, creation is not perfect in the beginning, but has to become perfect, and such fall as there is becomes, or may become, the means by which development is achieved. We can call this an evolutionary view of the creation, and it is characteristic of those modern theologies which are shaped by Hegelian and Darwinian influences. The weakness of this position is that it tends to minimise the problem of evil and so make the cross of Jesus redundant. It generates an eschatology of emergence, in which the end emerges from the beginning as a plant from a seed, or, in the more Hegelian form, as the result of historical dialectic.

Another view, which can owe something to both of the previous views, is what might be called a transformative or, perhaps better, eschatological view of the relation of redemption to creation. According to this, a form of which I shall advocate, creation is a project – that is to say, it is made to go somewhere – but by virtue of the fall can reach that end only by a redemption which involves a radical redirection from the movement it takes backwards whenever sin and evil shape its direction. Creation is that which God enables to exist in time, and is in and through time to bring to its completion, rather like an artist completing a work of art. Although Irenaeus is sometimes supposed to take the second of the views here sketched, he belongs rather in this third category. He has a strong doctrine of both sin and redemption, and an equally strong eschatological and transformational view of the process. I shall call the eschatology consequent upon this view one of completion, because it suggests that the end of redemption is not simply a return to a primal perfection, but a movement towards an end that is greater than the beginning. On such an account, redemption involves not only the defeat of evil, but its removal in such a way that the original direction or directedness of the created order is restored.

Sixth, it follows from a number of features of the above that no theology of creation is complete without attention being paid to the place of humankind in the project. According to Genesis 1:27, God 'created man in his own image . . . male and female he created them', and there has been in the tradition much discussion of what this means both for man and for his relation to the remainder of the created order. The traditional tendency to locate the image of God in reason or some other human endowment or quality is now much disputed in favour of a conception of the whole of human being as existing in relation to God, other human beings and the rest of the created order. The latter relation is described in Genesis as 'dominion', which means – as I shall argue during the course of the book – a calling to be and to act in such a way as to enable the created order to be itself as a response of praise to its maker. However, the distinctive place of the human creation cannot be understood apart from christology. Genesis makes the human race both the crown of, and uniquely responsible for, the shape that creation takes. By speaking of Jesus Christ as the true image of God, the New

Testament shows that this responsibility is realised only in and through him.

Seventh, and related to the previous section, the ethical dimensions of the doctrine must be mentioned. These have come into the centre in the light of recent concerns about the environment, but it must be remembered that sexual relations, abortion, genetic engineering and war are also among the human activities that involve the doctrine of creation, because they all concern relationships between created persons and between them and the material world. If God's purpose is for the redemption and perfection of the whole creation, then *all* human action will in some way or other involve the human response to God that we call ethics. It is part of our createdness that what we truly are and do is, or should be, shaped by our relations to our creator. Ethics, as encompassing not simply principles of action but a whole way of being in the world, is thus integral to a Christian doctrine of creation as distinct from a mere cosmology or ontology.

The ways in which an ethic of creation is approached tend to correspond to different conceptions of the image of God and of eschatology. Conceptions of the image as reason tend to correlate with an eschatology of return and a view of the material creation as instrumental to human salvation. A theology of the image which links more firmly mind and body tends to see the human task as more intimately bound up with the material world, and so to suggest an eschatology of completion. Are human destiny and salvation in some way *out of* or *along with* the material environment? The ethical dimensions of this are bound up with the way in which we should regard the material world. What kind of reality does it have in relation to ourselves? What does human 'dominion' of the world imply? The range of questions is so long and so complicated that it will be possible only to do anything like justice to them in the book as a whole, where the main concern will be to develop an understanding of what the doctrine of creation teaches in its various dimensions and relations. As we now move to trace some of the central historical episodes in the expression of the doctrine of creation, we shall find that all the themes here reviewed will figure in different ways at different times and in different contexts. But they are all involved in some way at every stage.

2

WHAT KIND OF WORLD?
THE BIBLE, THE GREEKS AND
THE QUESTION OF ONTOLOGY

—⁓⁓ᏆᎮ◎ᏌᏍᏍ⁓—

Some questions are perennial, however different the form they take in different cultures and eras. It is one of the illusions of the modern age that we are in every way different from our predecessors, particularly because the worlds revealed by the sciences are apparently so radically different from those of the ancient texts, of whatever form. In this chapter we shall examine one of the questions that recur in every era. It will begin with an account of theologies and theories of the creation in the ancient world. These are interesting and important in their own right, because the past influences our understanding of the world today, for instance in the way we understand science to have its roots in ancient thought, whether Greek, biblical or a combination of the two. But they are also interesting as they reveal that a real and continuing question underlies them. Does the world come from another, a creator, or does it in some sense create itself? This question is raised by the differences between Greek and biblical thought, and recurs in some of the recent writings on the nature of being in the shadowy and increasingly well populated no-man's-land between science and religion.

I THE BIBLE: (1) THE OLD TESTAMENT

We enter a minefield when we approach a discussion of the place of the

Bible in the doctrine of creation. For the most part, more heat than light is generated by recent – and not so recent – debates about 'creationism', by which is often meant a belief in the literal, absolute or 'scientific' truth of the first chapter of Genesis. We must be particularly aware that there are dangers in the discussion of individual texts of scripture, and perhaps none more so than those of the creation narratives. It is surely significant that Irenaeus showed little interest in disputing the interpretation of individual texts with his opponents.[1] He refers to Genesis very little, and rightly, for his concern is with the theology of creation as an interpretation of the first article of the Christian creed, which is itself a summary of the teaching of scripture as a whole on divine creation. Yet because this text has bulked large in the tradition, and because its interpretation often provides an indication of the theology of its user, I want to say something about it in order to indicate the kind of questions with which we are concerned, before moving to more strictly theological matters.

(1) 'In the beginning, God created the heaven and the earth.' The first verse of Genesis is clearly crucial, though perhaps its interpretation does not provide as significant a test as some of the later ones. Attention should not centre primarily on the question of whether 'in the beginning' teaches or implies creation out of nothing. Westermann's contention that this is not the kind of question one may appropriately ask of the writer, along with Gerhard May's argument that the doctrine of creation out of nothing emerges only as the result of the church's struggle with Platonism and its extreme form, Gnosticism, suggests that one should in this case leave the question on one side.[2] Yet the theological function of the expression is clearly similar to that which the doctrine of creation out of nothing was later to perform. It is to show that the world in which we live is established firmly by the action of God, and it is therefore right to consider this as an action in our past, something once for all. Whether we can be as sure as Pannenberg what the author intends, we can agree with his general point when he says that, 'what the two Genesis accounts are really seeking to describe is the normative and

---

1. For example, in *Against the Heresies*, 1. 18, he rejects Gnostic allegorising, but does not offer a counter exegesis. His concern is for a more broadly based doctrine of creation than one derived from proof texts.
2. Claus Westermann, *Genesis 1–11. A Commentary*, translated by J. J. Scullion (London: SPCK, 1984), p. 100; Gerhard May, *Creatio ex Nihilo. The Doctrine of 'Creation out of Nothing' in Early Christian Thought*, translated by A. S. Worrall (Edinburgh: T. & T. Clark, 1994).

abiding basis of creaturely reality in the form of depiction of the initial event.'[3]

Of greater historical importance is the interpretation of the words 'heaven and earth.' Clearly intended to be a way of saying 'everything', it provides, as we shall see, a field day for platonisers and allegorisers of all kinds, all those indeed who would contend that some dimensions of the created world are more real and significant than others. Because the verse is often interpreted as teaching that the material world is in some way ontologically inferior to the 'spiritual' world – that the 'heavenly' realm in some sense precedes the 'earthly' – in interpreting it we should remember also those verses which affirm the goodness of all realms of the creation – the earth (v. 10), the heavenly bodies (v. 18), the creatures of sea and air (v. 21), the beasts of the earth (v. 25) and, finally, after the creation of the human race, come the words, 'God saw everything that he had made, and behold, it was very good' (v. 31).

(2) What is the status of the 'days'? Did the author mean a literal day? Whether or not we should accept the contention, sometimes made, that literal days cannot be meant because there were no days until the sun and moon were created to mark them, this feature of the text has always been an embarrassment for a certain kind of theologian. Embarrassment derives from two directions: the scientific or philosophical – and it is significant that many modern supposedly scientific objections to this way of speaking are of the same kind as those made by ancient philosophers – and the theological. Various attempts have been made to allegorise the feature, for example that of Augustine, which we shall meet below. Like other features of Augustine's thought, this derives from a refusal to recognise the self-limitation of God in creation, the fact that he can be conceived to 'take his time.' For Augustine, creation 'must have been' instantaneous, and the days only introduced as a concession to human limitation. It is with this theologian that there comes into theology the notion of creation as the product of a kind of abstract omnipotence, inadequately related to the economy of salvation. The latter dimension of Christian theology, however, is precisely what provides the demonstration that in other respects, too, God allows time for his purposes to work themselves out, and that therefore temporality is an indispensable feature of God's interaction with the world. Basil of Caesarea's interpretation of the days many years before Augustine is more instructive. When scripture says 'one day', he says, it means that it wishes to establish the world's relation to eternity, and is depicting 'distinctions between various states

3. Wolfhart Pannenberg, *Systematic Theology* 2, translated by G. W. Bromiley (Edinburgh: T. & T. Clark, 1994), p. 34.

and modes of action' – that is to say, different ways in which God acts towards and in the world.[4] Similarly, the great tradition of mediaeval treatments of the Hexaemeron shows that these writers, too, were not 'literalistic', but treated the days as a structuring principle for the created order.

(3) 'The Spirit of God was moving over the face of the waters . . .' (Genesis 1:2). While we cannot say categorically that this refers to the Spirit we know as the Holy Spirit, we should not be afraid to understand it trinitarianly in the light of later thought. This is justifiable particularly in view of the fact that other uses in the Old Testament of the same expression clearly refer to the Spirit, so that the possible rendering as 'wind of God' is less likely in view of the fact that it would be unique. 'Whatever may have been said in traditions from which the priestly writers drew, it is quite inconceivable that the shapers of the *canonical* text can have written *ruach Elohim* and not thought of "God's Spirit".'[5] Despite that, many have conceived the inconceivable, and not only recently. A remark made by Grosseteste in the thirteenth century suggests that the perennial appeal of myth may be somewhere in the background. An appeal here to wind would complete the ancient quartet of earth, air, fire and water, for the other three are mentioned elsewhere in the chapter.[6] In any case, there are limits to what should be made of one verse, whatever it is. We are concerned not with what can be wrung from a single verse, but with what scripture as a whole enables us to say about the part played by the Spirit of God in creation in the light of the whole sweep of his dealings with it.

(4) Verses (14–18) whose early interpretation is pregnant with menace for the future are those describing the creation of the two great lights, 'the greater light to rule the day, and the lesser light to rule the night'. It must be one of the disasters of theological history that the lessons of this verse for the doctrine of creation were so long in the learning. Do we have here an early attempt at what can be called a kind of demythologising? There are traces of the ancient view that the sun and the moon are deities – do they not 'rule' the day and the night? – but more significant are the differences. Westermann contrasts them with the Babylonian creation myths: 'What distinguishes the priestly account of creation among the many creation stories of the Ancient Near

4. Basil *Hexaemeron*, 2. 8.
5. Robert W. Jenson, 'Aspects of a Doctrine of Creation', in *The Doctrine of Creation. Essays in Dogmatics, History and Philosophy* (Edinburgh: T. & T. Clark, 1997), pp. 17–28 (p. 22)
6. Robert Grosseteste, *On the Six Days of Creation*, translated by C. F. J. Martin (Oxford: Oxford University Press for The British Academy, 1996), p. 79.

17

East is that for P there can be only one creator and that all else that is or can be, can never be anything but a creature.'[7] Everywhere else in the ancient world the sun and moon – and it is significant that here they are not named, but simply described as lights – were at least semi-divine agencies, who ruled the earth, but not in the merely subordinate way they are here allowed. In this text they are, to use one robust way of putting it, 'Gods nothing! Lamps and clocks that Jahve made and hung up there.'[8] Christian theology had to come to terms with the ancient assumption of the divinity of the heavenly bodies in a somewhat more sophisticated form, that of ancient Greek teaching of the perfection, eternity – and therefore uncreatedness – of the heavenly bodies. It was what theologians made of this teaching that determined much of the character of their theologies of creation. This point becomes particularly important in the light of the history of the relation between the doctrine of creation and the rise of modern science, for if the heavenly bodies are ontologically different from the earthly realm it is unlikely that they obey the same laws as earthly matter.

If we return to the second and several other verses of the chapter, a similar point can be made about the water, which was, for the ancient world, the origin and habitat of the gods of chaos and disorder. Water remains for the Bible a symbol of evil and destruction, as the story of Noah reveals. That story is also testimony at once to God's dominion over the water and his use of it as a medium of judgement and salvation. As merely H_2O, it remains subordinate to the creator. The rainbow in Genesis as a symbol of both irrigating water and ripening sun serves to represent the providential stability of creation, that creation's bounds are maintained by the creator. Baptism similarly uses the water that drowns as the vehicle of saving judgement, and as a promise that evil will be overcome: 'and there was no more sea' (Revelation 21:1).

(5) What is to be made of v. 27, 'So God created man in his own image . . . male and female he created them'? Without needing to go into the history of the interpretation of this verse, and particularly into the question of whether human sexual differences are here meant to be in some way constitutive of being in the image of God, we can at least say that our *material* constitution is in a central way important for the writer, as it is for the rest of the Old Testament.[9] The general point is

7. Westermann, *Genesis*, p. 127.
8. R. W. Jenson, *Story and Promise. A Brief Theology of the Gospel about Jesus* (Philadelphia: Fortress Press, 1973), p. 22.
9. See Hans Walter Wolff, *Anthropology of the Old Testament*, translated by Margaret Kohl (London: SCM Press, 1974).

that Genesis represents the close relations of the human species with God, on the one hand, and with nature, on the other. The human creature is created in *continuity* with the other creatures, yet is in some way, under God, also above and responsible for them. Once again, what is made of this in the tradition is of incalculable importance for future theological accounts of human being, because, as we shall see, any tendency to spiritualise the verses tends to accentuate our discontinuity with nature at the expense of our continuity. Gnosticism was an extreme example of this tendency, but it has also marked the pages of more orthodox theology.

It is also important to remember that there is much other Old Testament material that is relevant to the doctrine of creation, and in particular Psalms 33, 104 and 139 (see v. 13 for the depiction of creation as a continuing divine act). In addition, it is worth remembering that Proverbs and the Wisdom literature as a whole contain many representations of the world as the reliable and meaningful creation of God. Job 38–41, the speech of God from the whirlwind, contains a sustained celebration of the absolute sovereignty of God over the created order, and parallels some of its characterisations in the Psalms. Many of the passages so far mentioned derive from late in the Old Testament tradition, as does that in Isaiah 40: 28, where God is described as 'the creator of the ends of the earth.' But that passage from the prophet has its antecedents in the writings of the earlier prophets, with their assertions of the absolute sovereignty of God over the whole earth.

As we have seen, it is likely that the Old Testament did not teach what later came to be called creation out of nothing. It is not a biblical category, any more than are others of the concepts theology has had to devise in order to articulate and defend the biblical view of things. Yet the Old Testament came very near to later teaching both in its assertions of divine sovereignty and in affirmations like that of Psalm 104:5ff, that the earth has been established by God once and for all. As Francis Watson has pointed out in his treatment of the biblical doctrine of creation in his recent *Text and Truth*, this should not be understood in terms of the modern obsession with the 'dynamic' in preference to the 'static':[10]

10. Francis Watson, *Text and Truth. Redefining Biblical Theology* (Edinburgh: T. & T. Clark, 1997), p. 234: 'Capitalist ideology applauds dynamism, the restless dissatisfaction with the way things are and the quest for the new . . . to such an extent that that which endures and does not change becomes a troubling enigma that must either be passed over in silence or denounced as inflexible, outdated and dogmatic.' These discussions of the Old Testament material are succeeded by a wonderful passage in which the author shows how themes of Genesis 1 reappear in descriptions of Jesus' life and teaching in the gospels.

19

> The creation narratives in Gen. 1–2 represent God's activity in creation as belonging, in some sense, to the past . . . These narratives locate the time of creation in the past, 'in the beginning', precisely in order to understand the basic structures of present experience . . . What is valued in this all-encompassing present is its *stability* . . . 'I establish my covenant with you that never again shall all flesh be cut off by the waters of a flood . . .' (pp. 230–1)

The grounds for later doctrines of creation are undoubtedly present, particularly in the expressions of the freedom and sovereignty of God which are everywhere to be found. They are to be found above all in, first, the way in which the language of myth is transformed in order to remove any suggestion that this God, unlike the gods of other cultures, was in any way limited by any other reality; second, in passages like Isaiah 48:7, 43:19 and 45:7, where 'creation' language is used of God's redemptive action in history;[11] and third Ezekiel 37:1–14, where the Spirit of God is shown to be in sovereign interrelation with the created world. In that latter vision of the transformation of the dry bones, we read an anticipation of what was to find more systematic expression in New Testament and early theology.

II THE BIBLE: (2) THE NEW TESTAMENT

In the New Testament there are to be found a number of credal affirmations of the doctrine of creation in general. Some are almost certainly dependent upon Genesis 1, and it may be that it operates as an invisible matrix for one of them, Hebrews 11:3. The RSV translation brings out the point: 'By faith we understand that the world was created by the word of God, so that what is seen was made out of things that do not appear.'[12] Revelation 4:11 supplies what is the most clear credal expression of the content of the doctrine: 'For thou didst create all things, and by thy will they existed and were created'. The attribution of creation to God's will is most important for future developments, for it is the teaching that creation is freely willed by God that forms one of the distinctive marks of later doctrine, and is constitutive for what came to be distinctive about the Christian view of things.

The definitive New Testament contribution to the development of the

---

11. See Wolfhart Pannenberg, *Systematic Theology Volume 2*, pp. 11–12, for references to myths of chaos in Psalms 74:12ff; 77:12ff; 89:6f.

12. See also Heb: 4. 3b–4: 'although his works were finished from the foundation of the world. For he has somewhere spoken of the seventh day in this way . . .'

doctrine is to be found in its christological form. This is already indicated in the best known of likely allusions to Genesis 1, John 1:1, 'In the beginning was the Word . . . Without him was not made anything that was made.' The Word who, according to verse 14 of that passage, became flesh is the one through whom the whole creation has its being. But there is a case for saying that other New Testament passages indicate the wider christological basis of the teaching. 1 Corinthians 8:6, which, as John Gibbs has argued, is likely to reflect very early tradition as a confession of belief appealed to by Paul, sets the scene, placing Christ alongside God the Father as co-agent of creation.[13] 'There is one God, the Father, from whom are all things, and for whom we exist, and one Lord, Jesus Christ, through whom are all things and through whom we exist.' The later doctrinal tradition reinforces the christological claim. Colossians 1:16, in a passage of astonishing profundity - possibly anticipating Irenaeus' later attacks on theories that intermediate beings rather than God himself were responsible for the creation of the material world – describes Jesus Christ as the one in whom 'all things were created, in heaven and on earth . . . all things were created through him and for him. He is before all things, and in him all things hold together.' A similar form of expression is to be found in Hebrews 1:2f which speaks of: 'a Son, through whom (God) created the world. He reflects the very stamp of his nature, upholding the universe by his word of power.' This is a classical statement of the double function of Christ in creation, at once to mediate the creation of the world and to sustain it once it is made. It brings out again the point that Christian belief in creation is not a general product of reason, but a very specific credal affirmation which implies both origination and continuing interaction and upholding.

Here two points should be noted. First, the tensing: things both were created and (now) *hold together* in Jesus Christ. Tenses, we must never forget, are essentially problematic when we are speaking of the relation of eternal God and temporal creation. As these passages and the parallel treatment in Ephesians 1 alike indicate, neither 'past' nor 'present' of either Jesus or the world can be understood outside the eschatological context: that the world was created and is upheld by the mediator of God the Father's activity which embraces the tenses and holds in promise that what was once begun will through his mediation be perfected. Second, what is meant by 'in' Christ? Is he the 'container' of all the universe, and in what sense? We cannot make too much of one passage, but can at least signal a point to be developed in Chapter 6, that there

13. J. G. Gibbs, *Creation and Redemption. A Study in Pauline Theology* (Leiden: Brill, 1971).

is a world (*sic*) of difference between saying that the world is created in Christ and in God, *simpliciter*. Part of the point of christology in this connection is that it is possible to treat creation as externalisation – the creation of a reality outside the being of God – without the perils of deism. It is created in the past in such a way that already provision is made for a conception of God's continuing interaction with it. However it is to be taken, the notion that Christ is in some way the framework of all things is an important one, whose fate in future centuries is crucial for the way the doctrine of creation developed and was understood, as we shall see.

The background provided by the Synoptic Gospels, which were written, we must remember, for the most part later than the epistles, shows that their writers saw Jesus in intrinsic relation to the created order, though inevitably, in view of the difference of their interests, in a different way. 'Who is then this, that even wind and sea obey him?' (Mark 4: 41). Healings, the raising of the dead, the multiplication of the loaves and fish, show Jesus as not merely a teacher, but one exercising – or rather *reasserting* – God's lordship over the created order. The overcoming of the demons shares in this, if we understand demonic possession as a form of slavery endured by the created order, which is liberated to be itself by being set free by creation's Lord. In the light of the doctrine of creation it becomes clear that it is a mistake to distinguish between 'miracles' of healing, for example, that can perhaps be 'explained' in other terms, and so-called nature miracles. All are of a kind in the respect that they are concerned with God's sovereignty over the created order, its exercise and reassertion, in the interest above all of human healing and wholeness.

But if Christ is the mediator of creation, the Spirit is seen by the Bible as the one who both gives life to in the present and forms into their destined shape the things that have been made. Here, in view of the tendency of the New Testament writers to concentrate their attention on the new factor of Christ the creator, we should return first to the Old Testament to see something of the background. We have already alluded to the Spirit's work according to Genesis 1:2, 'the Spirit of God moved across the face of the waters'. The fact that this word is sometimes translated as 'wind' bears witness to the fact that the Spirit operates as a mysterious but effective power in and towards the world. Psalm 104 celebrates the Spirit as the giver of life – 'When thou sendest forth thy Spirit, they are created; and thou renewest the face of the earth' – while Ezekiel's vision of the dry bones returns to the wind as an image for the Spirit's free, unpredictable and uncontrollable power (compare John

3:8). There is in this passage a pun on at least three possible meanings for *ruach* – wind, breath and spirit: 'Come, wind, blow upon these slain, that they may live . . .' (Ezekiel 37:1–10).

The notes of life-giving, renewing and transforming are repeated in some New Testament characterisations of the work of the Spirit in relation to the created order. In Paul's treatise on the Spirit in Romans 8 the themes of renewal and transformation are both to be found. The allusion to the work of the Spirit as the one who 'raised Christ from the dead' brings us to this central theme for a treatment of the New Testament basis of the doctrine of creation. There is little doubt that a major impulse for the development of a christological and pneumatological treatment of creation came from the resurrection of Jesus from the dead. It suggests two things: first, the freedom of God's action in and towards the created order; and second that the fate or destiny of creation is in some way bound up with Jesus of Nazareth. That the body of Jesus is raised shows that God's redemptive activity is concerned with the whole of human life, not merely the 'moral' or 'spiritual', in the narrower sense sometimes given to the latter word. As we have seen, with particular reference to Ezekiel 37, 'spiritual' in the wider sense of meaning everything pertaining to the work of God the Spirit has undoubtedly a reference beyond the merely spiritual as it is often understood, because it has to do with the creation and redemption of the whole created order. Once again, as in christology, we are brought face to face with the intrinsically eschatological setting of the doctrine of creation.

This latter point is taken up by Paul in Romans 4:17, a text heavy with significance for the doctrine of creation, although, as May has argued, it does not necessarily teach creation out of nothing.[14] It is a basis for the latter in that it clearly shows the same divine sovereignty over the created order expressed in Genesis 1 and elsewhere. The context is the giving of a child to Abraham and Sarah, when for the purposes of reproduction they were effectively dead. But, 'in the presence of the God who . . . gives life to the dead and calls into existence the things that do not exist . . .', death is overcome. This verse inevitably also points us to a second eschatological feature, a more contentious item of Christian doctrine, that concerning Jesus' conception in the womb of the virgin. This teaching has a double significance, neither aspect of which has anything to do, as is sometimes suggested, with a negative evaluation of human sexuality, or indeed much to do with a miraculous proof of Jesus' divinity. Its interest lies in what it says about Jesus' humanity, which

14. May, *Creatio ex Nihilo*, p. 27.

is that on the one hand it is indeed a new and miraculous creative act of God, in continuity with those things promised as new creation in texts like that of Isaiah 43:19; while on the other, this new humanity is formed within the womb of Mary of earthly material in such a way that the creation is renewed from within.[15] The Spirit is thus active in the recreation of the fallen world through the incarnation of the Son of God in the flesh.

The twin biblical themes we have explored, of the creation formed through and upheld by Christ and the Spirit's free and transformative action within the world, encourage us to conceive God as personally involved in the creation, not simply a machine-maker operating 'from without.' He is clearly 'without' in the sense of being other, transcendent. He is creator and not creation, but he is also, in realisation rather than denial of that transcendence, one who in Christ becomes part of that creation, freely involved within its structures, in order that he may, in obedience to God the Father and through the power of his Spirit, redirect the creation to its eschatological destiny. It is because of this that we are able to look back at the Old Testament passages and see them as in their own way witnessing to the God made known in the revelation in Jesus Christ.

III THE GREEKS: (1) EARLY COSMOLOGY

The Greek philosophers provide important background to the Christian doctrine of creation for a number of reasons. In the first place, they asked some of the questions with which the doctrine engages, especially that concerning the nature of the world: of what kind of being it is; broadly, the question of cosmology. For the most part, questions of this kind remained unasked in the biblical writings, because the writers had different interests. In the second place, and this is a similar point, they provided some of the concepts with which the Christian writers expressed their teaching. Third, they contributed, as we shall see, aspects of the content of some of the thought of early Christian writers, especially perhaps Origen and Augustine. In sum, we cannot understand the Christian theology of creation except as in part a conversation between two different but interacting worlds, just as today we are bound to say

---

15. Paul Haffner, *Mystery of Creation* (Leominster: Gracewing, 1995), e. g. p. 71, attempts to combine this with a reference to the doctrine of the immaculate conception of Mary, but that undermines the point that for the creation to be renewed from within the saviour must not be shielded from full engagement with the fallen creation.

something in this context about the interrelation between theology and modern science.

The origins of Greek cosmology are to be found in a demythologisation of the gods of the ancient Greeks. That religion was polytheistic, attributing different functions to different of the deities, so that Poseidon was God of the sea and of earthquakes, Ares the God of war, and so on. In the Trojan War, as told by Homer, there is, corresponding to the battle on earth, a struggle for mastery between the gods on Olympus. This is not as naive or objectionable as we may think. As David Hume pointed out, there are respects in which polytheism makes better sense of our experience than monotheism.[16] In so far as gods and myths are the projections of aspects of human experience, Greek religion is a rational and intelligible enterprise. It represents among other things the essentially pessimistic character of much of the Greek response to the world, and it is worth noticing that above the gods there is a stronger force, 'fate' or 'necessity' to which they are subject. It is here that we reach the real distinction between all Greek theories and Christian teaching of a sovereign creator.

The Greek cosmologists began a rational critique of their polytheistic inheritance by removing from it what they regarded as its objectionable nature and seeking to develop a version of some of its underlying insights. Thales of Miletus (born about 624 BC) is generally recognised to be the father of Greek philosophy and science in his quest for the *arche* of all things, by which is meant both their originating state and their permanent ground of being: an account of where things come from, and what they finally consist of. His speculation that everything consists in some configuration of water, which is both alive and everlasting, was answered by the speculations of later philosophers extending this into the four elements of hot and cold, warm and dry, which by their eternal conflict achieve a kind of balance or 'justice'. On this understanding, the cosmos works by the perpetual dynamic of a conflict of the elements which constitute the eternal matter of things. This is cosmology rather than creation, in the use of the word 'cosmology' in this case to refer to the Greek tendency to attribute the meaning of things to eternal principles underlying an eternal world rather than to a personal creator of a temporal world. The same holds good of the more sophisticated speculations of Heraclitus, who wrote around 500 BC, and Parmenides (born about 515–510 BC). Heraclitus, whose philosophy is best known through his slogan that 'everything is flux', is the originator

16. David Hume, *A Natural History of Religion*, 9-12.

of the tradition of thought that sees reality as fundamentally 'many'. He is the philosopher of pluralism, at least if those interpreters are correct who understand his theory of the Logos as fire to imply that there is no underlying stable reality, but that the only reality is change. The world is a living and everlasting fire.[17] This world, it is important to see, is a philosophised version of the world of the Homeric gods. Just as the deities in the *Iliad* represent different actors in the struggle of people and states taking place in the world below them, so the conflict of opposing principles is written by Heraclitus into the very fabric of the universe. It is here most of all that Greek teaching echoes the Ancient Near Eastern creation myths which understand the world as the outcome of conflict.

The importance of the distinction of this way of seeing the world from biblical creation thought cannot be exaggerated. As Paul Ricoeur has written in reference to Babylonian creation myth,

> It will be seen what human violence is thus justified by the primordial violence. Creation is a victory over an Enemy older than the creator; that Enemy, immanent in the divine, will be represented in history by all the enemies whom the king in his turn, as servant of the god, will have as his mission to destroy. Thus Violence is inscribed in the origin of things, in the principle that establishes while it destroys.[18]

The biblical view that the creation has its origins in the covenant love of God is thus a way of understanding the world different in principle from both the myths of the ancient world and much of the Greek philosophy that has its roots in them. Consequently, as we shall see, it generates a different ethic: a different way of inhabiting the world and treating its inhabitants. The continuing importance of this contrast of world-views is to be found in the fact that the view of creation as deified conflict is perpetually renewed in human culture, most recently perhaps in Hegel and Marx, as well as in many of their disciples. Violations of the peace of creation are an offence against the God of the Bible, in complete contrast and opposition to the fact that they are a rational response to the gods of mythical and philosophical paganism.

However, the idea of creation as violence was not the strand which

---

17. W. K. C. Guthrie, *A History of Greek Philosophy* 1 (Cambridge: Cambridge University Press, 1962), p. 461.
18. Cited from Paul Ricoeur, *The Symbolism of Evil* (Boston: Beacon, 1969), pp. 182–3, by J. R. Middleton and B. J. Walsh, *Truth is Stranger than it Used to Be. Biblical Faith in a Postmodern Age* (London: SPCK, 1995), p. 125.

dominated later Greek cosmology, despite echoes of the old myths in Plato's *Timaeus*. It fell to Parmenides, writing in the next generation, to represent the opposing view of reality to that of Heraclitus, and at the same time to introduce the dualism that became in time such a stumbling block for Christian theology, especially as it was mediated by the platonists. In place of a conflict of equals, or near equals, Parmenides generated a dualism of higher and lower forms of being. For him reality was not flux, but by definition that which did not change at all. The real is the totally unchanging. It could be said that while Heraclitus observes the world and philosophises the change and decay that he observes, Parmenides seeks to tame the flux by looking for an underlying stasis (I am tempted to say, inertial system) which is discovered by applying a rational principle to reality. The key is twofold. First, he turns into a metaphysical principle the logical doctrine that what is is, and therefore eternally is. Ordinary things, the material world and its contents, cannot really be said to *be*, because they are subject to decay and destruction. (We should contrast this with the affirmative view of the writer of Genesis, for whom God sees all that he has made, and it is very good. In that respect, there is as absolute a gulf between Parmenides and the platonism which succeeded him, on the one hand, and on the other the doctrine of creation, as there is between that and the myths of violence.) The Parmenidean depreciation of the material world is based, second, on a dualism of sense and reason. The world of the senses, the *aistheton* – that which is perceived – is unreliable, and Parmenides' goddess tells him: '*not to trust the senses*, but instead to *judge by reason*.' Guthrie comments: 'Here for the first time sense and reason are contrasted, and we are told that the senses deceive and that reason alone is to be trusted. It is a decisive moment in the history of European philosophy. . .'.[19] Change, movement, becoming, are all taught by the senses. Only reason takes us to that which is truly real, the realm of the *noeton*, that which is thought. Therefore for Parmenides what is truly real is what is eternal, unmoving, one and continuous. Reality is therefore an undifferentiated continuum, with no past and no future. It just timelessly *is*. The universe is thoroughly homogeneous in every respect, and while there is thus a *cosmology*, a theory of the universe, there is no *cosmogony*, no theory of the universe's coming into being. For that, we must turn to Plato, who in his later work the *Timaeus* produced something that did cohere more nearly with Christian teaching.

19. W. K. C. Guthrie, *A History of Greek Philosophy* 2 (Cambridge: Cambridge University Press, 1965), p. 25, expounding Parmenides, Fragments 6 and 7.

IV THE GREEKS: (2) PLATO AND ARISTOTLE

The philosophy of Plato is heavy with significance for the later theology of creation. The history of the developments in the second century shows a progressive attempt by a number of theologians to extricate themselves from the grip of platonic ideas. At the heart of the matter, as we shall see, is the status of the material world. Plato's Parmenidean inheritance is revealed in his *Theaetetus*, where it is claimed that sense perception 'has no share in the grasping of truth'.[20] Among the reasons given is that the senses are bound up with matter, which is marked by particularity and change. Neither of these is conducive to rational truth, for, according to Plato, reason concerns itself only with the unchanging and universal. Matter is therefore intrinsically resistant to rational understanding. The importance of this cannot be overestimated, in view of the future development of science. It shows that this aspect of Plato's thought is something that had to be overcome before science, which is concerned with the intrinsic rationality of the *material* world, could develop.

However, the first thing to be observed about Plato is that in general he represents a modification of the Parmenidean philosophy. His doctrine of the forms, eternal realities which provide the models of everything in the experienced world, introduces an element of plurality into the otherwise unrelieved monism of Parmenides. The cosmological assumptions underlying his position emerge in the *Republic*, where there appears what is perhaps his most influential treatment of the forms. Despite the fact that the *Timaeus* was in many ways more influential in the development of the doctrine of creation, the *Republic* is the book which enables us to engage with Plato's view of reality in general. As will be pointed out repeatedly, this – ontology – is as important a dimension of the doctrine of creation as talk of 'beginnings'. In some contrast to the writings of many of the Presocratic philosophers, who use the language of 'justice' to speak more of the balance of forces in the universe than of relations in society, Plato's primary concern here is with social and political order. His quest is for that ideal justice, laid up in the 'heavens', to which the ruler can refer in quest of a model for earthly political order. The parallel to the observation of Schmid, referred to in Chapter 1, about ancient creation myths is surely here instructive. Plato's book is designed to perform some of the functions that myths did for ancient Near Eastern societies.

20. Plato, *Theaetetus*, 186e 4ff, the reason being that it has no share in being.

But the general theory of reality taught or supposed by Plato is also important, particularly in view of the function it was destined to perform as part of the structure of some theologies of creation. Two features must be observed. The first is that Plato appears to hold that not only moral qualities and natural objects but also man-made objects like articles of furniture have an eternal form to which they should correspond if they are to be what they should be. The famous example of the bed appears in Plato's discussion of art. According to him, art deals with the fundamentally unreal, and therefore has no place in a philosophically ordered society. When a carpenter makes a bed, he must hold in his mind's eye the eternal form of the bed. What he makes is only more or less adequate as a representation of reality, for all material expression is necessarily at one remove from 'true' reality.[21] The artist who draws or paints the bed produces something at one more remove still from the ideal. There is a trace of what can be called theology in Plato's discussion, for he describes the ideal bed as being made by *theos* or god, but the significance of this for our topic cannot be decided because of its vagueness, and because in general for Plato the forms are eternal. The chief point is that Plato is operating with a hierarchical conception of reality: at the top are the eternal and immaterial forms, below that their realisation in matter, and finally at the foot artistic representation.[22]

The second feature of the *Republic's* theory of reality can be outlined more briefly, and it appears to be – for here too interpretation is not unanimous – that material things are only half real, existing as they do mid-way between being and non-being. This means that the ordinary person, who believes that material things are real, is, according to Plato's vivid analogy of the cave, imprisoned in a world of illusion, like people who see but the passing shadows of things carried in front of them and take them for the whole of reality.[23] This picture, too, sits uneasily alongside the biblical affirmation that 'God saw all that he had made, and behold, it was very good' (Genesis 1:31), implying as it does the reality of the world in which we actually live.

The *Timaeus* gives a better impression than the *Republic* of a positive attitude toward the material world. It is an odd and difficult book, showing far more evidences of the mythological background of Plato's

---

21. See Plato, *Timaeus* 28: 'Whenever . . . the maker of anything keeps his eye on the eternally unchanging and uses it as his pattern . . . the result must be good.' Translations are from H. D. P. Lee, *Plato, Timaeus* (Harmondsworth: Penguin Books, 1965).

22. For the discussion, see Plato, *Republic* 10, 595–603.

23. Plato, *Republic*, Book 7.

philosophy than most of his other dialogues. It is also difficult to know whether he is simply experimenting with ideas, or meant the dialogue to be taken as a kind of cosmology.[24] Whatever be the case, because the *Timaeus* has been influential in the development of Christian doctrine, something should be said of what is to be found in it. First, Plato teaches that there is a two stage creation. First created is a timeless, perfectly circular sphere, constructed from fire, water, air and earth (32ff). This constituted a physical body, whole and complete. There was a soul both in the centre and diffused throughout the whole, producing a single spherical universe in circular motion: 'His creation . . . was a blessed God' (34). Then was created the world of time as 'an eternal moving image of the eternity which remains for ever at one' (37). This heavenly world supplies the pattern for our world, which is thus a kind of copy of a higher, divine world.

Second, it is asked whether the cosmos came into existence. The answer is that, yes, it did: 'for it is visible, tangible and corporeal, and therefore perceptible by the senses . . .' (28). Although it may not be clear on the surface, the way this is expressed effectively disparages the universe of our experience, because its perceptible nature is implicitly contrasted with the eternal world of forms and divinity. It is an inferior mode of being. The *Timaeus* therefore has a two-fold relation to the Christian doctrine of creation. On the one hand, there are clear parallels. The world is good, the nearest thing in Plato to an affirmation of the value of the created world (29). On the other hand, God on this account is not a creator out of nothing, but a demiurge who creates order out of chaos (30). *God made a world but did not create the universe.* This world, even as good, is secondary to the perfect Parmenidean world of the first creation.

Third, it should be noted that some of the background and reason for this cosmology is found later in the book, where its well known threefold world-view comes into prominence. In addition to the unchanging model and the visible and changing copy that we have already met, there is a third feature, what Plato calls 'the receptacle' (49). This is 'a kind of neutral plastic material on which changing impressions are stamped'. The receptacle is (like) 'the mother, the model . . . the father, and what they produce between them . . . their offspring' (50). Here is Plato at his most mythological, revealing how much of Greek philosophy is a philosophising of the ancient myths. And the philosophy emerges a

---

24. See Richard Sorabji, *Time, Creation and the Continuum* (London: Duckworth, 1983), chapter 17 for a discussion of different interpretations of the *Timaeus*.

little further on: there are three eternal realities, eternal form (the 'model'); the receptacle (unformed, shapeless, chaotic matter) and the demiurge, or divinity, who does not create but shapes that which is of equal eternity with him (52).

The fact that this speculative work is so unlike Plato's other writings indicates that Plato was here writing more as an explorer of ideas than a builder of a systematic world view. That activity was taken up by his successors, and in different directions. Especially important was his immediate successor Aristotle, who was unconvinced by the doctrine of forms, but adopted aspects of the cosmology from the *Timaeus* in a way that exercised a baneful influence on the subsequent history of theology, and especially its relations with science. So far as the latter is concerned, Aristotle has a double significance. First, his naturalism, involving as it did a stress on careful observation and measurement, is sometimes claimed to be of importance for the later development of modern science. As we shall see, it is undoubtedly the case that the rediscovery of Aristotle and the emergence of modern science took place at roughly the same time. But, second, while later scholarly opinion appears to agree with Luther in the view that Aristotle 'leaves unsettled the question of whether the world is eternal',[25] Aristotle took from Plato a belief in the perfection of circular motion and was in general responsible for handing on a doctrine of the divinity of the heavenly bodies.[26] This will bulk large in later developments. 'According to Aristotle', writes Thomas Kuhn, 'the underside of the sphere of the moon divides the universe into two totally disparate regions, filled with different sorts of matter and subject to different laws.' He cites Aristotle's *On the Heavens* to the effect that: 'the primary body of all [that is, celestial matter] is eternal, suffers neither growth nor diminution, but is ageless, unalterable and impassive.'[27] Another remark of Kuhn's, to the effect that Aristotle's conception of motion is effectively a transmuted animism, shows again how far less successful the Greeks were than the Hebrews in demythologising the ancient creation myths.[28]

25. Martin Luther, *Luther's Works*, 1, *Lectures on Genesis chapters 1–5*, edited by J. Pelikan (St Louis: Concordia, 1958), p. 3.

26. Alan Scott, *Origen and the Life of the Stars. A History of an Idea* (Oxford: Clarendon Press, 1991) summarises and cites the evidence, pp. 30–2.

27. Thomas S. Kuhn, *The Copernican Revolution. Planetary Astronomy in the Development of Western Thought* (Cambridge, Mass. and London: Harvard University Press, 1957), p. 91.

28. Kuhn, *The Copernican Revolution*, p. 97.

V LATER GREEK COSMOLOGY

Opinion is also divided on whether Aristotle's thought finally implies a pantheism, and it is certainly the case that no Greek philosophy is far from an identification of the world, or aspects of it, with the divine. It came more clearly to the surface in two later philosophies, those of Stoicism and Neoplatonism. To the Stoics we owe the development of some of the pantheistic ideas that are inherent in Greek philosophy. They tended both to understand the universe as an organism, a living being of some kind, and to draw on earlier traditions about its being shaped by the interaction of opposing forces – in their case, opposing active and passive principles. But this is much nearer to a monism than to the dualism of Plato:

> since the active principle, to poioun, is not spiritual but material. In fact it is hardly dualism at all, since the two principles are both material and together form one Whole. The Stoic doctrine is therefore a monistic materialism, even if this position is not consistently maintained.[29]

The inconsistency to which Copleston refers occurs chiefly in the teaching at once of materialism and that the universe was pervaded in varying ways by a cosmic spirit or pneuma, with the different degrees of its pervading accounting for the emergence of different kinds of entity. Yet although this plurality of beings mitigates the pantheism of the system, it is clearly difficult for Stoicism to distinguish between the divine and the non-divine, so close is their interrelation. The necessitarian nature of Stoic teaching is a symptom:

> This reign of necessity the Stoics expressed under the concept of Fate . . ., but Fate is not something different from God and eternal reason, nor is it different from Providence . . . which orders all things for the best. Fate and Providence are but different aspects of God.[30]

Some of the Stoics also held the view, which appears to have influenced Origen, that there was a cycle of universes, each identical with the last, and proceeding to eternity.[31] More clearly influential for future developments is their doctrine of the *logoi spermatikoi* or seminal reasons,

---

29. F. C. Copleston, *A History of Philosophy* 1 (London: Burns Oates and Washbourne, 1946), p. 388.
30. Copleston, *A History of Philosophy* 1, p. 389.

the seeds of all things which come to be, which become, in Augustine's theology of creation the *rationes seminales,* or forms of things whose creation precedes that of the material world.

The second later Greek cosmology at which we must look is that of Plotinus (possibly about AD 200–70), known as a Neoplatonist for his development of certain of his great predecessor's insights. The world in which Christianity grew to intellectual maturity was a highly religious world, in which platonic philosophy tended to be mined as much for its religious as for what we would now, probably wrongly, today consider its strictly philosophical content. Plotinus is of immense historical importance for the doctrine of creation because of the influence which his ideas, or ideas like them, had on Origen, Augustine, Pseudo-Dionysius and beyond – right up to the recent writing of Wolfhart Pannenberg.[32] From him not only comes the classical form of the doctrine of emanation, which is, as we shall see, to be strongly contrasted with that of creation, but he also raises in the sharpest possible form questions about the reality and status of matter.

Let us first outline something of his not altogether clear theory of reality. His is a hierarchical view of the world. At the bottom of the great chain of being is matter. To gain some apprehension of Plotinus' views, imagine some object, like a flower, and remove from it all its qualities – colour, shape, texture, mass, scent. What would remain? The answer of a later theologian, Basil of Caesarea,[33] as of a modern one, George Berkeley, would be 'nothing', but that is not Plotinus' view. There would, according to his discussion in the *Enneads,* remain pure, quality-less matter, a substratum or support for being without any characteristics. This is what Plotinus calls *to me on,* or nothingness, though by this he does not mean the absolute nothingness or non-existence implied by the other Greek negative, *to ouk on.* Matter exists, yet does not really exist: it is 'truly non-being; it is a ghostly image of bulk'; or, we might gloss, a mere parody of true being. This gives rise to the apparent paradox that matter is

---

31. For this account, I am dependent upon Copleston and Michael Lapidge, 'Stoic Cosmology', in *The Stoics,* edited by J. M. Rist (London: University of California Press), 1978, pp. 161–85.
32. Wolfhart Pannenberg, *Metaphysics and the Idea of God,* translated by Philip Clayton (Edinburgh: T. & T. Clark, 1990), pp. 75–8. I am not convinced by Pannenberg's attempt to find an orientation to the future in Plotinus' philosophy of time.
33. Basil believes that because God has made it, the creation is what it appears to be. 'Do not let us seek for any nature devoid of qualities ... Take away black, cold, weight, density, the qualities which concern taste, in one word all these which we see in it, and the substance vanishes.' *Hexaemeron,* 1. 8.

incorporeal (3. 6. 7). (It is only an apparent paradox, because it is the qualities which confer corporeality and thus thingness.) The point is that matter is a kind of being, but only of the lowest kind. It is a radical version of the platonist view that matter is less real than form. That is why it must logically be evil, although that evil is, if it can be so put, of a hypothetical kind: 'if it really participated and was really altered by the good it would not be evil by nature' (3. 6. 11). Clearly, then, as matter, it is evil by nature. Everything in this world is not created 'very good', or, indeed, created at all.

Just as matter is at the very bottom of the scale of being, so at the top is the One, which shares some of the characteristics of matter in the respect that it is absolutely indeterminate. It has no name or form and so is *amorphon eidos*, 'a formless idea' (6. 7. 33). It has no attributes, and is an entirely indivisible unity, an absolute oneness (rather like, it must be observed, the God of Arius, or, dare it be said, Origen). The One cannot really be described as an existing thing, because all existing things flow from it and it remains completely unaffected and undiminished by their outflowing (3. 8. 8–9). Thus in one sense it is absolutely transcendent and without past or future, but in another sense it is the maker or cause of all other being. Here there is a real contrast with Plato. The One is not a demiurge, a shaper of pre-given forms in the light of the pre-existent material, because it is the cause of the forms (5. 3. 17), as well as of all other things; it is Plato's form of the good and demiurge rolled into one and deprived of all personal characteristics.

How does the One give rise to other beings? To answer this question, we need to see something of the entities which people the intervening space between the One and formless matter. Immediately below the One in the hierarchy of being is Thought or Mind (*nous*). This represents the intelligible world, and in using the expression 'father of the cause' Plotinus suggests – but only suggests – Plato's demiurge. This is eternal and beyond time, but contains within it an element of plurality or multiplicity. It contains the whole multitude of ideas or forms, though it contains them indivisibly. Below this again is *psyche* or soul, which appears to be equivalent to the world-soul of the *Timaeus*. It is the connecting link between the higher world and the world of sense. It is a mediating reality, looking at once upwards and downwards. It has both higher and lower aspects, the higher oriented to the Mind, the lower, called nature or *physis*, to the soul of the material world. Human souls participate in both, and are thus the junction, so to speak, of the intellectual and sensible worlds. The human soul is pre-existent, and this means that embodiment is a 'fall', for it involves incarnation in that which is a lower order of being. This doctrine repeats something said by Plato, that bodily existence is the result of a fall of souls.[34] Indeed, Pannenberg points out that, according to one passage in Plotinus, the creation of the visible world is attributed to the fall of the world soul.[35] We shall learn some of the implications and impact of this when we come to study the theology of creation of Origen, a junior contemporary of Plotinus.

So far as the status of the actual material world is concerned, it receives, according to Plotinus, just as much reality as can be mediated to it through the higher realms of being. The best way to understand this is through the analogy of light. Light becomes dimmer the further it is from its source; and so does reality become less real the further it is away from the One on the great chain of being. But it must be remembered that in contrast to some of the Gnostics the attitude of Plotinus to the material is not entirely negative. In so far as there is form, there is also light. What we have in Plotinus is the world view of the *Timaeus* almost entirely freed of the mythical background which still pervades that work. It is the myth of the *Timaeus* turned into a hierarchical cosmological system.

How do the lower realms of being derive from the One? The answer Plotinus gives is by emanation, which is a metaphor derived from the flowing of a river. Creation flows from the One, which is like a spring which has no source outside itself (3. 8. 10). Commentators differ on whether the One can be conceded to be free in creating, and in what sense. Copleston claims that the system is necessitarian: the world has to flow from the One by an automatic process, although that is not necessarily to say that it is pantheistic. It is certainly to be distinguished from free creation out of nothing.[36] Rist on the other hand argues that although there is no willing or choice in what happens, emanation is spontaneous, in the sense that there is no external constraint. Quoting Plotinus' statement that 'The entire intellectual order may be figured as a kind of light with the One in repose at its summit as its king', he proceeds to argue that emanation is a 'kind of free will' (5. 3. 12).[37] The whole arrangement is summed up in Rist's characterisation of it: 'The One does not concern

---

34. Plato, *Phaedrus* 248c–d.
35. Pannenberg, *Systematic Theology* 2, p. 18, referring to *Enneads*, 3. 7. 11, where that seems to be suggested, though the passage is highly obscure.
36. Copleston, *A History of Philosophy* 1, p. 467.
37. J. M. Rist, *Plotinus: The Road to Reality* (Cambridge: Cambridge University Press, 1967), p. 72.

itself directly with the second hypostasis . . .',[38] nor with things below it, which simply flow from it as the result of its being the kind of reality that it is. Whatever the resolution of the difference of interpretation, we undoubtedly have both a contrast and a comparison with the Christian doctrine of creation. Like that, this view is strongly monotheistic, though it cannot be called trinitarian, despite the fact that the world is brought about by a kind of triad – the One, mind and soul – because the three form an ontological hierarchy, and not one God in three equally divine persons. The real contrast is between the flowing forth of the lower from the higher, in which the material order is grudgingly given a small place, and the personal act of creation which affirms the whole of the world, matter and spirit alike. It is between creation as the result of the One's concern with itself, and the triune God's love of that which is not himself.

Is Plotinus then a pantheist? The doctrine of extreme transcendence suggests not, while the logical and necessitarian relations between the One and the many implies it. At the very least, we might say that the concept of emanation raises the question of the way in which God or the divine transcends the world. Any doctrine of creation involves some measure of transcendence of God and the world; that is, some under-standing of a distinction and 'space' between creator and creation. If that were not the case, the world would simply create itself, and while Plotinus' teaching is therefore a kind of theory of creation, it amounts to a rejection of the doctrine as Christianity has understood it. A source and its stream are ontologically continuous, whereas the heartbeat of the doctrine of creation is that God and the world are ontologically distinct. The question to Plotinus is whether his doctrine of emanation leaves sufficient space between the two, and whether those who drew on him in developing Christian theology found an ally or a Trojan horse. Rist suggests that the question of pantheism is irrelevant, but it is clearly not. If the lower world flows from the being of God, it is continuous with him, and so in some sense or other divine. This raises the question of ontology, of the kind of being that the world is, and to this we now turn.

VI ONTOLOGY

The perennial questions about what kind of a world it is, and why, are raised by the interaction between the two very different ancient cultures, aspects of whose literature we have summarised. It will be with us until

38. Rist, *Plotinus*, p. 83.

the end of the book, and we shall treat different dimensions of it in different chapters. In this one is raised the most fundamental question of all: that of pantheism. Is the universe in some way divine, in the sense that it accounts of itself for the way that it is, or is it the creation of an agent who is other than it, and, specifically, personal? Once the Bible has made its impact on human thought it is a recurring and unavoidable question.

That such a distinction between two ontologies is inevitable is shown in the writings of some modern popularisers of science. It is often observed that in recent decades physics has tended to encourage an increasing openness to religious questions, and, indeed, in some writers becomes effectively a religion in itself. It is the biologists, although not only they, who are now carrying the burden of proclaiming science as an alternative to religion, taking up the tasks that once fell to the priests, at least as they sometimes see the matter. Yet as we read some of them it appears to be the case that when the being of the world is no longer attributed to the personal agency of God it is itself made the bearer of divine or creative powers. In other words, something like a pantheism is generated.

The roots of this modern pantheism are not in science itself but are in part to be found in a phenomenon we shall explore later, that western culture never succeeded in throwing off some of the features of Greek pantheism. A number of mediaeval writers, John Scotus Erigena (about 810–77) perhaps important among them, were virtual pantheists, while some late mediaeval mystics, like Jacob Boehme, appear to have been very influential in spawning modern idealism and pantheism.[39] The doctrine of creation was never secure enough in the West to prevent outbreaks of virtual pantheism, so that some commentators have even noticed pantheist logic in the thought of Thomas Aquinas.[40] That is to say, the doctrine of the creator God has always contained seeds of a kind of continuity between God and the world, with the result that a mind divided between Greek and Hebrew remains to this day.

Pantheism emerged into modern thought in the work of Baruch Spinoza (1632–77), whose system was an appropriately mechanised version of the doctrine: the universe is a timeless substance, at once God and the world, every one of whose events is absolutely determined by the state of the whole. More recent is the contribution of the post-Kantian

39. Thomas McFarland, *Coleridge and the Pantheist Tradition* (Oxford: Clarendon Press, 1969).
40. See below, chapter 5, section I.

philosopher Schopenhauer (1788–1860), whose interest in Eastern religions is probably significant. He understood the world as the product of a relentless, impersonal will, determining everything about the state of the whole. This is worth mentioning because it is likely to be at the root of some modern biological determinism, as revealed in the titles, let alone the contents, of books like *The Selfish Gene* and *The Blind Watchmaker*.[41] But the language of personal agency will out, and when it is denied of the creator it tends to be attributed to the creation in general. Thus, ironically, pantheists like Spinoza and Schopenhauer while claiming to be freeing the world of such anthropomorphism are in fact anthropomorphically transferring the language of creative agency to the world itself. What happens is that even while it is being denied, personal agency is by the nature of the language used effectively attributed to non-personal agents.

Thus the words 'nature' and 'evolution' are often hypostatised – and, indeed, capitalised – almost as if they are agents that achieve ends, and thus clearly operate as secularised versions of the doctrine of providence, which they displace. Peter Atkins, a chemist, is a particularly egregious proponent of the personalising not only of nature as a whole, but of parts of it. 'Once molecules have *learned* to *compete* and to *create* other molecules *in their own image*, elephants and things resembling elephants will in due course be found roaming through the countryside.'[42] (Just like that!) More is to come: molecules are 'equipped' (by whom or what?), they 'eat' other molecules, though we are not always sure which eat and which are eaten, they 'keep' less successful molecules 'in herds' and so on, and that is all by the second page of the book.[43] Mary Midgley draws on other parts of the same book to make a similar point. I quote her at length:

> Atkins constantly treats Chaos as a positive force guiding the world in a remarkably full sense, performing many of the roles formerly attributed to God, and seems to regard it as simply a form of Chance . . . [The] extraordinary mixture of strong teleological language with inflationary misuse of the concept of Chaos marks a fairly complete bankruptcy of real explanation.[44]

41. Richard Dawkins, *The Selfish Gene* (Oxford: Oxford University Press, 1989); *The Blind Watchmaker* (London: Penguin Books, 1991).
42. P. W. Atkins, *The Creation* (London and San Francisco: W. H. Freeman , 1981), p. 3. Italics added.
43. Atkins, *The Creation*, p. 5, though only the second page of the main text.
44. Mary Midgley, *Science as Salvation* (London: Routledge, 1992), p. 45.

How easily it happens that where God is no longer understood as the overall creator and upholder of the universe there is a reversion to the pagan attribution of agency to the impersonal worlds of molecules, evolution and chaos. The choice is inescapable: either God or the world itself provides the reason why things are as they are. To 'personalise' the universe or parts of it, particularly inert substances like molecules, is to succumb to crude forms of superstition.[45]

As we shall see, only a theology which distinguishes God from the world ontologically justifies the practices of science without succumbing to a pantheism or crypto-pantheism which effectively divinises the temporal. Once the universe or any of its aspects is divinised, an absurd attribution of 'creation' to that which is only creature eventuates: a strange reversal of the very process by which science freed itself from ancient paganism. Our material therefore imposes on us a clear choice between a biblical and a Hellenic ontology. Either the world creates itself, or it is the product of a personal creator. The choice between the two cannot be made on purely rational grounds because they are rival dogmas, to whose formation centuries of thought have been given, so that neither of them is irrational. Both are finally adopted by their various exponents on the basis of a wide range of considerations. But they are utterly contrary ways of interpreting the world in which we live, despite the attempts that have been made to combine them.

Part of the argument of this book is the cumulative one that attributing the world to a personal creator is more plausible than the various ways ancient and modern cultures have sought effectively to attribute personal agency to the impersonal. Of course, there are difficult objections to that view, none more so than the fact of evil. The mainstream Christian tradition has always held that evil is not part of the original creation, so that it in some sense represents the corruption of the world deriving from a source hostile or disobedient to the creator. As created, the world is good – a belief which is part of the inheritance of science also, at least in so far as Greek philosophies tend to trace evil to the materiality of creation, whose ontologically inferior status disqualifies it from being the object of scientific enquiry. The point for our purposes, however, is the fact that evil remains the chief objection to the Christian doctrine of creation. Yet for all that our confidence has been damaged in the last century or so, it is still a defensible position that the universe remains a place not finally hostile to the good, the true and the beautiful, that is, to the realisation of human moral, scientific and artistic values.

45. See below, chapter 8, note 14.

The sheer absurdity of some of the statements made in the name of science should therefore alert us to their desperate concern to establish the self-createdness of the universe against any suggestions of its creation by the God and Father of our Lord Jesus Christ. And the mention of that name should remind us that Christianity is not only a doctrine of creation. It is a doctrine of a creation whose ultimate perfecting is secured and guaranteed by the life, death, resurrection and ascension of the one who became part of the created order for the sake of its redemption.

3

TOWARDS A THEOLOGY OF
MEDIATION:
ASPECTS OF THE EARLY HISTORY

—◅◦◦◦◦◦◦◦◦◦◦▷—

I THE THEOLOGY OF CREATION

The move at the end of Chapter 2 from Greek philosophy into the world of modern science shows something of the modern equivalent of the ancient interaction of the Bible with Greek philosophical culture. Both ancient and modern worlds demonstrate that the theology of creation will always take shape in some relation with the culture of the day. In the previous section, we have noted something of the negative relations between the two worlds. But there is a positive side, too, that is of great importance, so that we should not understand the debate as a merely polemical one: that is to say, as narrowly a matter of a biblical against an alien world view of some kind. It is that in part, because Greek thought made, and some modern thought makes, assumptions which simply render an adequate doctrine of creation impossible. But it is also the case that there could be no doctrine of creation without the setting in which it was hammered out. Theology goes beyond the writings of the Bible, in seeking to say something of what is true of God and the world as a whole on the basis of the biblical teachings. It is to that extent an abstractive discipline,[1] abstracting the truth from its various

---

1. And only to that extent, for the discipline is also highly concrete in being concerned

expressions in the biblical witness to God the Father and his Christ; and in order to abstract in this way, a conceptual apparatus is needed. Those concepts are often provided by the world of philosophy in which theology takes shape. One example is 'nature', a Greek way of speaking about the way things are, that had to be both adopted and adapted if Christians were to speak Christianly about that same world.

It is further the case that because theology is often a response, on the one hand, to questions asked by the unbelieving, or half-believing, world, and, on the other, to crises of faith and practice within the believing community, it necessarily approaches general questions of truth and meaning that are different from those of the biblical writers, though they are often in continuity with them. Very relevant here, especially in view of the sillinesses or worse perpetrated in the name of the text of Genesis, is the fact that in Christian theology, as distinct from any religion which identifies the text with the words of God – as appears to be the case with some forms of Islam – there has nearly always been a recognition of a space between the Bible and itself. Theology has always involved more than simply a repetition of biblical expressions and teaching. But the space between the two is not an empty space which offers complete freedom of speculation. The relation between Bible and theology is an intrinsic one, without which a theology ceases to be Christian. There is, rather, a relative freedom, in which theological thought seeks, in obedience to the gospel, to find those words best suited to express the limited truth that is granted of the ways of God toward and in the world.

In this and the next chapter we shall examine some of the writings of those who have exercised that limited freedom in different ways, and so allowed the questions to be asked, and a theology of creation begun. They are all operating on land previously occupied by others, and particularly Greek philosophers, from whom they gradually, but never completely, disengage themselves. Out of that interaction there come both advances and what, with the benefit of hindsight, sometimes appear to us to be mistakes – mistakes which are serious because they have both distorted the doctrine and sometimes made theology's life in the world, particularly, in recent centuries, the world of modern science, more difficult than it might have been. In their different ways, these early theologians articulate something of what the doctrine of creation

---

with abstraction in order to provide a structuring for life in the world. The doctrine of creation has cosmological implications, but it is not cosmology in the sense of a theory about the nature of the universe.

is, indicate different aspects of the conversation between Bible and culture, and bring to our notice aspects of the theology of creation which are of perennial importance.

Just as in Chapter 2 the historical material was used both to show how things came in the West to be the way they did and to focus the question of pantheism, so in this we shall use the work of some early theologians of creation to bring into focus a number of questions which centre on what I shall call mediation. They are all closely related to one another, and are as follows. First is what can be called the hermeneutical question. How are we to understand and interpret the texts of scripture that bear upon the doctrine of creation? There has already been a summary presentation of some of the main texts, but in this chapter we shall examine something of the way in which ancient interpretation of these texts, and particularly of Genesis, has affected the theology of creation. Second is the epistemological question. How do we know about the doctrine, and, in particular, how are the contributions from Bible and philosophy – and, in the modern world, science also – to be related?

Third is the question of the relation of creation and other divine acts in and towards the world, and particularly to redemption or salvation. As is clear from the summaries that New Testament writers give of the Christian faith, the gospel is primarily a vehicle of human salvation. Paul summarises it in 1 Corinthians 15:3b–4, 'that Christ died for our sins according to the scriptures, that he was buried, that he was raised on the third day in accordance with the scriptures . . .'. But the gospel is secondarily and *consequently* many other things also. The allusion to the resurrection makes some reference to creation inescapable, so that the Christian scheme is more than simply an account of salvation, as it is also if we take into account features of the gospel accounts of Jesus' ministry. Redemption takes place in, and is directed towards, the inhabitants of the created order in such a way that their relations with that order are necessarily affected.[2] Fourth is a question we have met already, the ontological question. The theology of creation is, as we have seen and will increasingly see, not only one of beginnings, but of the kind of world that ours is if it is the object of God's providential and redeeming care in the present. In this context, I shall call this the cosmological question. All of these questions will be with us until the end of the book, but engagement with some early theologians will enable a first encounter with them.

2. I have sought to give an account of this in *Christ and Creation. The 1990 Didsbury Lectures* (Carlisle: Paternoster Press and Grand Rapids: Eerdmans, 1992).

II HERMENEUTICS: THE FATE OF GENESIS IN THE HELLENISTIC WORLD

The interpretation of scripture is a theological matter, in that the texts concerning creation represent it as the outcome of divine action. But whenever God's action in and toward the world is under review there are complications, above all because scripture has a disarmingly personal way of representing that action. To the philosophically trained mind that reeks of anthropomorphism, or the attributing to God of human forms of action not appropriate to deity. Despite its immense sophistication, Genesis therefore often appears naive and incredible to both detractor and exponent. That this is not simply a modern problem is clear from the fact that from the first century, in the work of the Jewish commentator Philo of Alexandria, there grew up a tradition of what is known as allegorical exegesis. Philo is of great interest as an early example of the interaction of Greek philosophy and biblical interpretation. It would probably be wrong to see him as setting out deliberately to combine the two; but, being a Jew of Alexandria who took the philosophical world seriously, combine them is what he did. That is to say, he saw the first chapters of Genesis through the eyes of a platonist, so that it seems to the later reader that he combined two rather diverse, if not indeed contrary, worlds.

Despite this, the first thing to say about Philo is that he had a strong belief in the inspiration of the Scriptures. As we have seen, Greek philosophy without exception held that the universe in some form was eternal; only in the *Timaeus* do we read a philosopher coming to terms with something like a beginning of things, and even there the talk is of the creation of this world, and not of the universe. In his *On the Creation*,[3] Philo rejects any suggestion that the world is eternal. 'There are some people who, having the world in admiration rather than the Maker of the world, pronounce it to be without beginning and everlasting . . .' (1. 7). He gives two reasons for this, one of which is worth mentioning here. Creation by God, he says, means 'origination' (*genesis*, 2. 12). 'In the beginning' means that God is the creator of time, 'which began either simultaneously with the world, or after it' (17. 26). This is very important in distinguishing a biblical view which attributes the creation of the world to divine action from a mythological or philosophical account which seeks to answer questions about how things come to take the shape that they do.

3. Philo, *On the Creation*, translation in F. H. Colson and G. H. Whitaker editors (Loeb Classical Library, London: Heinemann, 1929), volume 1.

Alongside his strong belief in inspiration, however, Philo also exhibits great freedom in interpreting scripture, and, in facing what have remained major problems of interpretation, became one of the fathers of allegorical exegesis. There are many ways of defining allegory. Allegory means 'other speech', and in that respect is a way of describing all attempts to make sense of a text by explaining it in words from without. It need not involve the imposition of alien meanings, though that is the way it is sometimes taken, and what has often happened. We might say that there is proper and improper allegory, the former being that which brings out the meaning of the text, the latter that which falsifies it in some way. To be sure, the distinction is not an absolute one, so that deciding which attempts at interpretation belong in which category is by no means easy. One example will suffice. It is reasonable to take it that by speaking of creation over six days either the writer of Genesis or we, his modern readers, cannot be taken to understand six literal days of the kind we experience. But what 'other reading' is ruled out? At one extreme, there are good grounds for excluding one which takes them to refer to stages in the spiritual life, as Augustine did. But could we rightly take them, in the light of modern theories, to be stages of evolution? Probably that, too, is imposing alien categories, rather than saying the same thing in other words. The fact remains, however, that there is no easy way to distinguish between legitimate and illegitimate interpretations.

Is it of the essence of allegorical exegesis to know more than the text itself – a form of eisegesis? Or is allegory perhaps that which necessarily emerges in the attempt to initiate a conversation between Bible and contemporary interests – in our age often scientific ones – and so to find a 'spiritual' interpretation that enables us to mediate the text in the culture of the day? In this case, much depends upon what is meant by 'spiritual'. If the notion is in some way controlled by a reference to God the Spirit, among whose functions is to relate us to Jesus of Nazareth, the Son of God made flesh for us, there is little objection. But 'spiritualising' is quite another matter, and this appears to have happened in much of the interpretation of Genesis that called itself and is called allegorical. Here spiritualising means the opposite, an evasion of the material meaning of the text, and we shall use allegory here in a pejorative sense to refer mainly to its evasion of the text's reference to anything concrete and temporal. It is that which above all indicates the chief weakness of the ancient allegorical interpretation of Genesis, beginning with that of Philo of Alexandria.

Philo makes a good and interesting start in saying that in view of the fact that the days cannot be literal days their function in the narrative is to show that 'for the things coming into existence there was need of order' (3. 13).[4] The difficulties begin when this free interpretation is combined with certain platonist assumptions which override essential aspects of the text, particularly its celebration of the goodness of the whole of the created order, material and 'spiritual' alike. When we examine Philo's interpretation of scripture in this light, we meet our first problematic interpretation of Genesis 1:1. Where the latter says that God created heaven and earth Philo understands it to refer to a two stage creation, with God creating first the intelligible world of forms (the heavenly or intelligible world) and then the material or sensible world. 'In the beginning' according to this scheme means not only origination but origination of a particular kind, entailing the ontological precedence of the incorporeal heaven over the corporeal earth. 'When He willed to create this visible world He first fully formed the intelligible world, in order that He might have the use of a pattern, wholly God-like and incorporeal' (4. 16). First, then, an ideal world is created, and only 'afterwards' – for God does everything instantaneously – the material world in its image. In sum, although he affirms, as we have seen, that 'in the beginning' involves the denial of any teaching that the world is 'without beginning and everlasting' (2. 7), Philo falls short of affirming what Christian theology was later to call creation out of nothing. 'Philo already knows . . . that God eternally creates the spiritual world, while the visible cosmos has a specific beginning.'[5] That is to say, already something is being said which appears to contradict the meaning of the text. However, if it is platonism, this is platonism modified under biblical influence: though they are in a manner eternal, the ideas are created. Further, Philo does not show the same tendency as the platonists to belittle the material world. As a faithful Jewish thinker, he believed that everything is created good by God and it is in the service of such an account of the text that his interpretation is devised.

There is one other place in particular where Philo misinterprets the text under platonic influence, and where he also bequeaths a legacy of incalculable effect. When he comes to interpret Genesis 1:26–7, on the image of God, he cannot find any place for the human body in the scheme. 'Let no one represent the likeness as one to a bodily form for neither is God in human form, nor is the human body God-like. No, it is in respect of the mind, the sovereign element of the soul, that the word "image" is used . . .' (23. 69).[6] This has proved an interpretation with

---

4. Compare what Basil said some time later, p. 71 below.
5. Gerhard May, *Creatio ex Nihilo. The Doctrine of 'Creation out of Nothing' in Early Christian Thought*, translated by A. S. Worrall (Edinburgh: T. & T. Clark, 1994), pp. 19–20.

a tenacious hold on the human mind. While many later theologians have attempted to maintain a place for the human body as in some way intrinsic to the conception of the image of God, what can be called platonic drag has always exercised its power. It is with us today in the widely shared view that if a computer were to be able to think, it would be a person. But is 'thought' alone that which makes us personal? What of love, let alone making music and gardening, two activities which involve us in the material world?

The matter of our humanity will return, but we must now summarise Philo's platonising interpretation of Genesis as effectively positing a hierarchy of createdness, with the lower preceded by the higher. In effect what emerged was a doctrine that while the material world was in every respect temporal, the heavenly world represented a kind of eternal creation. This undoubtedly represented a modification of Plato's views, and one which the philosopher would not have accepted, for he had held to the absolute eternity of the forms: they could not be created, because they existed timelessly, like the truths of mathematics. The forms were for Plato external to and ontologically co-eternal with the demiurge. By being transformed by Philo into part of the created order, they are reduced in status, and are brought from outside God into the divine mind, so that Philo can say that 'the universe that consisted of ideas' (literally, 'the cosmos of the ideas') 'would have no other location than the Divine Reason' (5. 20). But the transfer results in a compromise and an ambiguity which was to dog the tradition at least until the Reformation. Though the forms are created, they are eternally created, and consequently to a degree share divine status as part of the heavenly world, so that they maintain their superiority to matter. Thus matter is implicitly, if not explicitly, demoted to a lower order of being. All may be 'very good', but some things are more so than others, the outcome being that a dualism is built into the doctrine of creation. The spiritual or rational world is created, but created as eternal; while the material world is created with a temporal beginning, and therefore at a lower station on the great chain of being.

III GNOSTICISM

An extreme form of the dualism of mind and matter which we find in modified form in Philo is to be found in what is known as Gnosticism.

---

6. Contrast the observation made by Francis Watson, p. 200 below. It seems that for platonism, the forms are godlike, but the human person as a whole is not.

Gnosticism is more a collection of religions, some of them considering themselves forms of Christianity, than a consistent philosophy. Both their mythical theories of being and their allegedly libertarian morals stand in immense contrast to the austere thought and ethics of Plotinus, who opposed Gnosticism, at least in its 'Christian' form.[7] And yet there is a respect in which there are overlaps, and in this range of beliefs we do find an extreme form of some of the dualistic doctrines which mark the whole platonist tradition. As its name suggests, Gnosticism is a system of salvation by knowledge. The key to life is initiation into the teaching of who we are, whence we come and whither we are going. In the respects in which we are interested in it, it is a negation of the Christian doctrine of creation, because it holds that our destiny, if we are among the enlightened, is to be taken out of this inferior material world to which we do not truly belong. At the heart is a negative view of the material world, which led to a belief that Christ was not really human, but was only dressed in a seeming body. The high god could not demean himself by involvement in anything so messy as matter.

There are four features of Gnosticism's various understandings of creation which concern us. First is its view of the origin of the created world, which was attributed to a lower deity than the God of Jesus Christ. The God of the Old Testament was at best an inferior deity whose work had to be corrected by the God made known in the immaterial Christ. As Filoramo puts it, 'Jahweh, far from being the single Lord of creation, is its simple artificer, uncouth and ignorant.'[8] Second, and consequent on the first, was its view of the mediation of creation. Because the material creation was not the achievement of the highest god, it was understood as mediated by lower beings arranged in a hierarchy of some kind. Irenaeus' no doubt selective account of the views of some of his opponents presents a range of weird speculations which share this feature, that the mediation of what can scarcely be called the creation was understood as taking place through a range of agencies intermediate between the divine and the material.[9] This is being stressed here because of its contrast with Irenaeus' own view of mediation, which is also at the centre of his thought.

7.   J. M Rist, *Plotinus: The Road to Reality* (Cambridge: Cambridge University Press, 1967), p. 14.
8.   Giovanni Filoramo, *A History of Gnosticism*, translated by Anthony Alcock (Oxford: Blackwell, 1990), p. 78.
9.   Recent studies have shown that the more sober of the teachers generated sophisticated accounts of creation, at times coming very close to what was later to be called 'creation out of nothing'. See May, *Creatio ex Nihilo*, chapter 3.

Third, there is in Gnosticism an absolute dualism of creation and salvation. If the higher deity is concerned with spirit and not matter; if Christ is spirit but not truly bodily; if the creator god of the Old Testament and the saviour God of the New are other than one another, creation and salvation are so antithetical that creation can only be out of the material world, not in and with it. This is of particular importance for our age which is much occupied, by reason of its worries about the environment, with an ethic of the material. But the issue is wider than that, for it concerns the human estimate and use of the body also. It is significant that Irenaeus observes that the Gnostics derived two contradictory ethics from their dualistic theology. If the body is unimportant, one can draw either an ascetic conclusion – that the body must be suppressed in the interest of the 'spiritual' – or a recommendation of license, because if the body is not truly a part of the human constitution, what we do with and in it is irrelevant.[10] Both moralities derive from the same underestimation of the goodness of the creation.

Fourth, and in some ways most central of all for a doctrine of creation, is the question of evil. Christian doctrine, by stating unequivocally that the universe was created good, indeed very good, appears to make, at best, a rod for its own back, because it seems to contradict the manifest experience that there is immense evil in the world. As a system of salvation, Gnosticism had an answer to that. There is evil because the world contains matter, and therefore the source of evil is to be found in the created world simply as created. 'The world came about by a mistake. For he who created it wanted to create it imperishable and immortal. He fell short of attaining his desire.'[11] It is here that we see the gulf between Gnosticism and Plotinus, even though they share some assumptions. Both believe that the source of evil is to be found in matter, yet Plotinus rejects the Gnostic view of the unutterable evil and ugliness of the world as we experience it. Because the world flows from the One, and not from the clumsy efforts of a lower divinity, it is, as a whole, to be affirmed as beautiful and good. 'No one should reproach this world as if it were not beautiful or the most perfect of corporeal beings.'[12]

In sum, Gnosticism was – and, indeed, remains – a Christian heresy which fed upon Greek philosophical suspicions of the goodness and reality of the material world. Like many heresies, however, it provided

---

10. Irenaeus, *Against the Heresies*, 1. 28. 1–2.
11. *Nag Hammadi Corpus*, 2. 3. 75. 3ff, cited by Filoramo, *History of Gnosticism*, p. 54.
12. Plotinus, *Enneads*, 3. 2. 3, cited by Filoramo, *History of Gnosticism*, p. 55.

the spur to efforts to counter it, and in the process gave the church one of its greatest theological achievements. For Irenaeus' doctrine of creation was forged in opposition to each of the features I have outlined. We shall treat that after we have first reviewed something of the thought of his greatest predecessor.

IV EPISTEMOLOGY AND COSMOLOGY: JUSTIN MARTYR

The relation between biblical faith and Greek philosophy is focused in slightly different ways in the thought of Justin Martyr (died c. 165 AD), who enables us to move from the hermeneutic and cosmological questions we have met to a closer engagement with the epistemological and cosmological.[13] Justin and the other Apologists received their title from the fact that they were early defenders of the faith, especially in the face of philosophical objections. Justin was a convert from platonism, which continued to mark his thought. Indeed, it is sometimes suggested that his thought continues to be dominated by platonist categories. This is undoubtedly the case in one aspect of his teaching on creation, for, in contrast to those who were to teach that God created the world out of nothing, Justin was ambiguous; as Gerhard May says, 'in platonising phraseology Justin can . . . say "God in his goodness created everything from formless matter".'[14] But in other respects Justin modifies and even overcomes the standard platonism of that expression. In particular, he never attributes the origin of evil to matter, nor holds that God needs the mediation of the Logos in creating because he is unable to come into contact with matter.[15] 'Justin understands the process of creation itself as the shaping of a pre-existent unordered material. But after that the Platonist model no longer has any importance for him.'[16]

There is, however, more to be said for Justin's contribution than this. If we bear in mind that there are two central questions to be asked in this connection, that concerning the origin of the world and that concerning the source of our knowledge of the creator, we shall find that in the latter at least Justin has made a major contribution. Evidence for

13. See Richard Norris, *God and World in Early Christian Theology. A Study in Justin Martyr, Irenaeus, Tertullian and Origen* (London: A. & C. Black, 1966).
14. May, *Creatio ex Nihilo*, p. 122, citing Justin, *Apology* 1. 10. 2. Athenagoras also held that creation involved the shaping of unoriginate matter, May, p. 139, citing *A Plea for the Christians*, 22. 2.
15. May, *Creatio ex Nihilo*, pp. 125–6
16. May, *Creatio ex Nihilo*, p. 132.

this is to be found in the opening sections of the *Dialogue with Trypho*, in which Justin's encounter with a Jewish believer shows the former's commitment to a biblical understanding of the creation. He contrasts his earlier platonism with his later biblical faith. In the former, 'the perception of immaterial things quite overpowered me, and the contemplation of ideals furnished my mind with wings . . . and such was my stupidity, I expected forthwith to look upon God . . .'.[17] The old man who was responsible for Justin's conversion to Christianity posed for him a question that reveals the marrow of the dispute between the Bible and the Greeks. Is there between the mind and God the kind of continuity which platonism presupposes? 'Is there then . . . such and so great power in our mind? . . . Will the mind of man see God at any time, if it is uninstructed by the Holy Spirit? . . . What affinity . . . is there between us and God?'[18] Thus it comes about, argues Francis Watson, that 'philosophically-articulate Judaism confronts Platonism with a radical doctrine of creation and a critique of the myth of the uncreated and godlike soul.'[19]

Because, that is to say, Justin realises that the origin of his doctrine of creation is not that of his autonomous mind but has to come to him from without, his view of the relation between God and the world is beginning to be modified. Platonism tends to hold that the mind is continuous in some respect with the divine, while the bodily and material is at best irrelevant. That is the continuity between the contents of the previous section and this one. While for platonism the forms, with which our souls were acquainted before we were imprisoned in our material bodies, are the mediators of our knowledge of God, Christian theology, lacking such a view of the divinity of the mind, must be taught by the Holy Spirit. Although Justin does not yet draw against his philosophical master the conclusion that God is the creator of both matter and mind; and although he remains in the platonic world in which both are pre-existent, and shaped by God, yet the leaven of biblical teaching is beginning to permeate. The importance of Justin Martyr for our purposes, therefore, is that he enables us to see something of the development of the tradition in mid-course. Theology does not spring ready made from the mind, the text, or the Christian community, but takes shape as questions from within and without are raised, and as answers given in one generation are seen by another to require supplementation

---

17. Justin, *Dialogue with Trypho*, 2.
18. Justin, *Dialogue with Trypho*, 4.
19. Francis Watson, *Text and Truth. Redefining Biblical Theology* (Edinburgh: T. & T. Clark, 1997), p. 312.

and correction. The realisation of the requirement of a new epistemology eventuates – though not yet – in a new ontology. And so we reach naturally the one who owed much to Justin but was also driven by the needs of his situation in the church to develop the first thoroughgoing and expansive Christian doctrine of creation.

V TRINITARIAN MEDIATION:
IRENAEUS OF LYONS

In Irenaeus (died c. AD 202) we meet a theologian who understands that the Christian conception of salvation is inextricable from a proper theology of creation. He was enabled to make his great contribution, perhaps the greatest of all, to the doctrine of creation because of the crisis that met him in the form of those heresies grouped under the name of Gnosticism. As we have seen, Gnostics saw salvation in terms of the imparting of knowledge, and knowledge of such a kind as to require a radical distinction between the material and spiritual worlds. In contrast, Irenaeus saw it as the outcome of incarnation and its fruit in a life in community centred on the bread and wine of the Lord's Supper, a life which as a consequence embraced the importance of life in the body.

Out of Irenaeus' preoccupations there developed two motifs which set the tone for later developments. The first is his strong affirmation of the goodness of everything created by God, matter included. The Gnostics had in various ways denied the goodness of the material world. Although Irenaeus does not assert what we shall later describe as the ontological homogeneity[20] of the creation, he writes in opposition to platonist tendencies to teach that there are two entirely different kinds of reality, the spiritual or intellectual and the sensible or material. 'He (God) conferred on spiritual things a spiritual and invisible nature, on supercelestial things a supercelestial, on angels an angelical, on animals an animal . . . on all, in short, a nature suitable to the character of the life assigned them . . .'.[21] The basis of Irenaeus' affirmative attitude to the whole created order is christological. If God in his Son takes to himself the reality of human flesh, then nothing created, and certainly nothing material, can be downgraded to unreality, semi-reality or treated as fundamentally evil, as in the Manichaean version of Gnosticism.

20. That is the doctrine, not as tautologous as it appears, that all created things share the common characteristic of being – created.
21. Irenaeus, *Against the Heresies*, 2. 2. 4, compare 1 Cor. 15:39–41.

The second motif to be discerned in Irenaeus' theology of creation is his affirmation that God creates out of nothing. He was not the first to teach this doctrine, for as Gerhard May has argued, he was anticipated by Theophilus of Antioch,[22] and possibly by others; but our interest here is in the thoroughgoing use he made of the conception. Although there might be said to be some ambiguity in the preceding sections, in Book 2 of *Against the Heresies* he is explicit. 'While men, indeed, cannot make anything out of nothing, but only out of matter already existing, yet God is in this point pre-eminently superior to men, that He Himself called into being the substance of his creation, when previously it had no existence' (2. 10. 4). He is quite clear what he means by this, and the reason for it. He means that there can be nothing which exists prior to God's free act of creation, because, if there were, that would impose constraints upon God, and so conflict with his freedom and omnipotence (2. 5. 4). Yet Irenaeus' conception of omnipotence is not the kind of abstract teaching that appeals to the fact that God, being God, can do anything. The doctrine of omnipotence is a new arrival on the scene of history, at least so far as Irenaeus' cultural context is concerned. Greek gods were not omnipotent, but subservient to fate, chance and necessity. Irenaeus' God is known to be omnipotent for Christian reasons: by virtue of what happened in the incarnation, life, death and resurrection of Jesus. 'For this is a peculiarity of the pre-eminence of God, not to stand in need of other instruments for the creation of those things which are summoned into existence. His own Word is both suitable and sufficient for the formation of all things . . .' (2. 2. 4). Christology underlies this feature because Irenaeus' conception of God's sovereignty derives from his consideration of the implications of God's free relations with what he has made in Christ, particularly as that is demonstrated in the incarnation and resurrection.

We shall see more and more clearly as we trace episodes in the history of the doctrine of creation that the place given, or not given, to the Trinity is determinative of the character of any doctrine of creation. There can and have been doctrines of creation in the Christian tradition which have been scarcely trinitarian in their shaping, with the result that their articulation contains elements which tend to undermine essential components of the teaching. For Irenaeus, two aspects are decisive. The

---

22. Theophilus of Antioch, *To Autolycus* 1.4 appears to imply it: God is 'before the universe . . . creator (ktistes) maker of the universe . . .'. Compare 1. 8 and 2. 4, the latter of which is perhaps the most important argument: 'For if God is uncreated and matter is uncreated, then . . . God is not the maker of the universe.' The creation of matter is crucial.

first is that his trinitarian matrix enables him to develop a theology of mediation, always the heart of the matter. As is well known, Irenaeus frequently says that God creates by means of his two hands, the Son and the Spirit. This enables him to give a clear account of how God relates to that which is not God: of how the creator interacts with his creation. The second aspect reveals the other side of this same reality, the freedom of God in relation to the created universe. Because God creates by means of his own Son and Spirit, he is unlike the deities of the Gnostics and the One of neoplatonism in that he does not require beings inter-mediate between himself and the world in order to achieve his ends. That is, because the Son and the Spirit are God, to create by means of his two hands means that God is himself creating. This is accordingly a theology of mediation which breaks through Hellenic doctrines of degrees of being. There do not, on this account, need to be intermediate beings between God and the world, because the Son and the Spirit mediate between the divine and the created.

It is at this place that there emerges into history the classic Christian ontology: that there are no degrees of being but two realities, God and everything else that he has made, the created order. The creation is indeed real, because God makes it so; but it is so only in relation to the God who continues to uphold it by his 'two hands'. Thus is Irenaeus able to hold together both God's freedom in creation and an affirmation of the goodness of all that has been made. The following passage brings together these themes:

> It was not angels . . . who made us, nor who formed us . . . nor any one else, except the Word of the Lord, nor any power remotely dis-tant from the Father of all things. For God did not stand in need of these [beings] . . . as if He did not possess His own hands. For with Him were always present the Word and Wisdom, the Son and the Spirit, by whom and in whom, freely and spontaneously, He made all things . . . (4. 20. 1)

It is accordingly his trinitarianism which gives Irenaeus the confidence and the reason to affirm the doctrine of creation out of nothing. The economy of creation and salvation as it takes its centre in Jesus Christ's redemptive recapitulation of the human story demonstrates God's total sovereignty in and over against all the created order.

The argument that any reality co-eternal with God would undermine his sovereignty in creating continues to be of great importance in sub-sequent discussion of the doctrine of creation. It dominates Tertullian's *Against Hermogenes*, which is a sustained assault on the position that God creates out of matter which is both co-eternal with him and in some sense intrinsically evil. Similarly, the appeal to divine omnipotence which is implicit in the argument is very important for Augustine also, as we shall see. But in the later writers it tends to be deployed outside the trinitarian matrix which is so important for Irenaeus. This has one important and for the most part damaging effect. It tends to concentrate on creation as an act of will or power – as it indeed is for Irenaeus – but at the expense of conceiving it as an act in which God creates that which he loves and wishes to love for its own sake. The difference can best be seen in a contrast of the eschatologies of Tertullian and Irenaeus. For Tertullian, the fate of the creation is eventually to come to nothing: that which comes from nothing will eventually return there.[23] For Irenaeus, that which comes from nothing is destined to become *something*, and it is perhaps the notion of creation as that which is directed to an eschatological perfection which is one of the most neglected features of Irenaeus' thought.

Eschatology is important because it enables us to engage with what is both a crux of interpretation of the thought of Irenaeus and a major problem in the doctrine of creation. Irenaeus has been accused of inconsistency in his doctrine of creation in teaching both that creation is perfect and that it is imperfect:

> In his protracted rebuttal of gnostic sects, Irenaeus repeatedly emphasises the unqualified goodness of the creation. But in iv, 38 he springs upon the reader the surprising contention that Adam, as first created by God, was imperfect.[24]

Although, however, Irenaeus may appear sometimes to say that Adam was created perfect, sometimes not, there is a contradiction only on a rather static understanding of perfection. As we shall see when we come to treat the meaning of creation 'in the beginning', the doctrine of creation out of nothing does imply that creation is in one sense indeed complete. But it does not follow that it is perfect in the sense that it does not have to be perfected. The creation is, we might say, perfect in that it is destined for perfection. That is, it is relatively perfect: created for an eschatological perfecting. It is the eschatological destiny of the finite creation that makes a fall possible; in that sense, the creation is imperfect. As Douglas Farrow has argued, with particular reference to the passage

---

23. Tertullian, *Against Hermogenes*, 34.
24. Robert E. Brown, 'On the Necessary Imperfection of Creation', *Scottish Journal of Theology* 28 (1975), 17–25 (18).

on the basis of which Irenaeus is accused of contradiction, this theologian does apparently teach the imperfection of creation; but it is an imperfection which:

> makes the fall possible, not inevitable. The 'imperfection' is this: The love for God which is the life of man cannot emerge *ex nihilo* in full bloom; it requires to grow with experience. But that in turn is what makes the fall, however unsurprising, such a devastating affair. In the fall man is 'turned backwards'. He does not grow up in the love of God as he is intended to. The course of his time, his so-called progress, is set in the wrong direction.[25]

For Irenaeus, 'good' *means* precisely that which is destined for perfection.

On such an eschatological understanding, the relation of creation and redemption according to Irenaeus is clear in its basic outline, though complex in its outworking, because we are here concerned with the relation of time and eternity. Redemption or salvation is that divine action which returns the creation to its proper direction, its orientation to its eschatological destiny, which is to be perfected in due course of time by God's enabling it to be that which it was created to be. By virtue of their trinitarian mediation, both creation and its restoration in redemption are acts of the one God in and towards the whole created order. In turn, that means that Irenaeus must not be thought to operate with a naively linear conception of time. As Dr Farrow has shown, for Irenaeus the world is to be understood as process, but it is not - as in the contemporary process theologians - linear process.

> [I]t is one of Irenaeus' great strengths to have incorporated process as a positive . . . feature of his world-view. But the process in question is not a straightforward, linear one. Rather it involves a fraction, a breaking up. Worldly reality in all its aspects, the material and the immaterial, enters into a situation of fructification and endless bounty precisely by way of participation in the descent and ascent of Jesus.[26]

We shall return to the matter of how we are to understand the temporal world in the light of God's eternity below, but now, concentrating on the relation of creation and redemption, we move to something of a contrast.

---

25. Douglas Farrow, 'St Irenaeus of Lyons. The Church and the World', *Pro Ecclesia* 4 (1995), pp. 333–55 (348).
26. Farrow, 'St Irenaeus of Lyons', pp. 349–50.

VI CREATION, REDEMPTION AND COSMOLOGY: ORIGEN OF ALEXANDRIA

Origen of Alexandria (c. AD 185–254) belongs not only in the next generation after Irenaeus, but takes a decisively different direction. One can take different attitudes to his achievement. Either it is a step in advance of Irenaeus by virtue of his greater philosophical sophistication, or a step backwards because of a failure to preserve elements essential to the doctrine. The latter is the view to be taken in the following account, although it must be remembered that other commentators will take the former view. At the outset, however, Origen's firm adherence to the apostolic tradition must be documented. 'God is one, who created and set in order all things, and who, when nothing existed, caused the universe to be' (*On First Principles*, 1, Preface, 4).[27] As always in this context, what is interesting is what a theologian makes of the common tradition, especially at this time when the classical tradition was still only beginning to be formed.

Origen's distinction from Irenaeus is several fold. First, he takes a more sympathetic view of some of the Gnostic objections to Christian belief, and particularly their charge that the inequality of the distribution of good and bad fortune in this world presents a *prima facie* objection to Christian teaching of the goodness of the creation (2. 9. 5). One of theology's tasks, he holds, is to show that God cannot rightly be accused of injustice (3. 5. 4). Second, he has a far more positive attitude to the Greek philosophical tradition, and particularly to the religious versions of platonism that developed during the early centuries of the Christian era. He is in line of descent as much from his fellow Alexandrian, Philo, as from Irenaeus. Third, his doctrine of God is decisively different, in a way that has a considerable impact upon his doctrine of creation.

We shall approach Origen's theology of creation through the latter, crucial, topic. Origen's God is rather like a primary school teacher concerned with the limits of the size of class he can control, and this leads our theologian into a two-stage doctrine of creation, similar to but also different from that of Philo:

> In the beginning . . . God created by an act of his will as large a number of intelligent beings as he could control . . . He made . . . just as many as he could grasp and keep in hand and subject to his providence. (2. 9. 1)

27. Origen, *On First Principles*, edited by G. W. Butterworth (London: SPCK, 1936).

The first stage is the creation of a world of spirits, the *logika*, who apparently have a similar ontological status to that of the platonic forms in Philo. Although the details of this development are disputable, by virtue of both the insecurity of the text of Origen's work and the speculative character of his teaching, he appears to hold that the spirits are eternal, though not as eternal as God. They are eternal *as created*, and, because of God's need to exercise providential control, their number is finite. Whatever be the truth of that interpretation, Origen clearly holds, first, that everything other than God is created: 'By the world we now mean all that is above the heavens, or in them, or on the earth, or in what are called the lower regions, or any places that exist anywhere; together with the beings who are said to dwell in them'; but also, second, that there is a clear ontological hierarchy, like that in Neoplatonism, according to which some beings are higher, and so more real, than others (2. 9. 3). Certainly, Origen states that creative activity is necessary to God, and it would appear to follow that the *logika* are the eternal objects of this eternal creating activity. The teaching of the following passage was decisively rejected by later generations of Christian theologians:

> It is absurd and impious to suppose that these powers of God have been at any time in abeyance for a single moment. Indeed, it is unlawful even to entertain the least suspicion that these powers, through which we chiefly gain a worthy notion of God, should at any time have ceased performing works worthy of themselves and have become inactive . . . Whence it follows that there always existed objects for this well-doing, namely, God's works or creatures . . . It follows from this, that at no time whatever was God not Creator, nor Benefactor, nor Providence. (1. 4. 3)

Whether or not it can be decided that it is the *logika* who are the eternal objects of God's providential care, we do know something of what they were according to Origen. Because of their spiritual nature, these beings were essentially good, and their defining characteristic, what made them what they really were, was their freedom. There lies the root of Origen's doctrine of the creation of the material world. These spirits, called to live in eternal contemplation of God, fell away from him, and misused their freedom, so that they could be restored to unity with the divine only through the redirection of that freedom (2. 9. 6; 2. 6. 3). Origen, in the long line of those who have misused Genesis 1–3 for theological purposes, understands the first book of the Bible to be speaking not of an historical fall, but of one taking place before the time of the world we know. While it is difficult always to be clear about precisely what he means, he appears to take the whole of Genesis 1 and 2, or much of it, to refer to the first stage of creation, the making of the ideal world. According to him, Genesis 1:26 refers to the creation of pre-existent intelligences, and 'male and female' refers not to sexual differentiation but to the pre-existent Christ and his bride, the church.[28] Indeed, Genesis 2 is also understood to be concerned not with the first man and woman but with pre-existent spirits possessing 'ethereal' rather than material bodies.

Even the fall is pre-historical in Origen's account, for in attempting to defend the faith of the church against Gnostic charges about the unfairness of the distribution of human lots on this earth, he traces inequalities of fortune back to a pre-existent fall in which the spiritual beings lapsed from their contemplation of God.[29] To understand further the platonic pedigree of this reading of Genesis, it must be realised that the fall of the spirits is a descent into plurality and materiality. It also accounts for the creation of the material world, which is created by God the Father in order to bring back order to that which has collapsed into disunity and diversity. Our world is created out of nothing, but for a purpose, and its function is educational or pedagogic: for the training of the fallen spirits in virtue so that they are qualified to return to unity with the One.[30]

Origen was later condemned for teaching the eventual salvation of all things, but that is not the chief problem with his theology, which is that his eschatology, in contrast with that of Irenaeus, is one of return.[31] The material world is not created with an eschatological destiny, but to be made redundant as the spirits finally achieve re-integration with their original divine unity. Even the skins with which Adam and Eve clothe themselves are brought into the allegorical picture. They represent the earthly bodies which the human race must wear until it finally makes its way back to God, which for Origen means an ascension from materiality and plurality into the pure spiritual unity which is union with God. As Trigg has said, it is 'an eschatology more consistent with Platonism than

---

28. Henri Crouzel, *Origen*, translated by A. S. Worrall (Edinburgh: T. & T. Clark, 1989), p. 218.
29. Origen, *On First Principles*, 2.1: the variety and diversity is caused in the diversity of the fall of those 'who decline from unity in dissimilar ways.'
30. Not strictly for punishment, as Origen's critics charged. Alan Scott, *Origen and the Life of the Stars. A History of an Idea* (Oxford: Clarendon Press, 1991), p. 140. Origen was a liberal so far as the theory of punishment was concerned.
31. See above, p. 11.

the new heaven and new earth of the Bible.'[32] It is an eschatology of return according to which the material world is created as the instrument to an end. This is in considerable contrast to Irenaeus, whose christological orientation enabled him to say far more definitely that the material creation was destined to share in the redemption of the human race.

Part of the reason for the change is to be found in another aspect of Origen's doctrine of God. Origen's deity is transcendent in a rather different way from Irenaeus'. Irenaeus' God is ontologically transcendent, as creator of everything else that exists. But by virtue of his triune nature, God the Father is able to enter into personal relations with the created order by the mediating activity of his two hands, the Son and the Spirit, who are as truly God as he is God. Irenaeus' God is thus ontologically transcendent of the world – he is a different kind of being, creator as distinct from creation – but by virtue of his triune being able to enter into relations with that world. By contrast, Origen's deity is spatially as well as ontologically transcendent. He is a monad, 'incorporeal', 'a simple intellectual nature', incomprehensible, impassible and uncircumscribed (1. 1. 6). The eternal Son, who is indeed eternal – though as we have seen in connection with the creation of the spirits, who are eternal though created, there appear to be degrees of eternity in Origen – stands in some way *ontologically* midway between the transcendent deity and lower orders of being, rather than being, as mediator of creation, firmly on the side of both creator and creation, as he is in Irenaeus.[33] Irenaeus' christology enables him to affirm both the complete distinction from and involvement of God in the world; while for Origen, the distance of the Father leads to the creation of an intermediate world, in a platonic manner, rendering the material world less real and important than the spiritual.

Origen has, then, compromised the doctrine of creation out of nothing in its Irenaean form in several important respects. First, the notion of the eternal creation has introduced an intermediate world between God and the creation, similar to, though not as dangerously mythological as, that of the Gnostics. As we shall see, this contamination of the doctrine was to affect theology at least until the time of William of Ockham.

---

32. J. W. Trigg, *Origen. The Bible and Philosophy in the Third-century Church* (Atlanta: John Knox, 1983), p. 110.
33. 'The Son, being less than the Father, is superior to rational creatures alone . . . the Holy Spirit is still less, and dwells within the saints alone' (1. 3. 5). Note the restriction of the Spirit's action to the inner personal world, another deeply problematic bequest to the future.

Second, and at the same time, the two stage creation has downgraded the importance of the material world, which is mainly or even merely instrumental to the attaining of 'spiritual' salvation. At the very least, Origen's Holy Spirit is not as interested in the perfecting of the material order as was Irenaeus'; in any case, he was, for Origen, a *created* hypostasis. Part of the cause is the platonising elevation of unity over diversity, with its tendency to denigrate the material because that is the realm of variety and plurality. (In later theology we witness the return of the tension between what can be called a biblical celebration of diversity and materiality and a philosophical suspicion of them both.) And third, by speculating about the possibility of a plurality of possible worlds Origen sailed rather close to the wind of cyclical theories of the universe and, perhaps more important, called into question the uniqueness of this one.[34]

VII SYSTEMATIC QUESTIONS

All the developments we have met raise the question of mediation: that is to say, by what means do we understand God to have created and to uphold the world? As we have seen above, the epistemological side of that question was raised by Justin Martyr when he denied access to knowledge of the creator God to those who would bypass his biblical self-revelation. But as the chapter has progressed, attention has focused not so much on the basis of our knowledge of the doctrine of creation as on how we understand God's action to be mediated in and towards that which he creates. This question was raised already by Philo's interpretation of Genesis. There is, as Francis Watson has shown, a sophisticated theology of mediation in Genesis 1:

> God creates immediately by command and by fabrication, but he also and simultaneously creates mediately in employing one of his creatures as the womb out of which the others proceed . . . 'Let the earth put forth . . .' . . .
> The creation narrative thus makes use of three interconnected but distinct models in order to represent the act of divine creation. Each has a different role, but the full meaning of each emerges only in combination with the others.[35]

34. Origen, *On First Principles*, 3. 5. 3. See Hans Jonas, 'Origen's Metaphysics of Freewill, Fall and Salvation. A "Divine Comedy" of the Universe', in *Philosophical Essays: From Ancient Creed to Technological Man* (Englewood Cliffs: Prentice-Hall, 1974), pp. 305–23.
35. Francis Watson, *Text, Church and World. Biblical Interpretation in Theological Perspective* (Edinburgh: T. & T. Clark, 1994), pp. 142–3.

It is thus, and Watson draws out the point, incipiently trinitarian:

> This God is, first, transcendent, but the function of this concept is still to express something of the *relationship* between creator and creation, and not to postulate a deity who is so wholly other as to be incapable of creating. Second, this God is wholly involved in his creative activity, and his involvement takes the intimately bodily form of labour . . . Third, in the most intimate relation of all, this God indwells her creation, not in the form of a passive, static presence but in an active, dynamic, self-transcending movement towards the emergence and reproduction of life and breath . . .[36]

In contrast, Philo and Origen in similar ways subvert this conception of mediation. By interposing the platonic idea of a (semi-eternal) plan in the divine mind, Philo begins a process, whose development we shall follow in later chapters, of displacing biblical by platonic notions of mediation. By positing a world prior to and higher than the material universe Origen downgrades the part played in God's work by the one who became incarnate.

One of the effects of a platonising conception of mediation is effectively to displace the second person of the Trinity from his position as mediator of God's creating act. This invites the assumption that while salvation is christologically mediated, the same is not true, or not true to the same extent, with creation. We witness in Irenaeus a determined attempt to maintain the continuity of creation and redemption by means of a continuity of mediation and by an attack in its light on the Gnostic view that the God of creation and the God of redemption are effectively different. His defence of the goodness of the material creation is without equal in the history of theology, and the reason is that both creation and redemption are mediated by the two hands of God who are, as we have seen, God himself in action towards and in the world. When creation is mediated by the two hands of God, there is no need of intermediates like the platonic forms or their aristotelian equivalents.

Irenaeus thus moves things several steps forward beyond Justin Martyr. The latter had concluded that our knowledge of the creation was mediated by the Bible, not by pure thought. His successor, with his christological and pneumatological conception of mediation of God's action, is able to achieve the crucial breakthrough. Because God is lord of his creation, he does not need *intermediates* because mediation is achieved

36. Watson, *Text, Church and World*, p. 144.

through his two hands. We do occasionally find Irenaeus using platonic notions of modelling, but the overall conception is of God's transcendent power over the creation. Yet it is not a transcendence of distance, simply because it is made known from God's free and loving involvement in the world in both creation and salvation. Platonic intermediaries, including the decadent platonism of the Gnostics, are rendered unnecessary.

All this means that there is light to be thrown here, also, on the vexed question of the way we interpret the Bible in general and Genesis in particular. By allegorising the text because of their embarrassment with its concrete and metaphorical form, the platonisers fail to take with adequate seriousness the shape of the text. But Irenaeus shows that there is an alternative to literal and allegorical interpretation, and it is a properly theological approach to scripture as a whole. A so-called literal approach, which supposes the words to correspond directly to facts lying behind the words of the writers, is clearly ruled out for reasons *internal* to the text. That is to say, the sophistication and complexity of the writings make it clear that the authors, and that includes those who wrote the books in their canonical form, exclude – for example – any interpretation that insists that by the six days of the creation is meant six periods of twenty-four hours. But this raises the question of what kind of freedom the interpreter has in making theological use of the material. There is a strong case for saying that allegorical interpretation of the kind we have found in Philo and Origen, and which was later to be found in Augustine, falsifies certain important themes of the creation narratives, and particularly their characterisations of an involvement of God in the material world which shows no preference for a 'higher' non-material reality.

What, then, is to be understood by a theological interpretation? At the very least, we must essay an integration, if not systematisation, of the various biblical witnesses to creation, and not simply Genesis, in the light of the God made known in Jesus Christ and by the Spirit who relates the world to the Father through him. If we accept Irenaeus' strong contention that the God of Jesus Christ is the one who created in the beginning, we must interpret Genesis in the light of God's involvement in the material historicity of Jesus of Nazareth. This enables us not to read trinitarian themes directly into the book of Genesis, as if the author were in some way theologising in a consciously trinitarian way, but to understand the forms of divine action there depicted as the acts of the triune God. This is particularly well illustrated if we see that part of the divine engagement with creation in Genesis 1 involves the ministerial use of parts of the created order in the forming of others.

When God says 'Let the earth bring forth' we have a picture of divine action enabling the world itself to take shape in the way the sovereign creator intends. As we shall see, this has important implications for the way we shall understand the relation of creation and evolution.

A theology of creation does not in any case limit its biblical basis to Genesis 1, but is concerned with the meaning of the scriptural understanding of creation as a whole. Because Irenaeus' focus is incarnational he looks at the whole of scripture through what happened in Jesus Christ, and refuses to become preoccupied, as were some of his opponents, with the exchange of 'proof-texts'. This is not to say that we should hold that the biblical writers were consciously trinitarian thinkers. Clearly, they were not. The doctrine of the Trinity is a doctrinal development dedicated to saying something of who the God is who creates and redeems the world. In its turn and in its light, this enables an interpretation of the Bible's teaching as a whole. Thus, when Psalm 33:6 says that 'by the word of the Lord the heavens were made, and all their host by the breath of his mouth', we may recognise the adumbration of a conception which is later filled out by an understanding of the personal presence of God made explicit by Jesus Christ and the Spirit. As we have seen, the heart of the matter is the concept of mediation which the Bible makes possible, generating as it does its unique doctrine of creation out of nothing. This will be the subject of our next chapter.

4

CREATION OUT OF NOTHING:
ETERNITY, TIME
AND THE WILL OF GOD

The teaching that the creation is the outcome of God's willing is one of the most momentous developments in all the history of thought, affecting as it does the way in which the relation of God and the world is understood and, in the longer term, the development of science. We saw in the previous chapter that Origen shows relatively little awareness of a distinction between God's being and his willing: 'at no time whatever was God not Creator, nor Benefactor, nor Providence'.[1] The implication of this appears to be that in some way or other creation is necessary to God; he cannot but create. The objection to that notion is that it appears to generate a logical relation between God and the world, so that the existence of God in some way implies the being of a world. A theology of emanation is not far away. It is, on such an account, difficult to maintain the distinction between God and the world, or at least to be in danger of supposing that there is some continuity of being, ultimately subversive of a doctrine of creation, between the two.

As will become progressively clear throughout the course of this book, a distinction between God and the world is necessary not only to preserve the autonomy of God's action – its character as authentically

1. Origen, *On First Principles*, 1. 4. 3.

divine action – but also for the sake of the world. If the world is too closely tied to the being of God, its own proper reality is endangered, for it is too easily swallowed up into the being of God, and so deprived of its own proper existence. Such a consideration required the development of a distinction between the being and will of God, and it fell to the generations after Origen to provide it, not always unproblematically. God, it came to be concluded, is eternally triune, eternally a being in three persons, but for that very reason not eternally creator. Creation is an act of God, based in his very being; but it is not an extension of his being. It is, rather, an unnecessitated act in which something external to and ontologically other than that being is created. This distinction between being and act raises a number of questions, particularly about the relation of time and the eternal God, and a range of answers has been attempted. We shall examine some of them in this chapter, particularly as the early developments culminate in the definitive treatment by Augustine of Hippo. But before that, some stages along the way are worth mentioning.

I BEING AND WILLING: ATHANASIUS

Origen's ambiguous doctrine of God led eventually to the Arian controversy in the fourth century after Christ. At its heart was the status of the Son or Word of God. Origen taught, like Irenaeus before him, that the Son was eternally Son of the Father, but he was unclear about whether he remained a kind of creature, albeit the highest of them, or was fully divine. Later controversy necessitated a decision between the two possibilities, and it was the achievement of Athanasius (c. 275–373 AD) to articulate both what became the orthodox teaching on the divinity of Christ and some of the implications of christology for the doctrine of creation. Against the Arian view that God the Son mediates creation as the highest of the creatures – an apparently attractive position, because the Son's midway position appears to make him a link between creator and creation – Athanasius argued that the agency of the Son in creation is proof that he is not a creature.[2] Since God the Son is the mediator of the divine action in the creation of the temporal world, he must be eternal.

---

2. Athanasius, *To Serapion* 2. 2–4 contains a sustained attack on the Arian teaching in which all the attributes of God the Father, including omnipotence, are argued to belong also to the Son. PG 26. 609c–613b. Rowan Greer, *The Captain of our Salvation. A Study of the Patristic Exegesis of Hebrews* (Tübingen: J. C. B. Mohr, Paul Siebeck, 1973), pp. 74–5, refers also to Athanasius' letter *To the Bishops of Egypt and Libya*.

The outcome is to sharpen the distinction between God and the world, so that Athanasius placed the Son of God firmly on the side of God. This, indeed, Irenaeus had already done, although the later theologian did not stress so strongly as his predecessor the Son of God's human and so material involvement with the world. Athanasius' development facilitated the emergence of the crucial distinction between the being and the will of God. Because the Son is divine – and the same kind of argument served for the being of the Holy Spirit – God's eternal being is triune. That is to say, Father, Son and Spirit are necessarily related to one another, because, as the Cappadocians were to argue, they were mutually constitutive persons, and so together make up what it is to be God. But precisely because God the Father is thus intrinsically related to the Son and the Spirit, he is not bound always to have a world around him – as we saw Origen to hold – and therefore can be held to create freely. The outcome is that God's triune being is eternal, but not his willing of creation, which therefore becomes an act of free willing. This enables it to be said that the creation is contingent, in the sense that it does not have to be. It might not have been, or God might have chosen to create a different world.

The ontological distinction which is here implied between the creator and the creation had the effect, as we saw that it had in Irenaeus, of removing the necessity for beings intermediate between God and the world. There is thus developed what we can call an absolute ontological distinction between creator and creation, but one based on God's free personal relation to the world through his Son.[3] (This is to be preferred to the well-known and misleading expression, 'infinite qualitative difference', which implies something rather different.) As Athanasius had previously said, the one through whom the world was created in the incarnation came to his own realm in order that the Father's good pleasure for creation be not thwarted, and this saving *relation* between God and the world became the epistemic basis for the distinction between them.[4] That is to say, our understanding of God's free creating of that which is not God is based upon his free relation to it in Jesus. The incarnation implies a certain freedom in the relations between God and the world, and so is the basis of the doctrine that God creates 'out

3. See Oswald Bayer, *Schöpfung als Anrede* (Tübingen: J. C. B. Mohr, Paul Siebeck, 1990, 1st edition 1986), pp. 5–6. The 'address' of God *to* the creation has to be maintained alongside his freely chosen immanence *within* it if we are to avoid the twin perils of personalism and Spinozism in our conception of it.
4. Athanasius, *On the Incarnation of the Word*, 6–7.

of nothing'.[5] The act of creation is accordingly seen to be grounded in an anterior richness in God.[6]

Yet there are objections to Athanasius' rather exaggerated stress on the discontinuity between God and the creation, and indeed with all such conceptions. Unless it is allied with an equally strong – and Irenaean – stress on the affirmation of the material world, there is always the danger of taking away with the platonic left hand what has been given by the trinitarian right. There are traces in Athanasius of a tendency to deprive the created order of its temporal character,[7] and of so stressing the Son's *homoousion* with the Father that the humanity of the incarnate falls out of the picture.[8] If the willing is not conceived as the act of the God who is known through his involvement with the world in Jesus as well as in the inner-trinitarian relations, a dangerous abstraction threatens. We shall discover the outcome of this one-sidedness when we come to examine the main thrust of Augustine's doctrine of creation.

II THE ONTOLOGICAL HOMOGENEITY OF THE CREATION: BASIL OF CAESAREA

But before that, we must examine some of the many implications of the teaching that God created the world out of nothing through Christ. One of them was spelled out by Basil of Caesarea (c. 330–79 AD) in his exposition of Genesis 1, which is best understood in the context of a struggle with platonism, and particularly that of his predecessor Origen. As we have seen, there are in Origen a number of problematic features: a tendency to conceive of a two stage creation, with the intelligible world prior in both intention and time to the material; the concept of a pre-mundane fall, making the material world a place of reformation and education rather than of value simply for itself; and the stress on unity at the expense of plurality as a desirable feature of reality, leading as it

---

5. Athanasius, *Against the Arians*, 1. 24: 'that very earth . . . whereas it was not once, He has at one time made by His own Word'.
6. Athanasius, *Against the Arians*, 2. 2. Athanasius enquires how, if the divine being is barren, it can possess the framing energy to create. If that which by nature does not exist, how can that which is by will? The implication is that creation requires a living will.
7. Athanasius, *Against the Arians*, 2. 60, referring back to 2. 48. 'No one creature was made before another but all things originate subsisted at once together . . .'
8. See *To Serapion* 2. 3, PG 26. 612b–c, where Athanasius denies that there is anything *atrepton* or any likeness to the Son among the creatures, suggesting that Greer is right to suspect the influence of a platonising distinction. Greer, *The Captain of our Salvation*, pp. 74–5.

does to an eschatology of return rather than of perfection. As we saw with reference to Philo, one root of this rather platonising interpretation of the doctrine is to be found in a particular way of understanding Genesis 1. A tendency to allegorise uncomfortable aspects of the text leads to a relative devaluing of both the goodness and plurality or variety of the material world. What is interesting about the work of Basil is the way in which he struggles with and rejects some of these ideas, although many of them were later to receive a fresh incarnation in the work of Augustine.

The *Hexaemeron* of Basil is, as the name implies, a study of the six days of creation. There is much in the work that is dated, for it accepts a cosmology that would be rejected today on scientific grounds. But if we left it there, we would miss the chief contributions that Basil makes to the doctrine of creation. First, there is a series of arguments against the view that the world has existed for ever. Basil celebrates the infinity of God's creative power (1. 2) and distinguishes between different forms of creative activity: 'Not . . ."God worked", "God formed", but "God created" ' (1. 7). Moreover, if matter is uncreated, as the Greeks taught, it has the same honour as God, while the idea of judgement implies that the world must have an end (1. 4). There are, to be sure, platonising elements in Basil's account. Most significant in this respect is section 5 of the first homily, in which an Origenist meditation on what preceded the creation of the material world intrudes incongruously on the preceding sections: 'all the orderly arrangement of pure intelligences who are beyond the reach of our mind . . .' The end of that paragraph could have come from Philo: 'after the invisible and intellectual world, the visible world, the world of the senses began to exist.'[9]

However, of greater significance is Basil's ability to transcend his cultural context. For him, the visible world is not the place of disorder, as it was for so many philosophers, but of a wonderful order. At the very opening of the work we read, 'It is right that any one beginning to narrate

9. Thus although in many places there is no hierarchy of being in Basil, in 1. 6 he says that the visible and sensible things are there to lead the mind to the contemplation of the invisible. See also 1. 10; 3. 10; 6. 1; 8. 7. Similarly, although he says that the visible world is a school for souls, it is in general the case that the world has more intrinsic importance for him than it has for Origen (1. 5f). Significantly, A. Meredith suggests that the forms in mind of God are replaced by angels in Basil, *The Cappadocians* (London: Chapman, 1995), p. 120. This is a dubious development also, because Christ and the Spirit tend in much later theology to be displaced by the angels as mediators of divine action in the world. Evidence for this can be found in Augustine, *City of God* and in Aquinas' doctrine of providence, which we shall review below, Chapter 8.

the formation of the world should begin with the good order which reigns in visible things.' Moreover, he is positively enthusiastic about variety and diversity, which are not features of the world to be escaped so much as evidence of the richness of creation. He has an enthusiasm for the variety of species worthy of Darwin. Especially in view of the fact that the doctrine of fixed species helped to cause much of the strife between Darwinist and Christian, it is worth pausing to read at length Basil's disquisition on the variety of tree life:

> What a variety in the disposition of their several parts. And yet, how difficult is it to find the distinctive property of each of them, and to grasp the difference which separates them from other species. Some strike deep roots, others do not; some shoot straight up and have only one stem, others appear to love the earth and, from their root upwards, divide into several shoots . . . What variety there is in bark! Some plants have smooth bark, some have only one layer, others several. What a marvellous thing! (5.7)

And that is not all. Basil's enthusiasm for describing the wonders of the natural world nearly distracts him from his task ('But I perceive that an insatiable curiosity is drawing out my discourse beyond its limits', 5. 9).

Perhaps of equal importance, in view of the fact that versions of some of the arguments reviewed above were used by Irenaeus, are Basil's objections to Aristotle's argument that, because their motion was circular, the heavenly bodies must be eternal. Even circular motion, he argues, requires a beginning and therefore an end (1. 3). (We shall meet this question again in connection with Galileo's argument with the papal authorities). There are other arguments against the divinity of the heavenly bodies, and attacks on astrology. In 3. 9 for example, Basil rejects Origen's view that the stars are alive.[10] For good measure, he adds an attack on the allegorical exegesis on which this theory was based:

> Let us understand that by water water is meant . . . Although, however, waters above the heaven are invited to give glory to the Lord of the Universe, do not let us think of them as intelligent beings; the heavens are not alive because they 'declare the glory of God,' nor the firmament a sensible being because it 'sheweth His handiwork.'

10. Alan Scott, *Origen and the Life of the Stars. A History of an Idea* (Oxford: Clarendon Press, 1991), p.166.

Similarly, the heavenly bodies do serve as signs, but it is overstepping scripture to say 'that our lives depend upon the motion of the heavenly bodies' (6. 5). The sun is, like other things, corruptible (5. 1). Also of interest, in view of the later arid discussions, even until the time of Darwin and beyond, about the 'days' of Genesis' account, is Basil's view of the matter. When scripture says 'one day' it means that it wishes to establish the world's relation to eternity, and is depicting 'distinctions between various states and modes of action' – that is to say, different ways in which God acts towards the world.[11] Basil has a fairly sophisticated view of mediation, and accepts – as we have seen Francis Watson arguing to be the case with Genesis 1 – that God enables the creation to act ministerially ('Let the earth bring forth . . .'). 'He who gave the order at the same time gifted it (the earth) with the grace and power to bring forth' (8. 1). But in other ways, Basil, like Athanasius though in a different manner, also points forward to problems that are to come. He seems to overlook the role of the Son in creation, saying in 2. 7 that God creates by 'a single word', which he appears to equate with the will of God, rather than his Word. Similarly, there are only two references to the involvement of the Spirit in creation.[12]

But the section on Basil must end with a reference to a principle of crucial importance for which he must be given much of the credit. It is that of the ontological homogeneity of the creation. Now we have seen that in one respect the creation is for Basil far from homogeneous. He glories in the very variety and difference of things. What is meant by homogeneous here is that, by virtue of his belief that God is the creator of everything, Basil comes to the conclusion, against the assumptions of almost the whole of the ancient world, that there are no degrees of being: that is to say, that everything created has the same ontological status. Neoplatonism in particular held that reality formed a hierarchy or ladder, by climbing which it was possible to ascend to divinity. Thus one ascends through matter via higher forms of being like mind to the divine. This doctrine presupposed a fundamental dualism between the material or sensible and the spiritual or intellectual. It also presupposed the inferiority of matter to mind. Christianity's teaching of the incarnation of the Son of God in material reality was fundamentally opposed to this notion, although, as we shall see, it continued to die hard, and, indeed, still does. Basil's attack on the idea of the eternity or superiority of the

11. Cited above, pp. 16–17.
12. 'The Spirit which completes the divine and blessed Trinity' (2. 6). I owe the three latter references to Mark Butchers.

heavenly bodies had the effect of subverting the dualism in favour of a very different duality. The fundamental division in being is now between creator and created: God and the world he has made, continues to uphold, and promises to redeem. The creation is homogeneous in the sense that everything has the same ontological status before God, as the object of his creating will and love. All is 'very good' because he created it, mind and matter alike. (This is not to exclude the special place of the human race in the creation, as we shall see in a later chapter; but it is to lead to a particular way of construing it.)

The point of this doctrine is to enable a distinction to be drawn between hierarchy and difference, as is shown by Robert Jenson in connection with the doctrine of creation of another of the Cappadocians, Gregory of Nyssa:

> The ontology of late antiquity had as its key operating principle the idea of degrees of being, the idea that there are sorts of entities distinguished from each other by being more or less real, by reflecting God's nature at fewer or more removes . . . Gregory [of Nyssa] denies the whole principle. So far as 'being' is concerned, a thing either is or is not, and that is all . . .
>
> Eunomius shows how he can speak of degrees of being, when he calls 'being' a 'value-predicate' . . . Gregory is indignant at the notion that being is a value: 'Whoever thought such a thing?' he asks. Now of course the entire ancient world thought just such a thing . . .
>
> Thus the whole ontological scheme is redone by Gregory. There are no degrees of being. There are different sorts of being, distinguished not by degree but simply by difference.[13]

The odd, if not tragic, thing about the history of the doctrine of creation is that, with few exceptions, Basil was not heeded in the ancient world. The physicist and theologian, John Philoponos (c. 490–c. 570), along with Cyril of Alexandria and John of Damascus, shared Basil's attack on the Aristotelian view of the eternity of the heavenly bodies:

> Following his perception that God was responsible for the creation of the whole universe, Philoponos was convinced that the cosmos as a whole was composed of the *same kind of matter* and was subject to the *same laws*. Hence, in direct opposition to prevailing thought, he both rejected the dichotomy between the *finite earthly* and the

13. Robert Jenson, *God After God. The God of the Past and the God of the Future, Seen in the Work of Karl Barth* (Indianapolis and New York: Bobbs Merrill, 1969), p. 120.

infinite eternal heavenly realms and recognised the importance of earthly reality. Further, especially in contrast to the neoPlatonism of his day, Philoponos insisted that nature could not be understood as the finite representation of infinite reality but as real in itself. To understand reality one must make deductions based on observation. In contrast especially to Aristotle, he maintained that reality could not be apprehended by making deductions from *known principle.*[14]

In general, the tradition ignored this discovery until a movement of thought beginning about the twelfth century began to call it in question. The notorious struggle between Galileo and the papal authorities did not come out of the blue, but harked back to Basil and Philoponos. The latter thinker is remarkable in that he both denied the life of the stars and claimed, against Aristotle, that events in the heavens are governed by the same physical principles as those on earth.[15] But others had made similar points. In a fragment of his commentary on Galatians, Cyril of Alexandria had commented that Paul described the *stoicheia* as imperfect because they lack mind and life and sense.[16] On the verge, we might say, of the Middle Ages, John of Damascus is more enthusiastic about superiority of the heavenly realm to the earthly, yet like Cyril, and perhaps echoing him, he denies souls and senses to the heavenly bodies.[17] Such teaching began only to become noticed again in the twelfth century, although it did not convince Thomas Aquinas who continued to believe that the heavenly bodies had, in a restricted sense, rational souls.[18]

III AUGUSTINE OF HIPPO:
(1) CREATION 'OUT OF NOTHING'

The discussions of Athanasius and Basil prepare the way for the definitive but deeply problematic treatment – or rather treatments – of the doctrine of creation in Augustine of Hippo (AD 354–430). Augustine's contributions to the doctrine of creation are so various that it is difficult to know which of them to stress. As is well known, he came to Christianity after

14. Harold Nebelsick, *The Renaissance, the Reformation and the Rise of Science* (Edinburgh: T. & T. Clark, 1992), p. 13. The italics are in the original.
15. Philoponos, *Opif.* 6.2, cited by Scott, *Origen and the Life of the Stars*, p. 166.
16. Cyril of Alexandria, in PG 74. 952b.
17. John of Damascus, *On the Orthodox Faith* 2. 6, PG 94. 885ab. Biblical sayings attributing rejoicing to the heavens are, he says, figures of speech.
18. Richard Dales, 'The de-animation of the Heavens in the Middle Ages', *Journal of the History of Ideas* 41 (1980), 531–50.

a flirtation with Manichaeism, which is appropriately enough the heresy most closely related to the doctrine of creation. While the latter affirms the goodness of all the created order, material and spiritual alike, the former is represented by the youthful Augustine's revulsion from the material world, so well described by Peter Brown. Manichaeism was highly dualistic, and incorporated a strong view of the hostility of soul and body. Brown quotes in this connection a Manichaean verse: *I have known my soul and the body that lies upon it, That they have been enemies since the creation of the worlds.*[19] In this heresy, Irenaeus' battle for the Old Testament was fought all over again. 'In Manichaeism, the stern Jehovah of the Jews was rejected as a malevolent demon . . .'.[20] Augustine's conversion to Christianity meant a rejection of Manichaeism, but also a continuing struggle with it which marked many of his writings.

It is also important to realise that Augustine's conversion to Christianity was one that took place in stages, and that neoplatonism served as a stepping stone. Neoplatonism was in this process a mediating position, in that it rejected Manichaeism's absolute dualism while, as we have seen, very nearly identifying matter with evil. That distrust of the material world continues to mark Augustine's writing, and both this and another feature together distinguish his engagement with the topic from that of Irenaeus. In the fifth century, the dogmatic shape of Christianity was more or less formed. What was apparently required was the defence of certain doctrines of the creed against their philosophical opponents, and it is this which dominates Augustine's approach. To a certain extent, he receives the doctrine from the tradition. But he receives it in such a form that certain problems remain for him. In every case, they centre on his continuing adherence to platonic ways of thought, and in every case mean that certain points are problematic for him in a way that they were not for Irenaeus. Augustine is not moving from the incarnation to the goodness of the created order. He is defending a position once established by that means, but now tends to leave them firmly in the background. There is, however, a price to be paid. The altered method means that the doctrine of creation is mediated in a different way, and is decisively different in some of its content.

We shall approach Augustine's distinctive position by beginning with the crucial dimension, his treatment of creation out of nothing. There is a very brief discussion in the *Confessions*, which is, along with the *City of God*, the chief source for his doctrine, though there are also many

19. Peter Brown, *Augustine of Hippo. A Biography* (London: Faber and Faber, 1969), p. 49.
20. Brown, *Augustine*, p. 50.

treatments of the opening chapters of Genesis, with which Augustine could never quite come to terms. In *Confessions* 12. 7 he makes two points which he does not relate to one another. First is the christological. He argues that if creation is made out of God's own substance – which Augustine rightly sees to be the only real alternative to creation out of nothing – then it would be equal to God's only-begotten Son.[21] This is an interesting and important point, for it distinguishes creation from emanation for *christological* reasons. If creation is the imparting to the world of something from the being of God, then it has a measure of divinity in it, and Augustine realises that it would then be in that respect *homoousios*, of one substance, with God the Father. The doctrine of the eternal Son prevents this, because the Son's ontological but necessary relation to the Father grounds the world's contingency. This is one of the rare places where Augustine treats the doctrine of creation christologically, others being in the *City of God* – a rather vague reference[22] – and *On the Literal Interpretation of Genesis*.[23] However, what is manifest and crucial is Augustine's appeal only to the eternal Son; unlike Irenaeus, he shows no interest in the relation between the Son's becoming material and the status of the material world.

This absence helps to explain a tendency to be found not only here, but in many subsequent treatments of creation, to appeal to omnipotence when arguing for God's capacity to create out of nothing. It is the second point to be found in the passage from the *Confessions* with which we began. Augustine affirms that God 'must have created them from nothing . . . For there is nothing you cannot do.' An appeal to omnipotence is often a sign of weak theological argument, because it is abstract and a priori. While Irenaeus does appeal to God's utter freedom in creating out of nothing, his argument is derived from what God has in fact done. God has demonstrated in his involvement in the material order in Christ and the Spirit that he is able to act sovereignly towards the created order, and so it follows that he requires nothing in order to create.

21. See Augustine, *Confessions* 13. 33 also for the contention that the creation is from nothing, not from God's substance or some pre-existing matter, and also *Confessions* 13. 2 for vaguely christological elements.

22. '[W]e have the statement: "In the beginning God created heaven and earth", by which it can be understood that the Father created "in the Son" . . .', *City of God*, 11. 32 .

23. Augustine, *On the Literal Interpretation of Genesis*, 1. 3, cf 3. 6, an astonishingly complicated and contorted passage. The chapter divisions are those used by Roland J. Teske, editor, *St Augustine on Genesis. The Fathers of the Church. A New Translation* volume 84 (Washington: Catholic University of America Press, 1991), pp. 145, 148.

By contrast, Augustine's stress on God's willing of the world leaves little reason except sheer will. The biblical stress on will comes into the centre, but there is undoubtedly a move towards a later emphasis on naked will; what was to be called absolute in contrast to ordered power. Lost is the christological orientation to the love of God in creating, so that it is sometimes difficult to understand why this God should want to create.

The influence of neoplatonism on Augustine is to be found in his interpretation – or rather interpretations, for he worried about Genesis continually – of the first chapter of Genesis. Augustine's interpretations are far more controlled by the now well-formed tradition than Origen's, but this means that they are more dangerous, for it is easy to miss their Origenistic pedigree. Although there are continuities between Philo, Origen and Augustine, the distinctive character of the latter, especially in contrast with Origen, is that while Origen is a speculative theologian of reason, Augustine is a theologian of the will. After Athanasius' achievement in distinguishing God and the creation christologically, it was easier to rely on a distinction between the being of God and his will. This does not mean that Augustine is unwilling to rationalise; clearly, he does rationalise, just as he sometimes allegorises, albeit in a rather different way from his great predecessor. But he is far more willing than Origen to take the text literally, and there is now no more nonsense about a pre-temporal fall. Indeed, so far as Genesis 2–3 is concerned, Augustine tends rather to literalism, and is the fountainhead of that Western doctrine of original sin that attributes too much to a literal reading of the story of Adam and Eve.[24] Yet, like Origen, Augustine would prefer that human reproduction did not take the messily material form that it does, and this leads him to one of the spiritualising readings of Genesis to which we must refer. Augustine finds it difficult to believe that the instruction to 'be fruitful and multiply' in Genesis 1:28 really means what it says. It must, he says, ideally be taken of spiritual fecundity, and 'was changed into carnal fecundity [only] after sin' (*Against the Manichees*, 19). He cannot easily be affirmative of the bodily dimensions of our being, though that is not to say that he never is so.

But that is not the only problem that Augustine had with the first chapter of Genesis, which troubled him again and again. That his first attempt at a literal reading of Genesis 'remains incomplete', as his editor says, 'bears witness to Augustine's inability to offer a literal interpretation of the text.'[25] It is when he attempts a theological reading that the

24. Especially the latter, unfortunately.
25. Roland J. Teske, 'Introduction', *St Augustine on Genesis*, p. 3.

problems begin to appear, chief among them the fact that he is unable to interpret the text in the light of the economy, by which I mean generally God's actions taking place in time according to the biblical account. The result is that his understanding of divine action becomes abstract and essentially at variance with the spacious movement of the author of Genesis. If God is omnipotent will, Augustine seems to believe, he must create all things instantaneously. Here he was anticipated by Philo, who was also embarrassed by talk of the days.[26] 'The reason for [the six day creation] is that six is the number of perfection. It is not that God was constrained by the intervals of time, as if he could not have created all things simultaneously... No, the reason was the completion or perfection of the works is expressed by the number six' (*City of God*, 11. 30). Because God is timelessly eternal, nothing that he does can be understood to take time. That is not to deny that Augustine wrestles page after page with the meaning of 'in the beginning.' Never the less, the kind of questions that he asks indicate that he is unable to come to terms with an economic reading of the passage, suggesting as he does that the language of days is only there for the sake of 'weaker souls' (*Literal Interpretation*, 3, 7). Once again, allegory comes to his assistance, but at the expense of the text. In *Two Books on Genesis against the Manichees*, written in AD 388 soon after his conversion, Augustine treats the days as accommodation to human weakness, seeing them first as seven ages of the world,[27] and then as stages of the spiritual life.[28]

Also crucial to an understanding of Augustine's doctrine of creation, and perhaps indicative of a residual Manichaeism, is his view of a two stage creation, in which he is once again closer to Philo than to Origen. He believes that Genesis 1:1–2 teaches a creation in which there is a definite order, if not of time, then of ontology. Of the first verse, he says: 'Clearly the Heaven of Heavens, which you created "in the Beginning" . . . is some kind of intellectual creature' (*Confessions* 12. 9). In some way, although it is definitely created, this heavenly world partakes in God's eternity. It is also the case that Augustine believes in the eternity of the forms, though it is a created eternity (if that is not a contradiction):

26. 'We must think of God as doing all things simultaneously,' Philo, *On the Creation*, 3. 13.
27. Augustine, *Against the Manichees*, 23ff. In this, Augustine anticipates those allegorisers who seek to show that the six days can be made consistent with a kind of evolutionary picture.
28. Augustine, *Literal Interpretation*, 25. Luther is contemptuous of Augustine's mystical interpretation of the text, as well as of his and Hilary's view that God created instantaneously, *Luther's Works*, 1, *Lectures on Genesis chapters 1–5*, edited by J. Pelikan (St Louis: Concordia, 1958), pp. 4–5.

The ideas are certain original and principal forms of things, i. e., reasons, fixed and unchangeable, which are not themselves formed, and being thus eternal and existing always in the same state, are contained in the Divine Intelligence. And though they themselves neither come into being nor pass away, nevertheless, everything which can come into being and pass away and everything which does come into being and pass away is said to be formed in accord with these ideas.'[29]

Like Plato, Augustine believed that there are *eternal* forms of things; like Philo, and in a move in this respect only half way to the doctrine of creation out of nothing, he located them within rather than without the mind of the creator.

The second stage of creation on Augustine's scheme is a double one, involving first the creation of matter and then its shaping into forms in the light of the first creation. It is the latter which interests Augustine, so that at times the reader wonders, as does Augustine himself, whether he retains a residual Greek doctrine of the eternity of matter. He asks, 'before you fashioned that formless matter into various forms, there was nothing?' and answers that 'there was this formless matter, entirely without feature' (*Confessions*, 12. 3). But matter was not eternal: 'though all formed things were made from this matter, this matter itself was still made from absolutely nothing.'[30] But matter's creation out of nothing does little for its status; it is generally not of much importance, and indeed – echoes of Plotinus here[31] – scarcely in existence at all. For Augustine, the first two verses of Genesis produce a definite hierarchy of being: 'From nothing . . . you created heaven and earth, distinct from one another; the one close to yourself, the other close to being nothing . . .' (*Confessions*, 12. 7). In sum, first of all God creates 'a kind of intellectual creature' – a real echo of the *Timaeus* here – and only then the manifestly inferior material world (12. 9).

We cannot emphasise this too strongly. Matter is not 'very good', but 'close to being nothing.' Once again, it seems that if everything is very good, some things are definitely less 'very good' than others. This is to be observed particularly in Augustine's preferred interpretation of the

---

29. Augustine, *De Div. Quaest.* 83, 46, 2, MPL XL. 30, translation from *Saint Augustine. Eighty-Three Different Questions* by D. L. Mosher (Washington, DC: Catholic University of America Press, 1977), p. 80. We really must take extreme exception to a theology that speaks of entities other than God which are 'stabiles atque incommutabiles . . . formatae non sunt . . . aeternae ac semper eodem sese habentes.'
30. Augustine, *Against the Manichees*, 6, compare *Confessions*, 12. 8.
31. See above, Chapter 2, section V.

creation of light and darkness in the Genesis account. Although he confesses that this may refer to 'two divisions of the physical universe', he prefers that it describe the good and evil angels. That he is thus manifestly introducing an ontological hierarchy into his interpretation is indicated by his teaching of the eternity of the angels in *The City of God*. Similarly, the statement that 'he created man's nature as a kind of mean between angels and beasts', suggests the same drive to ontological hierarchy.[32] Basil's achievement in adumbrating a doctrine of the essential homogeneity of the creation is submerged in neoplatonic hierarchy. Once again we have evidence that the platonic pull on Augustine is very strong, and seriously distorts his reading of the text, which it effectively contradicts or at the very least subverts. There is a revealing passage in the *Confessions* where he takes issue with those who interpret the opening verses of Genesis in a way that may appear to us to be its manifest meaning, of being a brief and comprehensive preliminary characterisation of the whole of the visible world. He does not even take them seriously enough to think such opponents worthy of engaging in argument (*Confessions* 12. 17–18). Such, I suspect, may also be the judgement of future generations who will not be able to understand why we in our time are so obsessed with reading Genesis in the light of our current preoccupation with science.

Augustine's treatment of creation out of nothing is therefore ambivalent. Where Irenaeus and Basil had employed it to defend the goodness of the material word, albeit a goodness sometimes qualified by remnants of platonism, Augustine has taken a step back. Alongside his determined, if rather voluntarist, doctrine of creation out of nothing there is reintroduced a definite hierarchy of being. Augustine continued to be marked by the scars of the Manichaeism from which he was so desperate to be healed. Therefore, in the aspects of his teaching which we have so far reviewed, it is difficult to welcome Augustine's contribution wholeheartedly. In the next section, we shall look at the area where he made a notable contribution, but made it in such a way that there, too, a certain amount is taken away with the left hand because it is unable quite to appropriate the contribution of the right.

IV AUGUSTINE OF HIPPO:
(2) 'IN THE BEGINNING'

'[F]or Christian theology the notion of creation is not primarily concerned with a hypothetical act by which God brought the world into

32. Augustine, *City of God* 12. 16 and 12. 22 respectively.

existence at some moment in the past, but with the incessant act by which he preserves the world in existence . . .'[33] In making that statement, Eric Mascall shows the influence of Augustine's view of creation as a timeless act, appropriated as it is in his case from Thomas Aquinas. As we shall see, it is a view shared in more radical form by Schleiermacher, who used it as a reason to reduce creation 'in the beginning' to providence operating timelessly. To realise what is at stake in this inadequate view of the matter we shall prepare the way with an examination of some contemporary questions, where the matter is often seen quite otherwise. Today the orientation to, and primary interest in, the past constitution of the world remain at the centre of interest, so that a feature of recent discussion is the apparent reintroduction of arguments for the creating activity of God through tracing back to a beginning; to what the media, usually now without reference to God, call the moment of creation. Despite, however, the studied ignoring of the question of divine origins in most discussions, the discovery of the red shift and its apparent suggestion of the expansion of the universe from a primaeval atom has apparently raised again the theological question. If the universe is an immense particularity rather than some general and eternal process, is not questioning about the source of that particularity invited? If the notion of a steady state is refuted by recent discoveries, may we not ask the question of who or what put the primaeval mass there in the first place?

We may, but already the guns are being spiked, and it is here that Stephen Hawking's *A Brief History of Time* is worth a mention. It has among its aims the development of a view of the universe as finite but without boundary, to the effect that 'it had no beginning, no moment of Creation.'[34] Hawking's argument is designed to devise an understanding of the universe which makes irrelevant the question of a temporal origin. David Wilkinson's discussion of this question in *God, the Big Bang and Stephen Hawking* is here of interest, and some of the points I shall make are at least partly dependent upon him. First, it is clear that Hawking owes something to deism, as Wilkinson shows,[35] and this has the effect of making him believe that the only way to establish the relevance of

33. E. L. Mascall, *Christian Theology and Natural Science. Some Questions on their Relations* (London: Longmans, Green and Co., 1956), p. 132.

34. Stephen Hawking, *A Brief History of Time* (London: Bantam Press, 1988), p. 116.

35. David Wilkinson, *God, the Big Bang and Stephen Hawking* (Tunbridge Wells: Monarch, 1993), pp. 97f. 'Deism viewed God as the initiator or originator of the universe, but that was all. It was as if God lit the blue touch paper and then went off for a cup of tea to have nothing more to do with the universe.'

God is to demonstrate that the universe needs something to account for its beginning in time. Second, however, there is a sense in which, theologically, Hawking is right, and it is clear that, in alluding to Augustine, he does himself indicate one of the sources of his view of time. He speaks of 'the fallacy, pointed out by St Augustine, of imagining God as a being existing in time: time is a property only of the universe that God created.'[36] By restricting the language of time to the universe and avoiding the anthropomorphic attribution of time to God, he shows that there is a sense in which his physics leaves the question of God unanswerable by the methods of science. Both Augustine and Hawking show us that there is a sense in which tracing back chains of causality is irrelevant to the real *theological* question of 'in the beginning'.

This takes us to a topic that is a permanent concern of this book, and that is the distinction essential to a Christian theology of creation between time and eternity. When we speak of the universe and its creation, we must understand it in terms of time. It has a beginning, and will have an end, and this holds true whatever scientific discoveries are currently at the centre of interest. Some of Augustine's predecessors, as we have seen, had two arguments in particular which were used to justify the necessary temporality of the created universe. The first was the necessity of the world being limited in time because if it was not, then it was as old as God and therefore in some way imposed necessity on him. The only world compatible with the all-powerful God who had raised Jesus of Nazareth from the dead was one that had an absolute beginning. The other argument came from the other pole of the time-scale, and held that the reality of judgement presupposed an end of time. *And that which must come to an end necessarily had a beginning, for it is finite in time.* This was not simply the result of a naive belief that there had to be another era in which God could judge the quick and the dead, because platonists and others who held to a judgement in another life continued to hold to the eternity of the universe. It was rather that the notion of the resurrection of the dead established the necessity of an eschatology of the whole created order, and that requires the idea of the end of time.[37] This God judges both the quick and the dead, and it follows that the Christian doctrine of creation implies a universe limited in both time and space. If this universe has any infinite features, either of time or space, then they displace and in effect replace God the creator.

36. Hawking, *Brief History*, p. 166.
37. In *City of God*, 12. 14, Augustine uses the once-for-all death of Christ and his resurrection as an argument against cyclical theories of time.

The universe must therefore have a beginning, an absolute beginning, in time. It had a beginning and will have an end, just like us, because only God is eternal.

It does not, however, follow simply from this that the beginning is the same as that traced back by scientific thought experiments approaching as nearly as possible to the first however many split seconds after the initial explosion. 'Less than one millionth of a millionth of a millionth of a millionth of a millionth of a second after the moment of creation . . .' began one recent sentence in a newspaper article about the origin of the universe.[38] What, however, happens before the supposed origin is in principle unknowable by the methods of natural science, and remains a question also on Hawking's attempt to spatialise time and so make such questions irrelevant. The reason is that creation as divine act is the act of one not restricted to the before and after of the finite time-scale. From God's point of view, we might say, without presuming to share it, all merely scientific theories of the origins of things are of a piece. They do not touch the question of divine creation, even though we may instinctively feel that the big bang theory is more consonant with Christian theology. The reason is finely set out by Augustine in what from one point of view must surely be the definitive discussion. Let us listen to his words:

> The Bible says . . . : 'In the beginning God made heaven and earth.' It must be inferred that God had created nothing before that; 'in the beginning' must refer to whatever he made before all his other works. Thus there can be no doubt that the world was not created *in* time but *with* time. An event in time happens after one time and before another, after the past and before the future. But at the time of creation there could have been no past, because there was nothing created to provide change and movement which is the condition of time. (*City of God* XI. 6)

We have seen how Augustine argues that creation comes about by the free, and totally free, willing of God. The chief puzzle here is that willing something appears to involve an act in time. What, then, Augustine's opponents asked, was God doing before he willed the existence of the world? Irenaeus refused to speculate about this question, on the grounds that we are not given any information about it. Augustine argues that the whole question is philosophically illegitimate. God is timeless; therefore there is no 'before' and 'after' in him. 'If there was no time, there was

---

38. Tom Wilkie and Charles Arthur, *The Independent*, 2 March 1996.

no "then".' The important implication of this is that God is the maker of time. Time is created when the material world is created; it is created *with* the world.[39]

None of the arguments directed against this view of the relation of God and the world seems to me to succeed. In particular, biblical characterisations of God's freedom to act in and over against the world require an absolute qualitative distinction between creator and creation. That is the point of the teaching that creation is 'out of nothing': a creative act in the purest sense of the word, in which God brought it about that, when there was 'once' nothing but God, there is now God and a world other than he. So far, so good on the Augustine front. However, we should accept only that part of his argument that would distinguish divine eternity from worldly time. In other respects, Augustine's legacy has been more problematic, if not actually disastrous, and provides the conditions for the development of deism like Hawking's. It is when we pursue the question of the relation of God's eternity to worldly time that we again stumble on the contamination of Augustine's thought by his platonic inheritance. Because for Augustine God is by definition timeless, it becomes difficult to conceive of any involvement of God in time. While, as we have seen, the notion of timelessness enables him to make valuable contributions to the doctrine, it also means that his theology is in the outcome far more 'other-worldly' than Irenaeus', and less able to be affirmative of the world of time and space. His concern is not, as was his predecessor's, with affirming the worldly, but with solving the philosophical puzzle of how the temporal and changing can derive from the timeless and unchanging.

In sum, Augustine tends to conclude that because creation is the act of the timeless God, then all God's acts must be conceived to be timeless. The outcome for him is that God's act of creation is understood to be instantaneous, and the days of Genesis demythologised away. He would not have liked 'creationism' either. However, if the divine creation of all things is simultaneous, it is difficult to take the order of time and space seriously as the good creation of God. Symptomatic is Augustine's tendency to hold that the fact that activities and events take time is a sign of their fallenness, making a gnostic equation of materiality and fallenness dangerously close. 'The discursiveness of thought and speech, the necessary division of discourse into a temporal succession of a multitude

---

39. Augustine, *Literal Interpretation*, chapter 3. Richard Sorabji, *Time, Creation and the Continuum* (London: Duckworth, 1983), p. 235. In this, too, Augustine was not original: 'time there was not before there was a world', Philo, *On the Creation*, 7. 26.

of parts, stands as a testimony to the Fall and thus to the separation of the rational soul from the perfect unity of God.'[40] If we are not to fall into that trap, we must do what Augustine failed to do and consider more closely what might be the shape of divine action in time. There are a number of biblical models available, all in some way or other depicting divine action as historical. Central is the incarnation. We have seen that Augustine's christology is centred on the eternal Son, and is neglectful, in this context, of the incarnation. But to understand the relation of the eternal God to time and history, that is precisely what we cannot neglect. Here is the life of a man which, as a narrated whole, from beginning to end, is also, and without diminishing its character as human, also divine act. This is a divine act, an act of the eternal God, which is, so to speak, stretched out in time. In the light of this, we can interpret Genesis 1 as relating a series of creative acts which set the stage, so to speak, for God's continuing interaction with his world. That is also why we may, without being naive creationists, take with complete seriousness the narrative form of Genesis 1 and 2. God's action both in the creation of time and towards and in that time once created, is action that 'takes time', just as his inaugurated completion of that creation in Christ's recapitulation of it also takes time.

The temporal shape of God's acts of creation has important implications, particularly for our understanding of the status of matter. Rather than diminishing the importance of the material world, its importance in itself is shown to be established: it, and not some higher 'spiritual' world, is the object of God's actual willing. The fact that the act of creation is directed to the establishment of things whose rationale is their shaping as beings in time and space demonstrates the importance of the created world in and for itself. God's continuing relation with it, as is instanced in what happens with Abraham, Israel and Jesus, reinforces this fundamental affirmation of the created world. But it reinforces something that has been, and remains, established, as many of the Psalms, for example, celebrate. Equally crucial here is the covenant recorded before that made with Abraham, in chapter 8 of Genesis, after the havoc wrought by human sin and evil on the good creation: 'While the earth remains, seedtime and harvest, cold and heat, summer and winter, day and night, shall not cease' (Genesis 8:22). This reinforces the teaching of chapters 1 and 2 of that book, that divine creation is that action of the

---

40. W. J. Torrance Kirby, 'Praise as the Soul's Overcoming of Time in the *Confessions* of St. Augustine,' *Pro Ecclesia* 6 (1997), 333–50 (339).

eternal God in time which establishes regularities and reliabilities. That is why Barth can say both that 'Creation is not a timeless truth, even though time begins with it, and extends to all times . . .', and that:

> The statement that God has created heaven and earth speaks of an incomparable perfect, and tells us that this perfect is the beginning of heaven and earth. It is also true that this beginning does not cease . . . But this does not alter the fact that it is a perfect, referring to something which has happened, and happened once and for all . . . It is for this very reason that the creator cannot be turned into a world-cause, a supreme or first cause or a principle of being. All such concepts denote a timeless relationship. . . . That is, creation speaks primarily of . . . a unique, free creation of heaven and earth by the will and act of God.[41]

We conclude, then, that creation is an act of the eternal God, but it does not follow that it is rightly described as eternal act. A careful correlation of the perfect and temporal after the manner of Barth is the key to the matter.

However, many of the other recent objections to Augustine's absolute distinguishing of eternity and time hold that for various reasons the christologically based insight into the essential temporality of God's creating act should in some respect be read upwards, so to speak, into eternity, so that it becomes necessary to speak of God in some way or other being limited, or self-limited to time. It is particularly objected that to make God eternal and 'outside' the created order leads to determinism: some view that because God 'sees' the whole of time before his eyes, he must in some way determine everything that happens. On this account, genuine freedom is established only when God is in some way or other unable to transcend time completely. While I cannot here go into all the arguments, it seems to me that whether or not a doctrine of an eternal God operates deterministically has much to do with the manner in which we conceive both the eternity of God and the temporality of the world. We shall have cause to look again at aspects of this question, but why we should not simply import time into God's eternity will become clear if we take more seriously the reference to the Spirit of God in the second verse of Genesis 1: 'the Spirit of God was hovering over the face of the water'. Whether or not so much can be made of so elusive a

41. Barth, Karl, *Church Dogmatics*, translation edited by G. W. Bromiley and T. F. Torrance (Edinburgh: T. & T. Clark, 1957–75), 3/1, pp. 60, 13f.

reference, the fact remains that in the context of the book of Genesis as a whole, creation in the beginning is indeed a beginning of *something*, and the Spirit's activity is concerned with its shaping. There is a long tradition of seeing the Spirit as one who gives direction to the created order. In a passage that has already been cited, Basil of Caesarea, while affirming that the Holy Spirit is 'inseparable and wholly incapable of being parted from the Father and the Son', yet distinguishes: 'the original cause of all things that are made, the Father; the creative cause, the Son; the perfecting cause, the Spirit.'[42] If we hold in mind this idea of the Spirit as the perfecting cause of the creation – the one who, by relating the creation to God through the Son, completes that which is begun – some of the problems that have dogged our topic will appear less severe. That is to say, if the Spirit is the one who gives shape and direction to the creation – again, to the *material* creation – it is in pneumatology as well as christology that we shall find the clue to the relation between eternal God and temporal world, particularly with respect to the proper autonomy of the creation. The Spirit is the one who enables the creation to be truly spatial and temporal by relating it to God the Father through the one who took our time and space to himself in order to redeem it.

Determinism is accordingly best avoided not by reading time back into God but by focusing on the action of the Spirit who is the giver of freedom and the one who enables the created order to be itself: to become what it was created to be. And in that regard, a note of eschatology cannot be far behind. To speak of the work of the Spirit in relation to creation is to speak of the created order eschatologically: that is to say, to direct our thoughts to the end. And the point of this is that we cannot understand the beginning without some orientation to the end. Already on the seventh day of the Genesis account an eschatological dimension may be present, especially in the light of the fact that that day comes in later tradition to be treated as a type of the coming Kingdom of God. Creation in the beginning cannot finally be understood without its directedness to an end, because it has to be understood as God's project, a project in which he freely and graciously involves us, his personal creation. But at this stage, we are chiefly concerned with understanding the beginning, and in the next two sections we shall draw out some of the systematic implications of the argument so far. We shall return to the matter of determining and determinism in later chapters.

---

42. Basil, *On the Holy Spirit*, XV. 38.

V THE DOCTRINE OF CREATION OUT OF NOTHING: IMPLICATIONS

Because of the importance of the doctrine of creation out of nothing, both historically and dogmatically, we must here pause to consider how things stand at this stage of the history of thought. We have explored the emergence of two doctrines which are mutually supportive: creation out of nothing and the teaching that because it comes from nothing the universe is finite in time and space. It has an absolute beginning, and will have an end. We have concentrated on time rather than space because that is the most difficult relation to conceive, although we cannot completely neglect the matter of space, as we shall see. In this section we shall detail some of the implications of the doctrine and the achievements of its proponents, before moving in the next section to a review of outstanding problems.

(1) The distinguishing of the orders of time and eternity has the implication of establishing the relative independence of the order of creation. Because God creates the world as something distinct from him, it has its own reality, dependent as it is on his *personal* creating act. This has two implications for the interaction of theology and science. On the one hand, science, as the study of the created order in its own right, is a proper human activity, as are technology, art and the other human activities we call culture. God makes a world that, unlike him, has a beginning and an end, and it is therefore of interest in and for itself as contingent – which in this case means *relatively independent* – reality. It has therefore to be taken *seriously* in its actual temporal and material shaping – though that does not mean *solely* and *absolutely*. But, on the other hand, particular scientific discoveries are, at the very least, of limited relevance to the doctrine of creation. I have already argued that however far back we trace the processes of cosmic evolution after the big bang, we shall in principle not be able to trace the hand of God. Similarly, the philosopher Peter van Inwagen opined at a recent conference that the truth or otherwise of the theory of evolution is irrelevant to the truth of Christian belief.[43] There is a certain desperation – and that means a capitulation to culture – in late nineteenth- and twentieth-century concerns to interpret evolution as in some way a function of God's continuous creation. It may be, but equally it may not. Darwin

---

43. See also Peter van Inwagen, 'Genesis and Evolution', *God, Knowledge and Mystery. Essays in Philosophical Theology* (Ithaca and London: Cornell University Press, 1995), pp. 128–62.

was himself more perceptive than many of his successors in noting the essential theological, indeed, moral, ambiguity revealed by his observations of the way things happen.[44] The shape of evolution can amaze with its demonstration of the emergence of richness and variety; or that same multiplicity may be seen as the source of pain and waste. This does not prevent us from appealing to such things as the universe's fine-tuning and the failure of all steady-state theories to convince in order to make the occasional point against those who try to show that the world in some way explains itself. It remains the case, however, that any theory or observation merely of finite entities is at best ambiguous. It is a function of the doctrine of the otherness of God – an otherness which, as we have seen, establishes the absolute ontological distinction between creator and creation – that the world is to an extent left, or, better, enabled, to be itself, while at the same time being drawn, contingently, to its proper end by the work of the Son and the Spirit.

(2) The doctrine of creation does indeed involve a particular claim about the past: not the past 'of God'[45] but the past of the world. We can indeed speak of a past act of God, for example, in the incarnation of his Son in Jesus of Nazareth at a particular time in history. Similarly, the establishment of a universe must be described as a past – and so, in a sense, complete – act of God – 'in the beginning'. Yet this past is not the same as that sought by the cosmologists, though there may be some overlap. Theirs is projected from the present rather than a seeing of the whole universe in the light of divine action. The point here is that the particular character of the cosmic past with which we are concerned cannot be understood without two equally essential theological perspectives which show that 'in the beginning' is as much an affirmation of a divine act as it is a statement about the existence of a finite world. They are the continuing action of God in upholding and directing the world he has made, and his action in completing that which was once begun. Here it is enough to reinforce conclusion (1), about the liberating function of affirmation of the past act of creation as establishing the world, as in one sense perfect – 'very good' – though in another not yet perfect, as not yet perfected. Again, this frees us from desperately seeking for divine creative action in the present. What takes place within the

---

44. Charles Darwin, *The Origin of Species*, edited with an Introduction by Gillian Beer (Oxford: Oxford University Press, 1996).
45. That expression can be used only in a tropic or rhetorical sense, because the unqualified use of tensed terms to God in his eternal being mistakes the categories of time and eternity.

realm of the created order is not creation proper. Even if scientists 'create life', as they sometimes put it, it will not be creation but the synthesising of given realities. Similarly, evolution is not creation but the rearrangement of what is given, even if 'higher' and more complex realities emerge during process of time. It also follows that biblical talk of 'new creation' is a metaphor: not creation out of nothing, but a radically new initiative within the structures of time and space. There is no more creation out of nothing, so in a sense no more creation, but simply what creator and creature alike and together make of what has been made.[46]

This has been finely and summarily expressed in two chapters of Oliver O'Donovan's *Resurrection and Moral Order*.[47] O'Donovan resists the tendency found in some recent theology to turn creation into history, arguing that the created order is that which establishes the possibility for history rather than being reducible to it. According to modern historicism, 'all teleology is historical teleology... Nothing can have a "point" unless it is a historical point; there is no point in regularities of nature as such' (p. 58). Against this, 'a Christian response to historicism will wish to make the ... point: when history is made the categorical matrix for all meaning and value, it cannot be taken seriously *as history*' (p. 60). It follows that, 'we must understand "creation" not merely as the raw material out of which the world as we know it is composed, but as the order and coherence in which it is composed' (p. 31). We must also understand the created order in both its vertical and its horizontal ordering. 'It forms, over against the Creator, a whole which is "creation"; and if there is any plurality of creatures within it, they are governed by this shared determinant of their existence, that each to each is as fellow creature to fellow creature' (p. 32).

> That which most distinguishes the concept of creation is that it is complete. Creation is the given totality of order which forms the presupposition of historical existence ... Because created order is given, because it is secure, we dare to be certain that God will vindicate it in history. (pp. 60–1)

(3) In all this, an eschatological perspective is central: not, again, a purely future eschatology such as those beloved of the cosmologists who seek to project to the end from their knowledge of the present, but the eschatology consequent upon and the implication of the resurrection of

---

46. Do we then need a doctrine of 'continuous creation' or would this not be better replaced with conservation, providence?

47. Oliver O'Donovan, *Resurrection and Moral Order. An Outline for Evangelical Ethics* (Leicester: IVP and Grand Rapids: Eerdmans, 1986), chapters 2–3.

Jesus Christ from the dead. This is an illustration of the peculiar character of Christian theology: that because it is concerned with the being of people and things in the light of the eternal God, abstractions to one time dimension without reference to the others distort the treatment of the topic under review. It follows that there is no 'in the beginning' without at least some reference to 'in the end.' This is because creation is 'project': it is something projected, as an act of God, into the future. It is a beginning which is to be perfected, again by divine action, but this time divine action involving the human. But, again, we must not confuse this simply with 'futurity' as we understand it. When we are speaking of the action of the eternal in time, we cannot remain content with our way of using tenses.

To explain what is at stake in this discussion, I shall develop a version of Paul Helm's view that we can understand the relation of eternity and time from two perspectives, that of the creator and that of the creation.[48] Because the creator is eternal – Helm would say timeless – we cannot predicate of him the time dimensions that belong to the creation. Creation out of nothing prevents us from either projecting God's eternity in some way on to the world, so that it is effectively deprived of its temporality, or from projecting the world's time into God, so that he is in some way limited by its temporal structures. The former is the danger of Augustinian doctrines, including that of Helm himself, because they tend to suggest that from the standpoint of an eternal God, time is unreal. Unlike some of his successors, Augustine is more careful. While accepting its force, he denies the contention of those who say, 'that the world is created by God, but refuse to allow it a beginning in time, only allowing it a beginning in the sense of its being created, so that creation becomes an eternal process.'[49] The outcome is an inference from the fact that creation is an act of the eternal to a view that creation is an eternal act.[50] I would not myself, therefore, speak of eternal creation, even in the carefully developed trinitarian approach of Alan Torrance.[51] While there may be merits in speaking of space-time as a single creation, this should

48. Paul Helm, 'Eternal Creation. The Doctrine of the Two Standpoints', in *The Doctrine of Creation*, edited by Colin E. Gunton (Edinburgh: T. & T. Clark, 1997), pp. 29–46.
49. Augustine, *City of God*, 11. 4.
50. The case has recently been argued in a second paper by Paul Helm, 'Eternal Creation. The first Tyndale Philosophy of Religion Lecture, 28 June, 1994', *Tyndale Bulletin* 45 (1994), 321–38.
51. Alan J. Torrance, 'Creatio ex nihilo and the Spatio-Temporal dimension, with special reference to Jürgen Moltmann and D. C. Williams', *The Doctrine of Creation*, edited by Colin E. Gunton, pp. 83–103.

not be done at the expense of the Irenaean teaching that creation is a project, to be perfected in and through time. A similar weakness is to be found in those who stress creation as ontological dependence rather than creation in the beginning; that is to say, the relationship of the created order to God now at the expense of a firm doctrine of the establishment of the order of creation in the past – our past, though not God's, because we cannot project our times into God – by divine action. The doctrine of creation is indeed concerned with the dependence of the world on God; but it is also concerned with the true temporality of that which is by virtue of God's creating act.

In sum, the strength of the Augustinian view is that it prevents God from being tied to the structures of time; its weakness that, unless it is carefully qualified, it risks depriving time of its true reality. Part of the way by which this is avoided is by maintaining Athanasius' distinction between the being and the will of God. If God wills the world freely, he wills something genuinely different from himself, distinctively real as the temporal and spatial order. But the problem remains of the apparent logic of creation by an eternal God. One way of circumventing this difficulty is that of Barth, who has qualified the view that eternity means timelessness. For him, eternity means neither endless time nor timelessness. Both views, he believes, represent a mythologising either of time or of non-time. Rather, the free involvement of God in time means that God, while not being tied to time, is not its negation either. What is needed is a view of God's eternity as, so to speak, directed to the creation of time.[52] The heart of the matter for Barth is christological, but to avoid some of the objections made against his position, we need again to add pneumatological considerations. Christologically, the point is clear. God is, indeed, involved in time, so that creation's reality is affirmed. But we should add that because the project of creation is realised as the Holy Spirit offers it, perfected, to the Father through the Son, the goodness of its extension in time is shown to be part of its essence. The eternity of the creator and the time of the creature meet in the incarnation, where in human time the ground of human time appears and its end is anticipated. Thus we are not here simply dealing with two perspectives, the divine and the human, but with two interrelated realms of being which bring with them two complementary perspectives, two ways of understanding the world as both the creation of the eternal God and a genuinely created reality.

The complementary tendency to read our time into God is more

52. Karl Barth, *Church Dogmatics* 2/1, pp. 615–8.

fashionable today, but is none the less to be excluded. There is a worldly perspective, so that we must understand the creation as that which is characterised by its finitude, its being in time and space. But if we view the relation of God and the world from the perspective of the created order, the danger is that God will be conceived by a process of abstraction from the world. Thus it might be argued that because the world's being is characterised by its temporal character, it will be tempting to say that God must be in some way temporal also, and a number of arguments to this effect have been produced in recent times, prominently in the Process theology of Whitehead and Hartshorne which argues to the effect that God's time is of the same kind as worldly time; its difference is that it goes on for ever. A number of more moderate accounts of what has been called temporalistic theism have been produced, sometimes in the light of this philosophy.[53] They all founder, I believe, on a version of Augustine's argument, that if God is the creator of time, then time belongs to the structure of created things, and accordingly not to God himself. This is also an implication of a point that has been made throughout this study, that the doctrine of creation, in teaching that it is one thing to be God, another to be the created order, rules out a simple, or even a complex, reading up of temporal reality into God. We require an eschatological as well as a relational conception of time. In sum, we should accept neither the timelessness nor the temporality of the being of God. We cannot but be apophatic, because no more is shown us. The work of Christ and the Spirit indeed indicate God's positive relation with time, demonstrating both his freedom and sovereignty over it and the fact that it is not entirely foreign to his being. But anything beyond that is necessarily mere speculation.

VI THE DOCTRINE OF CREATION OUT OF NOTHING: SOME REMAINING QUESTIONS

Our second concluding task is to indicate outstanding problems. From time to time two phenomena, which represent a continuing presence of contaminating features from the antithetical world of philosophical dualism, have been noted: the transfer of the platonic forms into the mind of God and the continuing tendency to attribute some form of superior,

---

53. For an argument not so dependent, see Richard Swinburne, *The Coherence of Theism* (Oxford: Clarendon Press, 1977) chapter 12. The arguments are reviewed in Sorabji, *Time, Creation and the Continuum*, chapter 16.

even divine, status to the heavenly beings. Both tend to subvert the doctrine of creation out of nothing in both the epistemological and the ontological realms. Ontologically, as we have seen, there are posited beings which, because they are nearer to the divine sphere, are of a higher mode of being than the material world. Could Irenaeus have described the material world as 'close to being nothing'? That it could be said is clear evidence of a contamination of the Christian doctrine of creation by Greek teachings of the ontological inferiority of matter. That which Irenaeus had spent every effort to expel creeps back into the theology of creation. As we have seen, the seriousness of this contamination is shown by Augustine's treatment of the book of Genesis. Like many a rationalist, past and present, he did not know what to make of this book, convinced as he was that God, being omnipotent, must have created the world instantaneously. He cannot therefore accept what I believe to be the message of that chapter, that it depicts God as 'taking his time' in a way similar to that revealed by his patient treatment of the erring world in Christ. Thus it is that the created world is project – something projected into and through time – and so something which is real and good precisely because it, too, takes time to become what it is created to be.

But the contamination also has a serious impact on Augustine's view of time. Here again, we are concerned with a divided mind, rather than a straightforward denial of the doctrine of creation. In his writings a number of various strands jostle for primacy. First, there is the view we have met that because time is created with the world, its reality is in some way tied up with it. If we may look forward a little here, we may anticipate the trouble that Newton's view that time and space exist absolutely was to cause for both science and theology. Augustine's account in the *Confessions* bears at least the seeds of a view that time is relational, not absolute: that is to say, it is a function of there being a world. According to such a concept, the world does not then take shape in time as an absolute given, as Newton, or at least Newtonianism, was to hold. Time is rather, as Einstein was to discover, a function of the way things are related to each other in the universe. It is created, and therefore not of platonic status as something belonging to a higher world, like the forms in the mind of God. 'Time', Augustine says, 'is constituted by the changes which take place in things as a result of alterations and variations in their form . . .'[54] This would be more than adequate were

---

54. *Confessions*, 12. 8, cf 12. 11: 'without change of movement there is no time.' In 11.24 Augustine appears to deny this view, saying that it is wrong to hold that 'time is constituted by the movement of a material body.'

Augustine not to take time's constitution by change to be a sign of its inferiority as an order of being. His main view of time is therefore quite different, and an anticipation of the subjective theory which later emerged in the thought of Immanuel Kant, one of the philosophers of Newtonianism. Augustine's tendency here too is platonic, for he holds that the problem with time is that that which partakes of it 'tends towards non-being'. The result is that when Augustine comes to analyse his experience of time, it disappears from before his very eyes. As he reflects about it, 'time' seems to be a vanishing point where the future moves into the past: 'no one would deny that the present has no dura-tion, since it exists only for the instant of its passage' (11. 28). It seems that both past and future can exist, because people apparently know the past and prophets foretell the future (11. 17). But where? 'I begin to wonder whether it is an extension[55] of the mind itself' (11. 26). Is Augustine suggesting that time is virtually the creation of our minds, rather than of God? He comes very near to saying so. 'It is in my own mind, then, that I measure time. I must not allow my mind to insist that time is something objective' (11. 27).

Similarly, Augustine's epistemology, which involves a continuing, if more restricted, role given to the platonic forms, posits a measure of continuity between the human mind and the divine world. That is to say, the mind is more truly oriented to the divine world than to the material. This is to be welcomed if it reminds us that the creation is not self-sufficient, but depends on God for all that it is. But its effect on the doctrine of creation has been to introduce a deep division – what can almost be called a schizophrenia – in the tradition of creation theology. It leads to the classical mediaeval view that we can know of the onto-logical dependence of the world on God by natural reason – whatever that is – while for the teaching that the world had a beginning in time, we require authoritative revelation.[56] Not only does this imply a diminution of the importance of the latter teaching, but also its relative irrationality, an implication that was to be ever more explicitly drawn out as modernity approached.

As we have seen, however, things are not so simple. The doctrine of creation was worked out in interaction with the thought world in which its exponents were set by means of a very complex range of arguments.

---

55. 'Augustine's notorious word, *distentio*, with its suggestion of *distortion*', Robert. W. Jenson, 'Aspects of a Doctrine of Creation', in *The Doctrine of Creation*, edited by Colin E. Gunton, pp. 17–28 (p. 26).

56. Aquinas, *Summa Theologiae*, 1. 46. 2.

The doctrine of creation out of nothing involves at once an appeal to christology and to 'philosophical' theories of divine omnipotence. Arguments are not 'natural' or 'unnatural' in themselves, but belong in particular settings. It follows that what we call revelation is what makes certain forms of argument possible. The early theologians were able to devise arguments for creation out of nothing and not merely assert it on authority, but only because of the revelatory divine action to which they oriented their thinking. Irenaeus had an authority: the inherited and shared confession of faith of the varied Christian communities of his time. But its meaning was contested, and argument was necessary for its further articulation and defence.

This point is so important that it should be repeated in another form. The doctrine of creation out of nothing is not a teaching which can be decided by reference to experience or philosophical argument alone, because only on the basis of a transcendent reference point provided by the action of the eternal God within time can it even be formulated. The doctrine of the absolute qualitative distinction between God and the created order depends upon an apprehension of the personal action of God in time and space. The reason, as I have argued elsewhere, is that without a personal relation centred on God's free involvement in the world in Jesus Christ, some logical or ontological – and hence necessitarian – link tends to be made between God and the world. This means that the difference between the view developed by the early Christian theologians and the view they opposed – that the universe is eternal in some respects at least – is a difference of fundamental belief and therefore not reachable by a process of neutral argumentation. Some affirm on the basis of their fundamental orientation on reality the temporal finitude of the world; others its infinity. However, it does not follow from this that neither position can be defended by argument. Arguments for and against both positions can be developed.[57] The sixth-century physicist and theologian Philoponos, among whose achievements was the anticipation of aspects of Galileo's dynamics, did devise an argument for the finitude of the universe which takes some overturning, although he devised it in defence of a belief which he already held because he was a Christian. He was thus able to produce arguments against the almost complete consensus of the ancient world, because he was a Christian believer.[58] Certain features of his situation, that is to say, made it possible

57. Kant, as is well known, believed that demonstrative arguments could be formulated for both sides of fundamental metaphysical disputes, the reason why, for him, metaphysics of this kind is impossible. Immanuel Kant, *Critique of Pure Reason*, Second Division, Transcendental Dialectic.

for him to think certain things which until now had been unthinkable. But those things were defensible by argument, for they accounted for dimensions of the created world not otherwise decidable.

Against Aristotle's view that time must necessarily be infinite, Philoponos devised an argument that can best be illustrated by a modern variation. If the universe were infinite in the sense that the number of stars it contains is infinite, the light emitted by them would be infinite, and therefore there would be no dark spaces in the universe. But there are dark spaces, and therefore the universe is finite. In a similar way, Philoponos argued that there must have been a first moment in time for there to be time at all. It is summarised by Richard Sorabji as follows: 'Philoponus' great achievement was to find a contradiction at the heart of pagan Greek philosophy... What [he] pointed out was that the universe would have had to pass through a more than finite number of years if the pagans were right that it had no beginning.'[59] This contention that revelation enables the construction of arguments rather than being an alternative way to truth relativises disputes like those of some mediaeval theologians concerning whether it can be established by argument that the world had a beginning in time.[60] It suggests that it both can and cannot, depending on what is meant by argument. It is impossible by argument alone to prove that the universe had a beginning in time (Aquinas); but, given belief that it had, it is possible to give reasons in defence of the doctrine (Bonaventure, in the tradition of Philoponos).

The main point with which to end this chapter, however, is to note that this thirteenth-century dispute was a sign that the topic of creation out of nothing had recently come into prominence after centuries of relative neglect. The main contention of the next chapter, already signalled in this one, is that Basil's and Philoponos' contributions were effectively ignored, so that for centuries the doctrine of creation was displaced by something that took away its real power, which lay in its trinitarian construction and mediation. In place of creation through the Son came a conception of creation through the eternal forms of classical Greek philosophy, so that the doctrine enters a long 'Babylonian captivity'.

---

58. Richard Sorabji, 'John Philoponos', *Philoponos and the Rejection of Aristotelian Science*, edited by Richard Sorabji (London: Duckworth, 1987), pp. 1–40. For the immense range of arguments about and positions taken on this topic both within and outside Christian theology, see Sorabji, *Time, Creation and the Continuum*, chapter 15.

59. Sorabji, 'John Philoponos', p.6.

60. For the dispute between Bonaventure and Aquinas, see Paul Haffner, *Mystery of Creation* (Leominster: Gracewing, 1995), pp. 54–5.

5

ARISTOTLE, CREATION AND
THE RISE OF SCIENCE

We saw at the end of the previous chapter the beginning of the divided mind of the West on the questions of both ontology and epistemology. In this chapter, we shall pursue the implications of this divided mind for the doctrine of creation in particular. This is not a book on the relations of Christian theology and natural science, but such of those relations as are relevant to the history and character of the doctrine of creation will be at least adumbrated, because we are in this chapter concerned with the era in which their relations are central. The interpretation of the history of ideas with which I am here operating is that modern science was not possible without some demythologisation of the heavenly realms such as had been espoused by Basil and Philoponos, and that the delay in its appearance is to be partly attributed to the effective sub-mergence of the kind of theology of nature implied by these theologians; in effect, by the virtual quiescence of the doctrine of creation out of nothing. In several respects, then, the doctrine of creation has endured a 'Babylonian captivity', some of the features of which we shall now examine. The main concern of this chapter is, then, with the effects of the long exile of the doctrine of creation, its effective submersion under foreign elements, and the beginnings of its return from exile.

Augustine is the dominating figure. His achievement was so to combine the classical inheritance with the Christian gospel that the theology of the Middle Ages, certainly until its waning, took the form of a synthesis of the classical and the Christian. Deep in the tradition is the teaching, stemming, as we have seen, from Philo that when God creates our world he uses the platonic forms as models. These are indeed transferred from the transcendent sphere into the mind of God, and so are part of the creation. Yet, as ideal and eternal, they give such priority to the intellectual over the material that it becomes difficult to take seriously the material as an object of independent interest and concern. Augustine continues that tradition, particularly with his dualism between the heavenly and earthly worlds. Neoplatonic elements were also introduced by Pseudo-Dionysius the Areopagite (early sixth century?).[1] The exclusion of christological mediation is definitive for the shape the thought of this era takes, because the structuring of the created order comes to be provided not by the one who became incarnate, *Christus creator*, but by *intellectual* forms or patterns.

Pregnant with threat for the future is the superior ontological status attributed to the heavenly bodies. As we shall see, the dogmatic belief in their superior status did much to provide the basis for the mistakes on the part of church authority which were ultimately to lead to the widespread view that science and theology are necessarily rivals of one another. With the hindsight that time gives, we are now able to see that theology in the time of Galileo made a double intellectual mistake: of hanging too much on the apparent cosmological implications of the book of Genesis – a mistake to be repeated in the controversies over Darwinism – and of tying itself to the essentially unbiblical cosmology of Aristotle. This is not, however, solely the wisdom of hindsight. Aristotle's critics in the early theology were there but not heard, while Augustine, for all the excesses of some of his allegorical interpretation, had at least taught the possibility of theological, rather than what we call 'literalistic' interpretation of the Bible.

1. Andrew Louth, 'Orthodoxy and Art,' in *Living Orthodoxy in the Modern World*, edited by Andrew Walker and Costa Carras (London: SPCK, 1996), p. 165, attributes this view to John of Damascus also, but the evidence appears to me to be ambiguous. Although John makes much play in book 2 of *The Orthodox Faith* with the creation of the angels, he attacks Origen's view of the priority of the creation of souls (2. 12). Louth cites *On the Divine Images* III 18–23, but only in 21 is there anything suggesting platonism. 'The fourth kind of image consists of shadows and forms and types of invisible and bodiless things which are described by the scriptures in physical terms'. Pseudo-Dionysius is another matter. *On the Divine Names* 5. 8 speaks of 'those principles which preexist as a unity in God and which produce the essences of things.' Pseudo-Dionysius, *The Divine Names*, v, 824b. The translation is from *Pseudo-Dionysius. The Complete Works*, translated by Colm Luibheid (London: SPCK, 1987), p. 102.

Additionally, we have to take some account of the work of Boethius (c. 480–524), the father of the Aristotelian method that so shaped the era of the schools.[2] With his dualism of reason and faith he at least encouraged the view, which was influential though not universal, that there are two parallel methods in theology, the philosophical and the theological. The doctrine of creation often came to be treated largely under the first, so that it almost wholly lost its trinitarian and so Christian form. This was not, then, a good era for the doctrine of creation, which tended to lose its integral relation to the doctrine of salvation, often, indeed, to be subordinated to it. Between them, the influential ancient writers most indebted to Hellenic ways of thought presided over an era in which philosophy tended to displace theology as the basis of the doctrine of creation. The outcome of this was not only the near-pantheism of an early mediaeval thinker like John Scotus Erigena, but also a deep ambivalence to be found in the thought of one of the greatest of mediaeval philosopher-theologians, Thomas Aquinas.

I THE HIGH MIDDLE AGES: THOMAS AQUINAS

As is often enough argued by his exponents, Aquinas (c. AD 1225–74) did believe in creation by the free will of God and he did aid the emergence of the sciences by his stress both on the reality of our perception of the world and on the notion of the world as an interrelated chain of causality. I have already hinted, however, that his continuing to hold to the Aristotelian cosmology militated against the doctrine of the ontological homogeneity of the created order. In addition, there are other features of his thought which maintain what I have called the Babylonian captivity of the doctrine of creation. The first is that despite assertions of creation out of nothing, there are still many traces of emanationism to be found. Neoplatonist thought influenced Aquinas particularly through Pseudo-Dionysius, whom he cites frequently. The theory of reality as forming a hierarchy is to be found underlying Aquinas' famous Five Ways, which set the scene for his theology. Causality is for Aquinas conceived not, as we tend to conceive it, temporally – B is caused by A which is before it in time; but vertically – B is caused by something higher than it in the order of being. The Five Ways are, as Robert Jenson has pointed out, interesting as ontological analysis,[3] and the

---

2. See Joseph Pieper, *Scholasticism. Personalities and Problems of Medieval Philosophy* (London: Faber and Faber, 1960) for an account of Boethius' influence on mediaeval thought.

ontology is essentially hierarchical in form.[4] It is, to be sure, a christianised neoplatonism, for God as creator is distinct from that which he creates, but neoplatonism none the less. This is shown by the fact that elements of continuity between the mind and the divine remain. The principle of like only being known by like, taken from Aristotle, is clearly influential. The material world becomes the instrument through which the (immaterial) mind rises beyond it to higher things.

A second point is that although it is not the case that trinitarianly conceived agency in creation is completely lacking from Aquinas' thought – he is in the tradition of Augustine in teaching that creation is the outcome of the free, personal willing of the creator – the act of willing is rather monistically conceived. The Trinity plays little or no constitutive part in his treatment of the divine realisation of creation, as is evident already in the Question which sets the scene for his treatment of creation, 44 of the first part of the Summa Theologiae, entitled, 'the first cause of things'. This question precedes the discussion of creation, which is thus introduced with a chiefly abstract and merely 'monotheistic' treatment of the status of God as first cause.[5] When we come to Question 45, 'Creation', article 7 is reached before there is mention of the trinitarian attributions, and there the distinctive forms of agency in creation are minimised rather than taken fully seriously. Despite a summary treatment of trinitarian creation in 1. 45. 6. ad 2, what emerges is a fairly strong conception of unitary divine activity, at the expense of mediation through the Son and Spirit.

Among the disturbing symptoms of the discussion is the rejection of Peter Lombard's view that power to create can be delegated to a creature which works ministerially, in apparent neglect of the pattern displayed in Genesis 1, where God does precisely that – 'Let the earth bring forth'.[6] In Aquinas, creation's relative autonomy is seriously understated.

---

3. Robert W. Jenson, *The Knowledge of Things Hoped For. The Sense of Theological Discourse* (New York: Oxford University Press, 1969), chapter 3.
4. Anthony Kenny, *The Five Ways. St. Thomas Aquinas' Proofs of God's Existence* (London: Routledge and Kegan Paul, 1969), shows that the proofs assume a conception of causality operating from above to below, higher being to lower being, not from past to present as tends to be assumed in modern notions.
5. I am here operating with one recent and pejorative use of the word 'monotheism.' See here Christoph Schwöbel, 'Monotheismus IV. Systematisch-theologisch', *Theologische Realenzyklopädie* XXIII, 1/2, pp. 256–62, for a demonstration of the variety of usage.
6. Aquinas, *Summa Theologiae* 1. 45. 5. See Francis Watson, *Text, Church and World. Biblical Interpretation in Theological Perspective* (Edinburgh: T. & T. Clark, 1994), p. 142, for the conception of mediated creation to be found in Genesis 1.

There are other problematic features, crucial among them two which threaten to undermine the distinct reality of the creature. First is a denial that God acts to achieve a purpose in creating – 'he intends only to communicate his own completeness';[7] and second is a denial that creation puts a reality into a creature except as a relation ('[Creation] in God is not a real relation, but only conceptual').[8] Both of these detract from the creature's value as creature, for they tie the creature too closely to God, and so fail to give it space to be. We might say that they detract from the proper substantiality of the creature.[9] Here it should be noted that there are two requirements for a satisfactory construal of the relation of God and the world: adequate conceptions of the continuing relatedness of the world to God and of that world's due reality – we might say due autonomy, better expressed as that is in the German *Selbständigkeit* – in its relation to God. It is not that Aquinas does nothing to ensure the reality of the creature; it is rather that the contingence of the creature on God (its dependence) is given more adequate weighting than its contingency: its freedom to be itself. 'The whole of what is genuinely real and true virtually exists in God though not in creation.'[10]

A third point concerns the continuing existence of the platonic forms – or the Aristotelian equivalent – in the mind of God. According to Aquinas, 'in the unique and most perfect act by which God knows himself are contained the idea of God and the ideas of all possible essences.'[11] The creation is already contained in God's eternal self-knowledge. This looks dangerously like a doctrine of eternal creation, and a necessitarian one at that. The world is indeed contingent for Aquinas, but there are many elements of his thought pulling in the opposite direction. This is the judgement of Adolf Harnack:

> Although Thomas rejected the pantheism of the Neoplatonic-Erigenistic mode of thought, there are still to be found in him traces of the idea that creation is the actualising of the divine ideas,

7. Aquinas, *Summa*, 1. 44. 4.
8. Aquinas, *Summa*, 1. 45. 3 ad 1.
9. For an account of this concept, see Colin E. Gunton, *The One, the Three and the Many. God, Creation and the Culture of Modernity. The 1992 Bampton Lectures* (Cambridge: Cambridge University Press. 1993), pp. 108–208.
10. 'virtualiter in Deo, sed non totum existit in rebus creatis.' Aquinas, *Summa*, 1. 19. 6. Much difference would be made by saying: 'really exists in the Son.' For Thomas' tendency to necessitarianism, see a sentence in the same question: 'An effect cannot possibly escape the order of the universal cause.' A similar, and stronger, point could be made against Schleiermacher's conception of the relationship of creation to creator as one of absolute dependence.
11. Thomas Aquinas, *Summa Theologiae*, 1. 15. 2.

that is, their passing into the creaturely form of subsistence. Further, he holds, on the basis of the Areopagite conception of God, that all that is has its existence 'by participating in him who alone exists through himself' (participatione ejus, qui solum per se ipsum est). But both thoughts obscure the conception of creation . . . [I]n the thesis of Thomas, that God necessarily conceived from eternity the *idea* of the world, because this idea coincides with His knowledge and so also with His being, the pancosmistic conception of God is not definitely excluded.[12]

That is to say, Aquinas' trinitarianism is not strong enough to extricate him from the danger of a slide into pantheism. In sum, Aquinas' theology of creation is symptomatic of the fact that in general in the Middle Ages, the Platonic forms or Aristotelian and Stoic *rationes* tend to displace Christ as the framework of creation. The effect is to replace something oriented to materiality with something at best ambivalent about it. Even in William of Ockham, who did so much to destroy the mediaeval synthesis, the christological silence is deafening.[13] The chief damage to the doctrine of creation, accordingly, comes from the institutionalisation of what we have seen to be the Achilles' heel of theology from Origen to Augustine, the positing of a nearly eternal creation intermediate between God and the material world. The effective quiescence of christology and pneumatology in the structuring of Western theologies of creation leaves a vacuum which non-biblical ontologies rush to fill.

II CREATION AND THE RISE OF SCIENCE: (1) HISTORICAL DIMENSIONS

The outcome of the uncompleted conversation between Christian theology and Greek philosophy is that the historical development of the doctrine of creation is full of paradoxes. So far as its relation to science is concerned, we are faced in it with a perplexing and difficult intellectual situation, which can be summed up in the following few claims: (1) It is now widely argued that without Christian beliefs and the institutions developed in Christendom, modern science would not have developed. (2) It is still widely believed that science and Christian faith are opposed in various ways, and particularly that science has replaced

12. Adolph Harnack, *History of Dogma*, Volume VI, translated by W. McGilchrist (London: Williams and Norgate, 1899), pp. 184–5.
13. See below, Chapter 6, note 16.

theology as a guide for life in the West. (3) It has become the case that approximately since the time of Newton the task of the doctrine of creation has largely been transferred from the theologians to the scientists. The reasons for this development are complex, but, I shall argue, it has much to do with the fact that during the period preceding the rise of science the task of the doctrine of creation was seen to be at least, if not more, the responsibility of the philosopher than of the theologian, or, better, constructed more with the tools inherited from Greek philosophy than with those made possible by the incarnation of the eternal Son of God in the material world. The situation parallels, indeed is partly the cause of, what Michael Buckley found to be characteristic of a later era. 'The absence of any consideration of Christology is so pervasive ... that it becomes taken for granted, yet it is so stunningly curious that it raises a fundamental issue ... To paraphrase Tertullian: How was it that the only arms to defend the temple were to be found in the Stoa?'[14]

According to Charles Norris Cochrane, the early church out-thought the decaying classical civilisation in which it lived by providing answers to certain questions which pagan antiquity was unable to answer. Prominent in the intellectual victory was the capacity to deal with aspects of reality which remained intractable on ancient assumptions. Cochrane's judgement on the achievement of Athanasius is that for trinitarian reasons he was able to think together what classical thought had always held apart:

> it becomes possible to envisage the divine principle as both transcendent and immanent, 'prior' to nature, the world of time and space in which we live, and yet operative within it ... [F]rom this point of view, the panorama of human history may be conceived as a record of the divine economy, the working of the Spirit in and through mankind, from the creation of the first conscious human being to its full and final revelation in the Incarnate Word.[15]

As we have seen, the incarnational interaction of God with material reality entailed an affirmation of the reality and importance of the latter. Cochrane proceeds in his remarkable study to associate Augustine with the same breakthrough, but, as we have seen, there are elements of Augustine's thought, and particularly his dependence upon neoplatonic

---

14. Michael Buckley, *At the Origins of Modern Atheism* (New Haven and London: Yale University Press, 1987), p. 33.
15. C. N. Cochrane, *Christianity and Classical Culture* (Oxford: Oxford University Press, second edition, 1944), pp. 367–8.

categories, which militate against the implications of the very doctrine of creation that he worked so hard to articulate. Other views of the influence of Augustine support the contention that his legacy was more problematic. Nebelsick quotes Jaspers, speaking of the Greeks, Augustine, and Neoplatonism in general: 'The material side of the world was neither knowable nor worth knowing'. To be any kind of Augustinian, and the Middle Ages was so universally, was to be in danger of pushing creation 'on the rim of the theological field of vision'.[16]

It remains the case, however, that the relation between Christian theology and the rise of modern science is far more complicated than the more old-fashioned type of secularist propaganda often supposes. The long and many-sided history chronicled by John Hedley Brooke shows that there have sometimes been positive relations, sometimes negative, and sometimes neutral relations between the two forms of culture.[17] As is becoming increasingly clear, modern science was not a return to Greek approaches suppressed during centuries of Christian darkness, but was prepared for by mediaeval Christian theologians who developed critiques of philosophical doctrines that stood in the way of science's development. In many respects, it does not matter whether, and in what respects, science was caused by the doctrine of creation. We must always bear in mind the cautionary note expressed by Amos Funkenstein, that one cannot draw necessary links between mediaeval theology and early modern science.[18] We must beware of the triumphalist note that is sometimes read in books claiming the truth of the thesis, even though they do serve to right a balance. What is more interesting for our purposes is that there is clearly an interaction. The situation is in some ways similar to that of the early developments of the doctrine of creation, which would not have taken the form it has received apart from the impetus and the concepts provided by the philosophers. Here, similarly, it was the rediscovery, in the middle centuries of the era, of the very Aristotle whose cosmology had to be defeated which provided the impetus for two, let us say, parallel developments: the development of experimental and mathematical science and the renewal of the doctrine of creation out of nothing.

16. Harold Nebelsick, *The Renaissance, the Reformation and the Rise of Science* (Edinburgh: T. & T. Clark, 1992), p. 17.
17. John H. Brooke, *Science and Religion. Some Historical Perspectives* (Cambridge: Cambridge University Press, 1991).
18. Amos Funkenstein, *Theology and the Scientific Imagination from the Middle Ages to the Seventeenth Century* (Princeton: Princeton University Press, 1986), p. 362.

It is this parallel that we shall examine, bearing in mind that the complications of the history are considerable. It may be that the parallel is more than that, for the questions must remain of whether the doctrine of creation, particularly with its christologically legitimated affirmation of the reality of the material world, makes it possible to think certain things that without it are unthinkable, or unlikely to be thought; and of whether it is indeed the case that science must necessarily displace the Christian faith, as is often supposed to be the case. The question is whether the coincidence at the heart of the history is one that is more than a mere coincidence: that both the early development of what came to be called modern science and the reaffirmation of the doctrine of creation out of nothing appeared on the scene at approximately the same time. Richard Dales has shown that it was not until the early twelfth century that the implications of Christian ideas for cosmology came to be worked out, and this is clearly the crucial time,[19] while it should also be noted that a century later the Fourth Lateran Council produced an ecclesiastical pronouncement of creation out of nothing, partly as a response to the growing influence of the revival of Aristotle's teaching that the universe was eternal. For our purpose, the following aspects need to be noted:

(1) The significance of the rediscovery of Aristotle is assessed differently by different historians. Some commentators claim that it was crucial for the advance of science, in that Aristotle's naturalism and stress on observation called attention to the natural world as it actually is, not as a ladder to the divine.[20] There must be something in this, for it cannot be irrelevant that the recovery of these texts at least opened up certain questions which had hitherto been relatively neglected in the more platonic world of the early Middle Ages. And yet even there questions must be asked. Some impulse was needed to achieve the realisation that the contingent material relationships between things were meaningful. By 'contingent' here is meant observed rather than thought; that is to say, what happens to be or to take place rather than what must take place. For all of Aristotle's interest in phenomena, it was what lay *behind* them that counted, rather than what gives them intrinsic meaningfulness. In distinction from Aristotle's, the implication of biblical teaching is the meaningfulness of the material rather than ideal or intellectual relations

---

19. Richard Dales, 'The de-animation of the Heavens in the Middle Ages', *Journal of the History of Ideas* 41 (1980), pp. 531–50 (p. 534).
20. Toby E. Huff, *The Rise of Early Modern Science. Islam, China and the West* (Cambridge: Cambridge University Press, 1993), pp. 228–9.

of things. That meaning was indeed given to things from without, but not in any way to the detriment of their own reality and meaning. Quite the reverse, for the doctrine of creation, in distinguishing God from the world, affirms the full reality of that world. Further, the key to later science is the combination of experiment and mathematics which goes ill with Aristotle's tendency to classify phenomena rationally. It is also clear that aspects of Aristotle had to be overcome before – to cite one obvious example – Galileo's denial of the eternity of the heavens could become thinkable.[21] At best, Aristotle's legacy is ambiguous.

(2) Another ambiguous event which is, however, generally agreed to be significant in this context, is the famous condemnation in 1277, by Bishop Tempier of Paris, of 291 propositions derived from Aristotelian philosophy. This, too, is variously interpreted. On a positive estimation of Aristotle, it is claimed that although the condemnation worked against the scientific developments of the time, it did serve to advance scientific thinking by encouraging speculation about hypothetical possibilities. Toby Huff's view is, generally, that Aristotle's materialism was an incentive to science. But:

> the condemnation . . . did not put an end to philosophical inquiry, but spurred philosophers to conduct a great variety of thought experiments, to imagine the impossible in the service of reconciling Aristotelian thought with Christian theology. This meant imagining non-Aristotelian possibilities, with the result that such speculations paved the way for the overthrow of the Aristotelian worldview in the sixteenth and seventeenth centuries.[22]

However, on a less positive view of Aristotle, an attack on the orthodoxy of his thought is likely to be beneficial to the development of science in more direct ways. This appears to be the more likely explanation, in view of condemnations 94 and 102, which reject the Aristotelian views that there are two eternal principles, the body of the sky and its soul; and that the soul of the sky is an intelligence. According to Klaaren, the 1277 condemnations served to establish, often against Aristotle, the doctrine of creation out of nothing and the contingency of everything, including the heavens. For him, it is the development of voluntarism that is crucial. That is to say, we observe at this time the beginning of a

---

21. When the matter is traced back to its beginnings in the twelfth century, it is clear that the intellectual battle was effectively won before Galileo, whatever was the actual shape of ecclesiastical dogma at the time.
22. Huff, *The Rise of Early Modern Science*, p. 339.

development to derive the origin of the world from the will rather than the reason of God. As has already been pointed out, even more rationalist theologians like Aquinas have a place for the will of God in creating. It is in part a matter of emphasis. However, while Aquinas gives rational grounds for why there should be only one universe, voluntarism allows for speculation about a plurality of universes, which in turn allows for a development of a notion of contingency by showing that this universe is not necessarily the only one, and could therefore be other than it is.[23] We shall examine the importance of contingency later, but here must indicate that others, particularly Roman Catholic interpreters, sometimes see the matter differently, pointing out that Aquinas held a doctrine of the contingency of the human mind and of nature, and taught that the universe was a network of rational causality.

(3) Another feature with ambivalent promise for the future was the replacement of an organic way of thinking about the world with one that was primarily mechanistic. While organism tends to suggest an intimate involvement of God with the world, sometimes, as in Stoicism taking a pantheistic direction, mechanism suggests an otherness between that which makes and that which is made. One early use of this analogy is to be found in Basil himself, in the use of a metaphor pointed out by Richard Dales, and it shows where in Christian theology itself is to be found the impulse which was later, in a different employment, to lead to the effective exclusion of God from the world. 'Like tops, which after the first impulse, continue their revolutions, turning upon themselves when once fixed in their centre; thus nature, receiving the impulse of this first command, follows without interruption the course of ages, until the consummation of all things.'[24] This has a remarkable similarity to the lesson Michael Faraday was to draw from Genesis in the nineteenth century.[25]

It is, however, only in our period in the Middle Ages that theologians begin to draw upon the metaphor of mechanism more widely. Huff cites the work of Benjamin Nelson to the effect that 'the idea, for example that the world is a rational and coherent order, that the world is a machine, that a divine being created the world according to "number, weight and measure," are all medieval themes enunciated by Christian clerics, cum natural philosophers, theologians, and even canonists.'

23. Eugene M. Klaaren, *The Religious Origins of Modern Science. Belief in Creation in Seventeenth Century Thought* (Grand Rapids: Eerdmans, 1977), pp. 32–52.
24. Basil, *Hexaemeron*, 5. 10.
25. See below, pp. 138–9.

'Indeed', he continues, 'the idea of laws of nature had Judeo-Christian groundings far stronger than any purely scientific arguments available at the time.'[26] Jaki similarly refers to 'Buridan's account of the world as a huge clockwork produced out of nothing by the Creator and put in motion by him. Buridan's disciple, Oresme, and many disciples of the latter followed suit.'[27] Every advance, however, brings its problems, and mechanism is a case in point. Many are the evils as well as benefits that have flowed from this metaphor, the chief one being that because the notion of a machine suggests a view of the universe as other than God it is but a small step to seeing it also as one that runs according to its own inherent logic, having no continuing relation to its maker. The reason why this abandonment of God was as easy as it was also lies in the deep history of the doctrine of creation, because the trinitarian mediation which distinguishes while relating God and the world had so long been left on the sidelines.

(4) But that was in the future. At the time, the development of mechanism was an essential part of what has come to be called the 'Copernican revolution', the change from an earth-centred view of the world to, first, one centred on the sun. It is often asserted that this change in the way of experiencing the world was of extreme signifi- cance psychologically for religious belief. Previously centred on a view of the universe circling around the earth, human beings were forced to reorient in a major way. How catastrophic one judges this first change of orientation from a geocentric to a heliocentric outlook depends in part on the way it is interpreted. It is an oversimplification to see it simply in terms of the opposition between a geocentric and a helio- centric view of things, as if all ancient creation views are alike in positing or assuming a geocentric universe. If we lay on one side the particular cosmological dress of the biblical creation accounts, we shall notice that their distinguishing feature is not this but their theocentrism. I repeat the fourth-century Basil of Caesarea's characterisation of the point of the days in the Genesis account, that they serve to establish the world's relation to eternity. In this context, we should also repeat a reference to his and other theologians' teaching that the heavens are not eternal because they are created. We have seen already that Basil and Philoponos taught the homogeneity of all created being, implying as it does the falsity of the dualism of material earth and higher heavenly sphere.

26. Huff, *The Rise of Early Modern Science*, p. 41.
27. Stanley Jaki, *Cosmos and Creator* (Edinburgh: Scottish Academic Press, 1980), pp. 80–1.

As Thomas Kuhn and others have shown, the doctrine of impetus, traceable to Philoponos, played an essential part in showing that the earth is a planet. Aristotelian dynamics presupposed that the earth could not move because if it did anything thrown straight into the air would come down in a different place from where it took off. By developing an alternative theory of motion, Philoponos and his mediaeval successors made it possible to hypothesise that the earth moved:

> In one way or another the impetus theory is implicated in most of the arguments, both medieval and Renaissance, that make it possible to move the earth without leaving terrestrial bodies behind.
>
> Some adherents of the impetus theory immediately extended it from the earth to the heavens. In the process they took a second long step toward the Copernicanism that was to come ... In Buridan's writings, perhaps for the first time, the heavens and the earth were at least tentatively subjected to a single set of laws ... [T]o conceive the heavens as a terrestrial mechanism ... is to break the absolute dichotomy between the superlunary and sublunary regions ...[28]

The Copernican revolution may indeed have been psychologically difficult for the religious to come to terms with, but many of its sources are in the Bible and the Christian theology of creation. There are, however, reasons for scepticism about even the psychological effect, especially about Copernicanism's implied reduction of the earth and human life within it to insignificance in the light of the vastness of the universe. R. G. Collingwood has pointed out that the theme of the insignificance of man in the vast cosmos was a commonplace in the Middle Ages, especially through Boethius' widely read *Consolations of Philosophy*, where the point was strongly made.[29]

(5) In his important study, Toby Huff has effectively made the point that this is not simply a matter of ideas and their influence, but is also

---

28. Thomas Kuhn, *The Copernican Revolution* (Cambridge, MA and London: Harvard University Press, 1957), pp. 121–2. Kuhn quotes Buridan: 'since the Bible does not state that appropriate [angelic] intelligences move the celestial bodies, it could be said that it does not appear necessary to posit intelligences of this kind. For it could [equally well] be answered that God, when he created the world, moved each of the celestial orbs as He pleased, and in moving them He impressed in them impetus which moved them without His having to move them any more except by the method of general influence whereby he concurs as a coagent in all things which take place' (p. 121).

29. R. G. Collingwood, *The Idea of Nature* (Oxford: Clarendon Press, 1945), pp. 96–7.

bound up with the development of institutions. After a close examination of Arabic and Chinese science in the period under review, he makes the point that although the former were, well into the Middle Ages, in advance of western science, neither civilisation had the institutions requisite for the development of a climate of free enquiry. Europe, with its particular system of law and the related distinction between church and state, provided the foundation in its universities for what was to come. Moreover, in view of the fact that it is often supposed, with particular reference to the Galileo affair, that science arose only in the teeth of ecclesiastical opposition, it is important to note that, according to Huff, the opposite is the case, and the treatment of Galileo is an exception to the general rule. 'The eruption of the Galileo affair is . . . an anomaly that occurred because of a variety of personal motives, personal vendettas, hubris and not a little malfeasance.'[30] We shall examine the intellectual aspects of this affair later, but here we note Huff's documenting of the general institutional support that Copernicus received well before the time of Galileo. In the light of the fact that he addressed his work to an ecclesiastical audience and dedicated it to the Pope, 'it surely seems that Copernicus believed that he had the intellectual space to freely present his new world system.'[31] The opposition, Catholic and Protestant alike, tended to come from those who had the kind of rigid approach to scripture which tied too much to inherited interpretations or details of ancient cosmology.

(6) Many interpreters hold that the Reformation was in most respects a positive force in the development of scientific practice and institutions. For some of them, the link is held to derive in part from the reaffirmation of doctrines that had tended to be submerged in the tradition. Again, because this is not chiefly a study of science, some of the influences, as they appear in Regin Hooykaas' important study, need only be mentioned, especially the Reformers' stress on the lay vocation, which encouraged a valuing of 'secular' work like science, and the recovery of the biblical affirmation of the importance of the work of the hands, in criticism of Greek intellectualism. The Reformation with its doctrine of the priesthood of all believers gave further historical impetus to the development of science, with its encouragement to the laity to become

---

30. Huff, *The Rise of Early Modern Science*, p. 353. For discussion of the complications of the affair, see also Brooke, *Science and Religion*, chapters 2 and 3, and Owen Gingerich, *The Great Copernicus Chase, and other adventures in astronomical history* (Cambridge, MA: Sky, 1992).
31. Huff, *The Rise of Early Modern Science*, p. 351.

'priests to the book of nature'. The two books – the book of the Word of God and the book of nature, a duality with a long history - were both open to be read by all, not just the priestly caste. Hooykaas appeals to the biblical insistence on what is given by God, which leads to the view that nature is the gift of God and therefore reliable. He cites Benjamin Farrington's opinion that the attitude of Francis Bacon in the matter of science 'might be summarized in the slogan: "out with Aristotle and in with the Bible".'[32] Similarly, doctrines like Calvin's of accommodation, by allowing that in them the writer is accommodating his language to the condition of the hearers, encouraged the notion of a space between the words of Genesis and their theological interpretation, and so freed from too 'literalistic' an approach to the Bible.[33] Above all, we find in the Reformers a return to a stronger form of the doctrine of creation out of nothing, as we shall see when we examine their contributions to the theology of creation proper. But what is it about that doctrine which can be conceived to be of relevance to the development of science?

III CREATION AND THE RISE OF SCIENCE: (2) INTELLECTUAL CONSIDERATIONS

Patristic writers like Basil and Philoponos employed the doctrine of creation in critique of Aristotelian and other theories of the divinity of the heavens, and it is now widely acknowledged that the defeat of pantheism is crucial to making experimental science thinkable. If the world as a whole is divine or the body of God, it is unlikely that anyone will think it proper to dissect it in a laboratory. However, with the exceptions of its tendency to deify the human mind and the heavenly bodies, Greek thought is for the most part not unrelievedly pantheist, so that the question of its contribution to modern ways of thought is a complicated one. This is recognised in one definitive early study of the intellectual relation between the theology of creation and the development of modern science, Michael Foster's 1934 paper, 'The Christian Doctrine

---

32. R. Hooykaas, *Religion and the Rise of Modern Science* (Edinburgh: Scottish Academic Press, 1972), p. 39. Hooykaas believes that it is no accident that Reformed believers were preponderant among the early modern scientists, giving the lie to the nineteenth century picture that science and religion are necessarily opposed, and that science happened in the teeth of theology. Quite the reverse is the case, certainly in the Protestant countries.

33. John Dillenberger, *Protestant Thought and Natural Science* (London: Collins, 1961), pp. 32–3.

of Creation and the Rise of Modern Natural Science'.[34] In it Foster argued that although there is in Greek thought a distinction between God and the world, because for Plato the sensible object is still the *appearance* of the divine, the necessary breakthrough to a view of the world as interesting in itself had not yet been made. That breakthrough is part of what is sometimes called the 'demystification of nature', by which is meant the critique of the doctrine that nature is in some way divine. We allude again to the ambivalence of the part played by Augustine. With his continuing to understand the temporal as the vehicle of the eternal, and with his continuing employment of the dualism of the sensible and intelligible, the father of western theology bequeathed to the mediaeval world a still hellenised version of the doctrine of creation, a version which survived virtually intact into the period we are reviewing. Science did not become possible until the distinctive rationality of the material world came into the focus of interest.

This takes us to the second point, which is that along with the demystification of nature, there developed a doctrine of the contingency of the world. Greek thought, as Foster shows, tends to be necessitarian: it seeks for forms, that is, patterns in reality that *have to be*, and that remains essentially the case with Aristotle, for all his naturalism. (Recall that according to the *Timaeus* both form and matter are eternal, and therefore necessarily what they are.) Scientific enquiry on this understanding becomes the quest for logical rather than factual links between things. In contrast to this, the world that results from a free act of creation does not have to be: it is therefore contingent. This contrasts with most Greek thought, for which contingency is essentially problematic: it is irrational because not necessarily and eternally true. A form of Gnosticism recurs in this context: truth is not to be found in material things, because that is the realm of the contingent. Therefore truth has to be sought somewhere outside the material world, in something or some principles underlying (or overlying) it. On this account, 'Objects are intelligible in so far as they are informed, sensible insofar as they are material.'[35] Contingency, and so materiality, is thus a defect of being. In contrast to this, in the words of T. F. Torrance, 'contingent rationality' is a quest for a rationality *inhering in* the order of space and time, not

34. Michael Foster, 'The Christian Doctrine of Creation and the Rise of Modern Natural Science', *Mind* 43 (1934), pp. 446–68, reprinted in C. A. Russell, ed., *Science and Religious Belief. A Selection of Recent Historical Studies* (London: Open University, 1973), pp. 294–315.
35. Foster, 'The Christian Doctrine of Creation', p. 310 of Russell edition.

beyond it. This, it is claimed, is the unique gift of the Christian doctrine of creation. The material world is contingent but rational.[36]

'Contingent' has a number of distinct but related meanings. In the first, we say that the created order is contingent because it is dependent on God for its being. In that sense, there is little disagreement between different versions of the theology of creation. In the second, it is contingent because it happens to be the world that there is, but might not have been created, or might be otherwise than it is. This is an implication of voluntarism and an encouragement to science because it focuses questions on what is actually there rather than on what is ideally true. The third sense, which is closely related, is that referred to by Professor Torrance, that because the structures of reality happen to be what they are – and are not necessarily what they are – in order to understand the workings of the world one is bound to explore its actual material regularities rather than enquire into its underlying rational structures, as is the tendency of all Greek thought, Aristotle's included.

The most notorious episode in the history of science makes better intellectual sense if we examine it in the light of this matter. The paradoxical fact about the Galileo affair is that from one point of view it is he, and not the authorities, who is defending the Christian theology of creation. Several features of the conflict between Galileo and the papal authorities make it theologically interesting. The first is that Galileo drew extensively on the work of a theologian we have already met, according to one authority citing him in his early writings more often than Plato, Albert or Scotus.[37] That Philoponos was an exponent of what I have called the ontological homogeneity of the creation is important here, for the second feature of the story is that the church had, in ignoring the theology of such theologians as Basil and Philoponos, tied itself to an essentially Hellenic theory of the eternity of the heavenly bodies. Thus it was that when Galileo observed through his telescope the surface of the moon, and was able to observe that the moon was of a similar substance to the earth, he appeared to be discovering something contrary to Christian belief. The example he takes in *Dialogue Concerning Two Chief World Systems – Ptolemaic and Copernican* is of the way in which observations of changes taking place on the surface of the sun disprove

36. T. F. Torrance, *Divine and Contingent Order* (Oxford: Oxford University Press, 1981). The argument has been reinforced by Nebelsick, *The Renaissance, the Reformation and the Rise of Science*.
37. Richard Sorabji, 'John Philoponos', *Philoponos and the Rejection of Aristotelian Science*, edited by Richard Sorabji (London: Duckworth, 1987), pp. 1–40 (p. 34).

Aristotelian beliefs in the changeless divinity of the heavenly bodies.[38] Even though it may well be the case that discussion of scripture would have been dangerous for him, it is clear that much of his polemic was directed against Aristotle rather than what in this book is being proposed as the Christian doctrine of creation. It is the dualism of celestial and elemental substances that provokes repeated attacks in this dialogue. As we shall see also in the case of Darwin, relatively peripheral matters are often at stake rather than orthodox Christian conceptions of the origin and nature of the world.

There was no essentially doctrinal dispute between Galileo and the authorities. One recent account goes as follows. It is quoted at length, because the story is now so often read in the light of the mythical doctrine of the eternal war between science and theology:

> A personal precept was put upon Galileo not to teach certain opinions, but Bellarmine, the cardinal who in a private interview communicated the precept to Galileo, himself declared in a letter . . . in 1615: 'If there was a real demonstration that the sun is in the centre and that the earth goes round it, then one would have to proceed with much care in expounding the places of Scripture which seem to be contrary to that, and it would be better to say that we do not understand them than to declare that false which has been demonstrated.' The lesser theologians whose opinions weighed with the Roman tribunal in 1616 were not so careful, and *the theological climate of the times, when any suggestion of a blemish in the Scriptures was likely to upset the faith of the uneducated*, did not admit much latitude of opinion. In China, whither the missionaries had brought the theories of Galileo, no such restraint was imposed, and the missionaries joyfully reported that with the hypothesis of Galileo they had made correct calculations for an eclipse . . .[39]

The passage in italics brings us to the third and in some ways crucial feature of the dispute, and it was the part played by scripture. As we have seen, the early theologians wrestled with the meaning of the first chapters of Genesis, and, for all their differences, shared a view that their literal

---

38. Galileo Galilei, *Dialogue Concerning Two Chief World Systems – Ptolemaic and Copernican*, translated by Stillman Drake (Berkeley and Los Angeles: University of California Press, 1962), p. 51.
39. F. J. Crehan, 'The Bible in the Roman Catholic Church from Trent to the Present Day', *The Cambridge History of the Bible* 3, edited by S. L. Greenslade (Cambridge: Cambridge University Press, 1963), p. 225. Italics added.

truth – whatever that may mean – was not the heart of the matter. The fact can be reiterated: belief in the doctrine of creation has never officially required belief in the literal truth of the book of Genesis. But in the early modern era, partly as the result of the disputes following the Reformation, the churches moved towards a much more rigid teaching about the nature of the text's claims. It is one of the most unfortunate aspects of history that in each of the great disputes between theology and science the waters were muddied by an unnecessarily rigid view of biblical inspiration.

In taking up again aspects of the Fathers' teaching, Galileo can be said to have been responding to a more authentic understanding of the doctrine of creation. This emerges in his advocacy of mathematics rather than logic as the key to science. Mathematics enables a greater openness between the mind and the world than logic, and indeed is more compatible with observation and experiment than thought alone, which tended to be the way of a Greek rationality, as we have seen.[40] This consideration enables me both to summarise the position so far and to say what is not being claimed. The fact that mathematics, first a Greek and then an Arabic discovery, bulked so large in the movement with which we are concerned should make us remember that we are here dealing with a very complex development in which many impulses joined to create what, after Tillich, we might call the kairos, the confluence of different cultural streams into a unique and historic configuration. Huff has shown very clearly that until about this time Arabic science was well in front of developments in the West, so that Muslim thinkers made contributions that were essential to the overall development. The Christian commentator, Harold Nebelsick, has reinforced the point. It was the Arabs who preserved and eventually transmitted Greek astronomy and science to the West. Their achievements in mathematics were also of major importance.[41]

It was, however, when the Christian doctrine of creation, particularly in its implied, and eventually its actual, critique of Aristotle, came into

---

40. In these respects, too, Galileo was assisted by mediaeval predecessors. Studies of medieval science are uncovering all kinds of anticipations of later discoveries, for example that the experimental method was being advocated by Roger Bacon (c. 1219–92) who, 'in his conception of the immediate use of science . . . had almost the outlook of the nineteenth century.' A. C. Crombie, *From Augustine to Galileo. 1 Science in the Middle Ages* (London: Heinemann, 1959), pp. 69–70. Funkenstein makes the point, *Theology and the Scientific Imagination*, p. 13, that Galileo's mathematical apparatus was anticipated by the fourteenth-century *calculatores*.

41. Nebelsick, *The Renaissance, the Reformation and the Rise of Science*, pp. 2–6.

the field that the historic breakthrough became possible. It was, especially in making the idea of the rational contingency of a world distinct from God, undoubtedly a necessary although not sufficient condition for the rise of science. But if this was the case, why did it appear necessary for the child to renounce its parent? The reason is to be found in the effective submergence of those very elements which were recovered about the same time as modern science emerged. It appears, especially in accounts influenced by anti-Christian propaganda, that science developed in the teeth of theological opposition. In fact, as we have seen, the doctrine of the superior status of the heavens and the inferiority of the material world were contaminations of the doctrine of creation which had been adopted into the tradition. They derived from its 'Babylonian captivity' to a non-trinitarian theology in which God the Son and God the Spirit were crowded out by a pagan ontology, so that God the Father was transmogrified into a monistically conceived deity owing much to Greek negative theology. Philo's introduction of the forms into the mind of God, adopted by Origen and reinforced by doctrines of the eternity of the heavenly bodies, generated a hierarchical view of being which, by minimising the importance of the material world, took attention away from that world within whose very structures the Son of God condescended to live, in a body shaped for him by the Spirit of God the Father. More than that, the platonic forms effectively displaced the eternal and incarnate Son as the means by which God the Father was related to the world. The outcome was that God was conceived to be related to the world by an immaterial structure rather than by the one who became flesh. The effective exclusion of the doctrine of the Trinity from the structuring of the Christian doctrine of creation is therefore at the root both of its Babylonian captivity and of the apparent mutual exclusion of theology and science.[42]

---

42. For another discussion of the same syndrome from a slightly different perspective, see Gunton, *The One, the Three and the Many*, chapter 2.

6

A NEW THEOLOGY OF NATURE:
FROM SCOTUS TO KANT

—·₩₩₨₨₨₨⑩₨₨₨₨₩₩·—

I THE LATER MIDDLE AGES:
(1) JOHN DUNS SCOTUS

In Chapter 5, the pronouncement of the Fourth Lateran Council on creation out of nothing was taken to mark the return of this until then marginal doctrine to the centre. To understand something of the dogmatic significance of the changes that took place – changes that were centred on questions about creation – we need to make a further observation about one side of Augustine's legacy. For Augustine, Anselm and Aquinas, God is understood very much as supreme *rationality*, and his reflection in the order of things construed in terms of the logical relations which shape the structure of things. The characteristic way of couching this relationship was one of cause and effect: God is the one who, as cause, imparts to the world a structure of causal relations, hierarchically conceived. These causes tend to be understood on the pattern of logical relations, so that 'A causes B' tends to be assimilated to 'A entails B'. It is true that another Augustinian note, God as creating *will*, was never absent, but it had taken a back seat. Modernity happens when the will moves into the driving seat, prepared for as that is by many earlier developments.

The later Middle Ages witnessed, particularly in the work of John Duns Scotus (c. 1266–1308) and William of Ockham (c. 1285–1347), a greater stress on creation out of nothing, deriving from a reinforcement of a voluntarist understanding of creation, and the correlative stress on the contingency of the created world. It was an era which closed with the latter philosopher-theologian's extreme voluntarism, which played the will of God against an earlier stress on the divine reason, but at the same time tended to lose the most central affirmation of all: that creation is the outcome of the love of God, freely willed indeed, but willed for the sake of the creation itself. The outcome, as in the earlier period, is ambivalent: consisting in a shift towards a more adequate doctrine of creation accompanied by its effective subversion, marked as that is by the fact that in the early modern era it is the scientists who take upon themselves the mantle of being not only philosophers of nature but theologians of creation, often displacing the theologians in the process.

Duns Scotus emerges out of the Middle Ages as the critic of some of its earlier teaching, and through three shifts of emphasis represents a move towards a new stressing of the doctrine of creation out of nothing. First, there is a move from intellect or cause to will, with God being seen as one who wills rather than as supreme reason. This is in effect to reassert the patristic doctrine of God as the source of the world's contingency. As the product of free personal willing the world does not have to be. There is, to be sure, only a relative difference from his predecessors. There is much appeal to omnipotence in Thomas and intellect in Duns, according to whom 'God wills in a most reasonable and orderly manner', because he is not an arbitrary deity.[1] But there is a real change in the way the platonic forms, or Aquinas' *rationes aeternae*, are understood. According to Efrem Bettoni, Scotus 'does not like, so to speak, the logical priority that possible essences obtain in this theory over the act of the divine intellect.'[2] The shift to an emphasis on the divine will means that for Scotus God is the creator both of things and of their forms. Forms are not so much in the divine mind, so partaking of a form

1. Efrem Bettoni, *Duns Scotus: the Basic Principles of his Philosophy*, translated by B. Bonansea (Westport, Connecticut: Greenwood Press, 1978), p. 161, citing Scotus, *Oxford Commentary*, III. 32. q. unica n. 6.
2. Bettoni, *Duns Scotus*, p. 154. Bettoni puts Scotus' relation to the scholastic tradition politely but firmly: 'Scotus is not completely satisfied', and makes the point that he was dissatisfied with the divine mind's passivity towards the *rationes aeternae*. He cites the *Oxford Commentary*. I. 35, q. unica n. 5: 'This seems to vilify the divine intellect, which in this case becomes passive in regard to the objects known through these *rationes*. The knowledge of these rationes on the part of the divine intellect would be determined by the presence of the objects.' That is the crucial objection to the location of semi-eternal forms in the mind of God.

of eternity, as more clearly a part of the created world. This, in turn, leads to a new stress on particularity, with all its long-term epistemological implications. Scotus' doctrine of *haecceitas*, or 'this-ness', implies that the ultimate reality of a thing is to be found in its being what it is rather than in its instantiating general notions or forms. This means, as T. F. Torrance has pointed out, that a knowledge of particulars is prior to a knowledge of abstractions.[3]

The second achievement is the move from a conception of being as analogous to a conception of its univocity. Put simply, this means that when we say that something *is* we are simply ascribing existence to it and not placing it on a scale of being. As we have seen in the discussion of Plotinus' ontology, for Neoplatonism all being was on a hierarchical scale between mere matter and pure mind, so that to predicate being of anything involves a judgement also of its place in the 'great chain of being'. On such an account, science is more concerned with placing a reality on a *logical* hierarchy than tracing its 'horizontal' interactions with other entities in the same world. The doctrine of the univocity of the concept of being is in certain respects the logical aspect of the ontological implications of the Christian doctrine of creation which have been stressed previously. It derives from the fact that everything that is not God is characterised by the common predicate of createdness: what we have called its ontological homogeneity. It is important for our purposes to repeat that this does not imply a teaching of utter homogeneity, that everything is the same. We have seen already how Basil's reading of Genesis, which affirmed the createdness of everything that is not God, also gloried in creation's multiplicity and variety.[4] The point is rather that being is not an analogical concept, but simply the predication of existence.

It is this patristic insight which Scotus restores in face of the massed opposition of his mediaeval predecessors. To say that the world is and that God is, is not to make two kinds of judgement, but one. That is not to say that the statement is ontologically neutral. As Gilson has shown, Scotus' development involves a re-establishment of the centrality of the will of God:

3. T. F. Torrance, *The Hermeneutics of John Calvin* (Edinburgh: Scottish Academic Press, 1988), pp. 4–5.
4. The abolition of the mediating function of the Platonic forms means that there can be a re-establishing of the diversity of things, in their own right, because the focus of attention is turned away from the eternal world to this one. 'God saw everything that he had made, and behold, it was very good.'

The God of Scotus is a necessary being because he is infinite being. Now, between infinite being and finite beings all ontological relations are radically contingent. In a doctrine which is based upon univocal being and not upon analogical acts of being, a dividing line other than the act of being must be drawn between God and creatures. The role played in Thomism by the existential purity of the divine Act of Being, is played in Scotism by the divine will.[5]

In turn this clearly involves a radical rejection of the pantheist under-tow of Aquinas' thought. It is a reaffirmation of the teaching that God and the world both exist, but are different; in other words, a reaffirmation of the fundamental distinction between creator and creation which had always been in danger in any thought influenced by Neoplatonism, even Aquinas', as we have seen. Scotus makes against his tradition the same kind of point that Irenaeus made against the Gnostics: there are no ontologically intermediate beings between God and the world. Indeed, Hans Blumenberg has made the point that the outcome of the development which was completed in Scotus' successor, William of Ockham, was a second overcoming of Gnosticism, although he draws rather more secularising lessons from it.[6]

This means — and it is our third point — that any mediation between God and the world derives not from the Platonic forms or their Aristotelian equivalents, but from christology. The link between God and the created world is God's eternal Son and Word, the one who became incarnate for the redemption of the world. Reference is made by Scotus to the subordinate authority of Jesus Christ in creation, with allusion to the dialectic in John 5 of Jesus' being able to do nothing of himself, but doing what the Father has given him to do.[7] By contrast, Thomas virtually never appeals to New Testament creation texts, nearly always to the first verse of Genesis alone. When he refers to the action of the Word, he tends to mean the *Logos asarkos*, out of the context of the confession of the incarnate Jesus Christ.[8] The point of all this is not

5. Etienne Gilson, *History of Christian Philosophy in the Middle Ages* (London: Sheed and Ward, 1955), p. 460.
6. Hans Blumenberg, *The Legitimacy of the Modern Age*, translated by R. M. Wallace (Cambridge, MA, and London: MIT Press, 1983), Part II, chapter 3, speaks of a second, and this time successful, overcoming of Gnosticism.
7. John Duns Scotus, *God and Creatures. The Quodlibetal Questions*, 8. 1. 17, translated by F. Alluntis and A. B. Wolter (Washington: Catholic University of America Press), p. 211.
8. There is little or nothing in Thomas' text here to provide support for the editor's

simply to assert the impropriety of all doctrines of the unfleshed or preincarnate Word, but to make the point that much Western theology has worked with a highly abstract theology of the second person of the Trinity, with the result that the New Testament linking of Jesus Christ and creation ceases to be determinative for the theology of creation. This contention can be reinforced by a more general one about Scotus' theology, as it is found in his famous disagreement with Thomas Aquinas over christology. As is well known, Scotus, in disagreement with Aquinas, taught that there would have been an incarnation even if Adam had not fallen. One of the reasons Aquinas gives for denying the speculation that the incarnation would have happened even if there had been no sin is that creation is *naturally* ordered to God.[9] Because he had Aristotle, Aquinas did not need a christological mediation of the doctrine of creation. Scotus' opposing view that Christ is definitive for the relation of God to the whole world at least opens up the possibility of a return to a christological mediation of creation.

II THE LATER MIDDLE AGES:
(2) WILLIAM OF OCKHAM

Not all of these achievements were maintained by William of Ockham, who is often linked with Scotus, though he is in many ways very different. Ockham represents some of the dangers of a one-sided assertion of the doctrine of creation out of nothing when it is developed in abstraction from the enquiry into the kind of being that the world is. They are, first, the appearance of arbitrariness and therefore irrationality: God simply wills things, for no reason and with no end in view; and, second, the assertion of immediacy, that God creates things so directly by command, without a structure of mediation, that something virtually

---

assertion that 'St Thomas' doctrine of creation is Christocentric and Scriptural, heir to the tradition . . . that God created in Wisdom and the 'word'. This does not appear in the foreground of most of the discussions . . . The weight St Thomas attached to a topic cannot be judged by the number of words he devoted to it . . . In the present case, unless the doctrine of *Colossians* 1, 15–23 is seen as central to his thought, he is no more than a religious philosopher who is the peer of Avicenna and Maimonides.' St Thomas Aquinas, *Summa Theologiae*, volume 8 (London: Blackfriars/Eyre and Spottiswoode, 1967), editorial note, pp. 87–8. Clearly, Aquinas does believe in creation as a triune act; see *Summa* 1. 45. 6. The question is rather whether such a conception is constitutive for his teaching, and it clearly is not.

9. Thomas Aquinas, *Summa Theologiae*, 3a. 1, 3, ad. 2, emphasis added. In this essentially unitarian mode of thought, it does not seem to have occurred that the creature might be 'naturally' ordained to God *through Christ*.

equivalent to pantheism results, a cosmology in which the world is simply a function of the divine will, with no freedom to be truly itself.

As we have seen, Scotus is a conceptual realist, at least to the extent that particular things appear to be linked together by universals of some kind. Against this, Ockham taught that universals do not exist, even for God, and so are entirely the product of the mind. Ockham's ontology, therefore, implies not only that only particulars exist, but that no real thing participates in the nature of any other things. The contrast with Aquinas' world of interrelated causes could not be greater. It is arguable, however, that Ockham is not a forerunner of David Hume in holding that relations between things do not exist, but was denying, as Berkeley was to do before Hume, that causality is absolute, after the manner of logical inference. On this understanding, 'A causes B' does not mean 'A entails B', but that B follows from A as an observed matter of fact. The laws of nature are, on this understanding, what happens to be regularly observed; they are conventional descriptions of contingently observed states of affairs.

Ockham is therefore by no means denying the doctrine of creation – that the world is made and held in being by God – as some of his successors were to do. Rather, he is making two points. The first is that nature is uniform, but not in an absolute sense, implying judgements of the kind: 'All individuals of the same kind are so made as to have effects of the same kind on an object of the same kind in the same circumstances.' Compare with this David Hume's later reduction of causality to the tendency of the mind to expect that if one thing regularly follows another, then it will do so again.[10] Second, it has been suggested that universals are not simply, for Ockham, psychologically formed convenient fictions, but exist as proper human attempts to generalise about the world. There is still a reality claim. Relations, such as causality, thus have 'no objective reality apart from the individual perceptible things between which the relation was found.'[11] This can be understood as a more radical version of Scotus' transfer of the forms from the mind of God to the created world, but it is not a Humean denial of causality. Belief in the doctrines of creation and conservation really do make a difference to the way the world is conceived!

What, then, is the chief difference between Ockham's doctrine of creation and that of the mediaeval mainstream? Ockham is far more

10. David Hume, *An Enquiry concerning Human Understanding*, 7. 2.
11. So Harold Nebelsick, *The Renaissance, the Reformation and the Rise of Science* (Edinburgh: T. & T. Clark, 1992), p. 58.

interested than Aquinas in the doctrine of creation out of nothing and the distinctive conception of contingency it generates, one very much derived from a stress on the free willing of the creator. It is thus a conception of contingency from above, rather than one from below of the kind Aquinas uses as the basis for an argument for the existence of a first cause. We might say that Ockham's scepticism about the latter has enabled him to move to a stress on creation as an act of free and personal divine willing. Ockham is celebrated, in works on the history of science, as one who, by stressing the contingency of creation, helped to lay the ground for that celebration of the distinct reality of the world which did so much to further the advance of modern science.[12] The outcome is that in this case the concept of will has come to predominate over that of cause, so that causality's tendency to suggest logical links between God and the world is replaced by one suggesting freely willed personal creation.[13] As Oberman comments in connection with Biel's similar epistemology, a demonstration of the deficiencies of the natural knowledge of God enables an elimination of Anselmian necessity, without losing the faith seeking understanding.[14] What this enables Ockham to do is to establish, in some contrast to Aquinas, a central place for the doctrine of creation out of nothing.[15]

But, and here the similarities between the two mediaevals present themselves to view, the matter is not so straightforward as the foregoing contrast between the two thinkers might make it appear. Certain concepts

---

12. Nebelsick, *The Renaissance, the Reformation and the Rise of Science*, pp. 52–63, and referring to such classics of the history of science as A. C. Crombie, *Augustine to Galileo* (London: Heinemann, 1959), volume 2, pp. 43–45 and 79. For Ockham's conception of the contingency of the divine act of creation, see, for example, William of Ockham, *In Librum Sententiarum* LI. D17. Q1, *Opera Philosophica et Theologica* (New York: St Bonaventure University, 1981), *Opera Theologica* vol. III pp. 453f: 'quidquid Deus contingenter creat, potest contingenter illud adnihilare quandocumque placet sibi.' (Whatever God creates contingently he can annihilate contingently whenever he wants.) That is voluntarism at its most stark.

13. Indeed, Ockham's is, as is often enough noted, a highly voluntarist conception of deity, and he holds against Scotus that the divine essence cannot be distinguished from the divine will; 'essentia divina nullo modo distinguiter a voluntate divina sed omni modo identitatis quo essentia est eadem essentiae etiam essentia est eadem voluntati.' (*Opera Theologica*, volume IV), p. 663.

14. Heiko Oberman, *The Harvest of Medieval Theology* (Cambridge, MA: Harvard University Press, 1963), p. 41.

15. 'Creatio est simpliciter de nihilo, ita quod nihil extrinsecum et essentiale rei praedicat; similiter in adnihilatione nihil remanet; igitur si aliquid essentiale rei creabili et adnihilabili praecedat et remanet non adnihilabitur nec creabitur.' Ockham, *In Librum Sententiarum* LI. D2. Q4, *Opera Theologica*, vol. II p. 116.

of will are as problematic as certain concepts of cause if they fail to leave space for what I have called the *Selbständigkeit* of the created order. The other desideratum for a doctrine of creation, a satisfactory conception of the continuing relation of creator God to created world, remains lacking. There is in Ockham contingency, but little account of the stability which derives from a continuing dependence of the world upon God. He continues to couch his discussion in terms of causality, rather monistically conceived, and so is unable to prevent the emergence of a conception of divine causality whose final outcome is an inadequate conception of creaturely reality. In that respect, the significant feature of Ockham's discussion of creation is the entirely non-trinitarian treatment of creation, perhaps best exemplified in the fact that he can refer even to the opening verses of the Gospel of John without noting the part played in its conception of creation by the mediation of the Word.[16] The danger is a monism of a particular God conceived in simple juxtaposition to a particular world, again without christological mediation.

Once again, the chief dogmatic deficiency of the doctrine is that the power or will of God is stressed at the expense of his ordering love. Aquinas himself had distinguished between God's absolute and ordained power: what we might call his theoretical omnipotence and his actual employment of it in the economy of creation and redemption.[17] Ockham is a theologian of the former, or rather of the latter subordinated to the former. The creation is the outcome of God's sheer will to create: it is a conception of radical theological voluntarism. The contrast with Irenaeus is instructive. As we have seen, Irenaeus' deity is the utterly free Lord, who creates out of nothing. But that conception is drawn not from abstract doctrines of the divine will, but from the freedom and love with which God has shown himself to work in the economy through his 'two hands'.

The outcome is that for Ockham, human reason has the power to perceive neither the logical nor the mediated, but only the contingent, structuring of reality. The effect in theology is, as Torrance says, that 'man is thrown back upon revealed truths which God provides by his absolute power.'[18] In other words a total disengagement of faith from reason is threatened. This has a twofold effect. On the one hand, it liberates

---

16. *Quodlibetal Questions* 2, Q4. Art. 2. Ockham understands John 1:3 to mean that God made all other things through himself (omnia alia a Deo per ipsum facta sunt), *Opera Theologica*, vol. 9, p. 215.

17. Aquinas, *Summa Theologiae*, 1. 25. 5. ad. 1.

18. Torrance, *The Hermeneutics of John Calvin*, p. 19.

'scientific' reason from theological. The world is able to be observed in its own right, as a contingent reality, so that theology and science are from now on free to pursue each its own field of truth. On the other, because God and the world are finally given no rational relation, Ockham 'detached knowledge of God from its own proper rationality' also.[19] In other words, the rationality of theology is undermined when the will of God is stressed at the expense of reason and love. Belief is made to be simply arbitrary, taken on authority. The evidence suggests that Ockham's nominalist theology served finally to subvert rather than to establish the doctrine of creation, because it ultimately caused the displacement of the centre of meaning and truth from the divine to the human creator. This is well illustrated by the thesis of Hans Blumenberg that modernity arises when the basis of rationality is displaced from divine to human agency.[20] The arbitrary will of the Ockhamist deity comes to be metamorphosed into the arbitrary will of the human agent. Thus Ockham represents a paradox. By cutting the claims of reason down to size, Ockham opened the way not – or not chiefly – for a renewed theology of creation, but for the rationalist reductionism that was to shape the development of modernity.

III THE LOSS OF THE DOCTRINE OF CREATION IN THE MODERN WORLD

Here we shall leap over the Reformation, to take up that side of the story in a later chapter, and explore something of the fate of the doctrine of creation in the centuries when the impact of rationalistic Ockhamism was most strongly felt. After the Reformation comes the time when, apparently, theology and science begin to go their separate ways. So far as the doctrine of creation is concerned, however, this means that it becomes essentially a function of science. The scientists of the modern era are effectively the theologians of creation, at least so far as the main stream of Western culture is concerned.[21] The development with which we are concerned centres on the thought and impact of Isaac Newton, but takes its beginning before that, in the side of Galileo that we have not yet explored. By moving towards a mechanistic conception

19. Torrance, *The Hermeneutics of John Calvin*, p. 22.
20. Blumenberg, *The Legitimacy of the Modern Age*, pp. 219–20.
21. Early modern science is the era of lay, or, as Funkenstein calls it, secular, theology. Amos Funkenstein, *Theology and the Scientific Imagination from the Middle Ages to the Seventeenth Century* (Princeton: Princeton University Press, 1986), pp. 3–10.

of reality, Galileo took a fateful step which was to have incalculable consequences. In introducing the fundamental distinction between primary and secondary qualities he generated a version of the deep-seated Western dualism which has dogged our culture until today. Primary qualities are the qualities things are supposed really to have: in Locke's later formulation, they are the qualities of 'solidity, extension, figure and mobility' which really inhere in the objects, while such qualities as colour, taste and smell are in some way the outcome of the configuration – which means mechanical interactions – of the primary qualities.[22] All other qualities are secondary, in some way not really in the object, but dependent upon arrangement of the primary qualities. This is in effect to imply that a thing's mechanical arrangements are more truly part of its nature – what belongs to it intrinsically – than other qualities, like colour, taste and the rest. But what reason is there for the distinction except a belief that the mechanical is more real than anything else?[23]

The dualism introduced by the distinction between primary and secondary qualities was reinforced by Descartes (1596–1650) with his distinction between mind and matter. He understood matter as 'extension' – filling space – and mind as that which is not extended. Once again, the effect is to elevate the mechanical, and thus to hold geometrical relations – Euclidean geometry – the key to the material world.[24] Now it must not be supposed that the effect of the metaphor of mechanism was entirely negative. Theologically, its long-term effect was disastrous, but in the short term it was encouraged by a theology which taught the scientist to take the created universe seriously in itself, and not as interesting only as pointing beyond itself to another, eternal world. The mechanistic model encouraged investigation into the actual spatial relations in the universe, and assisted the emergence of the great classical physics associated with Isaac Newton. The danger of Descartes' dualism, however, is also apparent, of cutting off mind from matter, God from the universe. Descartes' philosophy, along with Galileo's, contained the seeds

22. John Locke, *An Essay Concerning Human Understanding*, 2. 8. 9.
23. Berkeley was later to show at length that all the arguments which served to establish the relativity of the secondary qualities also served for the so-called primary ones. See especially the brilliant reductive arguments in *Three Dialogues Between Hylas and Philonous*.
24. '. . . all things which . . . are comprehended in the object of pure mathematics, are truly to be recognised as external objects . . . As to other things . . . such as light, sound, pain and the like, it is certain that although they are very dubious and uncertain, yet on the sole ground that God is not a deceiver . . . I may assuredly hope to conclude that I have within me the means of arriving at the truth even here.' Descartes, *Meditation* 6.

of deism. And that this is not simply a theoretical matter is shown by the fact that our theologies of nature affect our behaviour to the world. Along with a mechanistic metaphysic goes a tendency to treat the world as if it is merely or chiefly a machine, and to Galileo also is owed the notion, that was to reappear in Kant, that the scientist has to torture nature to extract her secrets.[25] From one inquisition to another, we might say.

Though he took over and developed the mechanistic approach, Isaac Newton was on the whole less rationalistic than Descartes, more concerned on the one hand to advocate experiment and observation, and on the other to avoid what he took to be the atheistic tendency of Descartes' dualism. Like Descartes, he was also a theologian, and much concerned to maintain the importance of God in his system of nature. God was required in his world in two respects. First, he was the creator; that is to say, the one needed to account for the existence and rationality of the universe. The regularity and harmony of the world requires God as an independent, voluntary creator to account for them. In this respect, Newton drew upon the traditional theology of creation out of nothing, stressing as it did the freedom and transcendence of God. Second, God was required as the one who conserved the order of creation. Like Descartes, Newton believed that the world depended on God from moment to moment, and was not simply a machine made to go its own way. On the whole, the mechanistic view resists any continuing involvement of God, for it does not seem to need it. If the machine is perfect, what more is required? For Newton, however, God was needed to iron out the irregularities and maintain continuing harmony of the world.

Moreover, underlying Newton's theology is not simply a god-of-the-gaps theology, as has often been supposed, but a much more determinative belief in God. Behind this world is a divinity without which it cannot be itself. This emerges in Newton's conception of time and space, which is crucial for so much of what came after him. Newton believed that there exist two orders of time and space, first relative time and space, which is what we experience in our day to day lives; and second

25. The charge against Galileo is made by J. Ratzinger. Galileo 'said that if nature did not voluntarily answer our questions but hid its secrets from us, then we would submit it to torture and in a wracking inquisition extract the answers from it that it would otherwise not give.' *In the Beginning. . .' A Catholic Understanding of the Story of Creation and the Fall*, translated by B. Ramsey (Edinburgh: T. & T. Clark, 1990), p. 35. Compare Immanuel Kant, *Critique of Pure Reason*, B. 13: 'an appointed judge, who compels the witnesses to answer questions which he has himself formulated.'

absolute time and space which in some way underlie the relative world. This geometrically ordered time and space form the container in which things happen. They are the absolute, God-given, framework for the world mechanism. Absolute space is empty, infinite, homogeneous and geometrical: 'always similar and immovable.' Absolute time is similar: 'absolute true and mathematical time . . . duration.' It 'flows equably without relation to anything external.'[26] The contrast between absolute and relative time is stated by Newton himself: 'All motions may be accelerated and retarded, but the flowing of absolute time is not liable to any change.'[27] What is the evidence for the existence of these absolutes? According to one historian, Newton simply assumed that they must be there; he never argued for them.[28]

A more satisfactory way of putting this, however, would be to say that Newton had theological reasons for positing these unknown realities. Time and space are for him God's *sensorium*, the sense organ with which God perceives the universe. In a paper on 'God and Natural Philosophy' (what we would today call 'natural science') Newton says that God is the one who constitutes duration and space 'by existing always and everywhere.'[29] Space and time are thus the 'places' where God is omnipresent to the world: the focuses of mediation where God at once creates and experiences the world. This theology is not as deistic as later criticism has often held. As Wolfhart Pannenberg has argued, such criticism oversimplifies, because Newton's theology of nature is more complex and sophisticated than often appears. Taking up Koyré's observation that 'Newton confronted with deep distrust the mechanical world-view of Descartes', Pannenberg points out that it is wrong to say that for Newton space is an organ of perception for God. The important point is this: 'God does not rule the universe as a world soul but as the Lord of all things.'[30] Similarly, as Robert Jenson has claimed:

> Jonathan Edwards, a far more careful reader of Newton than all his contemporary vulgar Enlighteners put together, proposed that the physical world is the intersubjectivity of universal personal

---

26. Isaac Newton, 'Scholium' to *Principia Mathematica*, in H. S. Thayer, editor, *Newton's Philosophy of Nature. Selections from his Writings* (London: Collier-Macmillan, 1953), p. 17.
27. Newton, 'Scholium', Thayer, p. 19.
28. Funkenstein, *Theology and the Scientific Imagination*, p. 92.
29. Isaac Newton, 'God and Natural Philosophy', in H. S. Thayer, editor, *Newton's Philosophy of Nature*, p. 43.
30. Wolfhart Pannenberg, *Toward a Theology of Nature. Essays on Science and Faith*, edited by Ted Peters (Louisville, Kentucky: Westminster/John Knox Press, 1993), p. 60.

communion between God and created persons and between the latter, that the physical world is what God thinks in order to think a community that can include others than himself. Edwards argued that such an interpretation sticks closer to the actual features of Newtonian science than does interpretation by the metaphor of the machine, which was dominant around him.[31]

Whatever the truth of all this, it shows that Newton resisted for good theological reasons the direction in which the mechanical philosophy appeared to be leading. But it could not be resisted, and for a number of reasons. Among them is the fact that the conceptions of absolute and relative space and time are deeply problematic, for they introduce, by the back door, so to speak, another form of the very dualism that had marked the earlier Babylonian captivity of the doctrine of creation. The idea that there is, behind the world as we experience it, another 'absolute' world, introduces a breach in our experience. The world we experience and experiment with is not the finally real world, which is something there but unknown and unknowable. Einstein was later to see that this was the Achilles' heel of Newton's philosophy. '[T]he concept of absolute space, which comprised that of absolute rest, made him feel uncomfortable; he realised that there seemed to be nothing in experience corresponding to this last concept.'[32]

Despite the nuances of Newton's theology, later generations witnessed the apparently irresistible transformation of the metaphor of mechanism from its use as a heuristic principle on the basis of which to explore dimensions of physical reality into an all-encompassing philosophy. The long-term effect of Newton is shown in the fact that 'at the very time when scientists such as Newton had begun to be suspicious of the need for a philosophical heritage, Newtonianism arose as a philosophical position.'[33] Newtonianism represents the entrenchment of certain aspects of Newton's position, and perhaps especially its dualism, in an ideology or world-view which excluded all others, and especially classical Christianity. It is surely no accident that this reintroduction of

---

31. Robert W. Jenson, *Essays in Theology of Culture* (Grand Rapids: Eerdmans, 1995), p. 173, citing Jonathan Edwards, *Miscellanies*, p. 926.
32. Albert Einstein, *The World as I See It*, translated by Alan Harris (London: John Lane the Bodley Head, 1935), p. 135. See T. F. Torrance, *Transformation and Convergence within the Frame of Knowledge. Explorations in the Interrelations of Scientific and Theological Enterprise* (Belfast: Christian Journals, 1984), p. 52, note 106.
33. John Dillenberger, *Protestant Thought and Natural Science* (London: Collins, 1961), p. 173. For the rise of Newtonianism, see Harold Nebelsick, *Theology and Science in Mutual Modification* (Belfast: Christian Journals, 1981).

a form of dualism deriving ultimately from the Greeks distorted both science – as Einstein suggests, and, as we shall see, Faraday demonstrates – and theology. There can be no satisfactory natural philosophy or theology of nature while this part of the Greek heritage continues to reign, even – perhaps especially – when it is transmuted into mechanistic form.

The development of ideological mechanism can be observed by the way in which John Locke in the seventeenth century, by extending Descartes' account of matter in his elaboration of the distinction between primary and secondary qualities, entrenched the view that only the mechanical qualities of things are truly real. Added to this is the fact that he also institutionalised in philosophy the breach which Newton had introduced between the world as it really is and the world as it is experienced. This he achieved by his definition of substance, a word used to refer in philosophy to that which is both the ultimate constituent of reality and the object of naming or reference. According to Locke, substance is the unknown support of the things we actually experience: 'something I know not what.'[34] The difficulties of Locke's position were exposed first by Berkeley, who attempted, vainly, to put something in place of the problematic qualities and substance, and then by Hume, who combined agnosticism with a dogmatic mechanism.[35] Berkeley is in some ways a most creative figure, to whom some allusion will be made below. But the crucial influence at this stage was Immanuel Kant (1724–1804), who attempted to pull together the threads he found hanging out all over the place.

IV IMMANUEL KANT

Kant had, on the one hand, an enormous respect for Hume, as the one who liberated him from what he believed was an unscientific philosophy. He was convinced by Hume that speculation about the origins of and relations between those impressions which were received by the human senses was illegitimate and impossible. On the other hand, however, Kant also had a reverence for Newton, whose science appeared to imply

---

34. John Locke, *An Essay Concerning Human Understanding*, 2. 23. 2.
35. This dogmatism is revealed in Hume's argument, in the second half of his chapter on miracle, that even were sufficient evidence to be evinced in support of a miracle, we would not believe by virtue of the impossibility of a miracle's taking place. See Hume, *An Enquiry concerning Human Understanding*, 10. 2. 96: 'what have we to oppose to such a cloud of witnesses, but the absolute impossibility or miraculous nature of the events . . .'. Thus is a problem solved by definition.

the opposite, that physics does teach us to know the world as it really is. The resolution of the impasse between Hume's agnosticism or scepticism about knowledge of the world and Newton's realism was by means of a theory of startling genius but, it must be said in the light of what has happened since, destructive falsity. Kant maintained the essentially platonic view that there are two worlds, what he called the noumena or objects of thought and the phenomena, or things that appear. The former world was the cause of the latter; in other words, the metaphysical or higher world – the vanishing remnants of the ideas in the mind of God – was the cause of this one. As Locke had held, our sense experience is caused by something we know not what. But two candidates for who or what this ultimate cause is, God and substance, are now ruled out, at least in the sense of *known* causes of the way things are. Both concepts are necessary, but only as regulating our thought – enabling it to know this world better. Of what they are in themselves, nothing can be known, because there is no way in which the mind can penetrate beyond appearances into what is really there. Thus Kant combines a platonic two-world theory of being with complete agnosticism about what the underlying world really is.

How, then, can the phenomenal world, the world of our experience, be known? According to Kant, only as it is structured by the mind. This solution to the problem, in a dogma that the mind structured our knowledge of the world which remained in itself essentially unknown, helped to entrench a certain form of Newtonianism in the thought and culture of our era, for it taught in effect that the mind is necessarily Newtonian in its structure. Because according to this way of seeing things Newtonianism's mechanistic metaphor is not metaphor but absolute truth, the mind is bound, if it is to know the real world, to construe it in Newtonian categories. The reason for this is that the mind supplies the concepts by which it knows the world, and these concepts are mechanistic in character. We are bound to use this set, just as we are bound to see the world as green if we wear green tinted spectacles.

(1) Crucial for our purposes is Kant's conception of space and time, which were for Newton, as we have seen, absolutely, objectively there. For Kant, they were absolute in another sense, as conditions for any experience of the phenomenal world – the world given to our senses. There cannot be absolute or even objective space and time, or, if there are such realities, we cannot know whether or what they are. They are, rather, subjective in the sense that they are conditions supplied by our minds to make experience of the world possible. They belong to the subjective constitution of our mind, 'apart from which they could not

131

be ascribed to anything'.[36] That is to say, the concepts of space and time are not derived from experience, as both Locke and Newton appear to have held, but brought to it — imposed upon it. Space and time are not objectively existing realities, but are the conditions of having any experience at all. Augustine had, after all, wondered whether time was simply an extension of his mind; here we find that particular chicken coming home to roost with a vengeance. Thus it is that the theology of creation of one era becomes entrenched in altered form in the philosophy of nature of the modern world.

(2) Another set of concepts, the twelve categories, are supplied by the mind, not this time to make any experience possible but to make our experience of the world possible. Two examples will serve to make the point: substance and causality. They were the problematic concepts for Hume, because in no way can they be established empirically: we cannot see or touch either of them. But it appears that the problems are solved if the mind orders its experience with concepts which are, so to speak, built into its very structure. The mind orders experience according to patterns of cause and effect, for example. This is the very place where Kant canonised the thought of Newton, for he believed that the mind is *bound* to order its experience according to the mechanical laws of motion. Newtonian mechanism, becomes, that is to say, the only 'scientific' way by which understanding of the world can be rationally ordered. It follows that to use non-mechanical concepts is to be 'unscientific'. If it is not mechanistic, it appears to follow, it cannot be known.

The general effects of Kant's views so far as the theory of knowledge of God and the world is concerned are as follows. First, they encouraged scepticism and idealism: scepticism because, as in Newton, it appears that the underlying real world cannot be known at all, only the world appearing to our senses; and idealism because the weight is placed not on knowledge of the world, but on the contribution the mind makes to ordering knowledge. This is a paradox, if not worse, in view of the fact that science appears, and, it may be said, more than appears, to be a way of ordering human knowledge of the real world. That, at any rate, it receives from the teaching that God places us in a real and good world. We must concede to Kant that the mind is creative in supplying and developing concepts. But the way Kant expressed his theories is wooden, and in two respects. First, he believes that all minds have built into them the same unchanging set of concepts, so that it is Newton and

---

36. Immanuel Kant, *Critique of Pure Reason*, B38. Kant there puts the matter interrogatively, but the answer is to be 'yes'.

only Newton. Second, rather than understanding the relation between the human mind and the world as a kind of interaction, in which, so to speak, the mind questions reality and listens to it, there is a far more limited view of the possibilities. To look ahead, we can say that post-Newtonian science developed when Newtonian concepts were found to be inadequate to encompass aspects of reality which were thrown up by developments in science. They took knowledge so far, but only so far.

The second effect of Kant's idealism was, in effect, to drive God out of the world. God on Kant's account belongs to the noumenal world, the real but intellectually shadowy world underlying this one; in fact, he belongs so completely to that world that there is no way of bringing him rationally into relation with it, by, for example, developing proofs of the existence of God from the world. Kant never denied the existence of that world beyond; what he denied was that there could be real knowledge of it. God is useful, indispensable even, as a regulative concept, giving us an idea of the unity of things and thus a motive for science. But the overall effect as the years passed was progressively to exclude God from the world. The outcome is symbolised by two features of the work of the French scientist Laplace (1749–1827). The first is the famous story of the presentation of his account of the solar system to Napoleon. Pressed to explain, so the story goes, why there was no place for God in his model of the solar system, unlike Newton's, he is alleged to have replied: 'I have no need of that hypothesis'. The second is his conception of the work of the scientist. According to this, the scientist is one who sets out to know everything: to be omniscient, and so to know as God might be supposed to know. As Polanyi has pointed out, however, this is not only impossible, but would in fact make science impossible, because science is a pursuit for which the prior identification of particularities remains an essential precondition.[37]

The result of the development we have traced was that the fate of the theology of creation came to be decided on ground chosen by the deists: those who held that the only believable God is one discovered by reason alone, and whose relation to the world can be none other than that of machine-maker to machine. Deism has an important range of relationships with the doctrine of creation. One the one hand, it can be understood as a rationalised version of the essentially non-trinitarian view of the relation between God and the world which held sway during the Middle Ages. The retrieval of the doctrine by the Reformers was for

37. Michael Polanyi, *Personal Knowledge. Towards a Post-Critical Philosophy* (London: Routledge, 2nd edition 1962), pp. 139–41.

all intents and purposes passed over. At the same time, deism translated into a temporal framework the essentially non-trinitarian conception it had inherited. What in Aquinas was understood in terms of a continuing hierarchical dependence of the finite on the infinite came to be understood as a relation of the present world to a past act of construction: the 'clockmaker deity.' The consequence was that those features of the doctrine of creation which had made it possible to conceive of a continuing relation of God to the world, and therefore continuing divine action in Christ, church, sacraments, etc., were excluded as the final outcome of that development in which the trinitarian foundation of the doctrine of creation had become excluded from the western intellectual world. The result of this was the progressive elimination of God from the world, the outcome exaggeratedly stated in John Dillenberger's remark that, 'the late nineteenth and early twentieth centuries may have been one of the rare periods in history in which theology was virtually impossible, when the crisis of language and imagination excluded the essential depth of both God and man.'[38] While there is no historical justification for so extreme an account of the situation, it does express how things sometimes feel. It certainly expresses the view put forward in many a work of popular theology on the current crisis of belief.

V THE NECESSITY OF A THEOLOGY OF NATURE

As has been said from time to time already, the doctrine of creation is concerned not only with divine action towards and within the creation, but with the kind of reality that the created order is. It is concerned with ontology, with an account of being; in this case, specifically with a theology of nature. On a definition of nature such as Collingwood's, that nature is 'that which is intrinsic to a thing', we can draw two conclusions.[39] The first is that the modern age replaced an essentially Hellenic philosophy of nature, according to which it is what it is by virtue of intrinsic rational powers and causes operating *above* material being, with one of contingencies consisting in patterning *within* it. This is accompanied by

---

38. John Dillenberger, *Protestant Thought and Natural Science* (London: Collins, 1961), p. 253.

39. R. G. Collingwood, *The Idea of Nature* (Oxford: Clarendon Press, 1945), p. 45. Thus does Ockham at once re-establish and subvert the Christian doctrine of creation, affirming contingency but at the expense of the world's foundation by God as 'that which shall not be moved'.

a philosophy of mechanism which tends to undermine it by returning to an idea of underlying rationality, in point of fact in a particularly rigid and deterministic form. The second is that on an Ockhamist account, according to which 'everything is due to an *ad hoc* act of an omnipotent God, then "nature" is denied.'[40] The outcome is that the theology of nature implicit in much science from Galileo to Newtonianism and beyond is problematic in a number of ways, so that science is both liberator and enslaver. Liberating from the dualism of eternal heaven and temporal earth, it – or its theorists – yet enslaves to alienating views, not only of the relation between ourselves and nature but also of that between different forms of human culture, broadly science, morality and art. It is only too obvious that our view of nature affects our attitude towards it and our behaviour to one another. If nature is mechanistic and empty of any other intrinsic meaning, then we are alienated from it existentially, and treat it not simply as another, but as a mere resource, or even an enemy. As we have seen claimed, it was Galileo who first used the language of inquisition in relation to the scientist's treatment of the physical world, and he was followed by another of modernity's patrons, Immanuel Kant.[41]

There are moments of truth in his contention. Nature does have in a sense to be subdued. In its present state, it does give up thorns and thistles rather than cabbages unless it is brought under the plough and weeded. It has to be made into a home, though that does not in any way imply ruthless exploitation so much as the freeing from alien control, a theme that is well expressed in Jesus' exorcisms when they are understood as the liberation of the enslaved creation from its orientation to dissolution rather than perfection. Moreover, if we are to take seriously the implications of the view that as human creatures we are both in continuity with and other than the remainder of the created order, we must explore the question both of our nature and of the non-human world's, as well as of the relation between the two. This cannot be done theologically without seeing both in relation to God. It is only the theological couching of the question which enables us to answer the question of what kind of otherness subsists between beings in their manifold relationships. If nature is a mechanism, and we are in some sense, as personal, other than machines – as is by no means evident on a mechanistic philosophy, whose implication might be that we are simply machines ourselves – then that is one form of otherness. But it is certainly not the

40. Collingwood, *The Idea of Nature*, p. 46.
41. Above, p. 127.

only conceivable one. We shall explore some aspects of this in the chapter devoted to the doctrine of the image of God.

Implicit in the question of the varying notions of the otherness of man and nature is the topic we have met in the outline of Kant's thought in particular, concerning the sense in which the world is knowable: what it is that makes it possible for human beings to relate with understanding to that which forms their environment. One aspect of the question recurs in the Enlightenment, in the dispute between Bishop Berkeley and his mechanist opponents. The thrust of Berkeley's polemic against those who would account for the way things are by the mechanical properties of 'substance' is that this is absurd. How can inert, impersonal matter, give rise to that most mysterious of all achievements, the human ability to know and perceive the world?[42] Berkeley argued that it is more rational to attribute our perception of the world to the direct agency of God than to inert substance. That Berkeley's own philosophy itself sailed close to the wind of pantheism is due to the fact that he lacked the trinitarian mediation whose absence we are lamenting. The problem of relating the one and the many tempted him to a concept of archetypal ideas which was never satisfactorily worked out because it was scarcely consistent with his main position.[43] Yet his formulation of the problem went to the heart of the matter: is impersonal matter or a personal deity the source of our personal knowledge? It is a repetition at another level of our recurring question: does the world create itself, or is it the product of personal agency?

Accordingly, some focus of personal mediation there must be if pantheism – too direct a relation between creator and creation – or deism – the lack of real relation – are to be avoided. If some account is to be given of the knowability of the world and the human capacity to know which gives due weight to each, a concept of mediation is essential. The question about the knowability of the world is and remains a real one, and was raised by one himself near to pantheism, Albert Einstein, when he said that the miracle is that there can be science at all: that our concepts can in some way, we know not how, engage with the world in such a way that its way of being can be known. 'The belief in an external world independent of the perceiving subject is the basis of all natural science.'[44] The concepts and theories by which we seek to understand this world

---

42. I have dealt with this question in detail in the opening chapters of *Enlightenment and Alienation. An Essay Towards a Trinitarian Theology* (London: Marshall, Morgan and Scott and Grand Rapids: Eerdmans, 1985).
43. George Berkeley, *Three Dialogues Between Hylas and Philonous*, 2.
44. Einstein, *The World as I See It*, p. 156.

'are free inventions of the human intellect, which cannot be justified either by the nature of that intellect or in any other fashion *a priori*.'[45] And yet they work. The miracle is that in some way or other they are seen to fit, as Riemannian geometry was found to fit with the world hypothesised by relativity theory.

Historically, as we have seen, the problematic step was moving from the metaphor of mechanism – of mechanism as a heuristic device – to a view that the universe is literally and only a mechanism. The metaphor did enable the liberation of thought from a pantheist or semi-pantheist view to one which is able to conceive of the world as creation: as other than the one who made it. But if pursued at the expense of other considerations, it strangely enough returns to a new pantheism, in which the machine serves effectively as the deity. This was the conclusion to which Coleridge came in his studies of the Newtonian tradition: that in effect mechanism and the pantheism which was being adopted by some of his contemporaries – and formerly by him – as a solution to its excesses were one and the same. Interestingly, this led Coleridge to the conclusion that there are, finally, only two alternative views of the world: trinitarian theism which enabled a distinction within relation between God and the world, and some form of pantheism in which worldly reality was swallowed up in that of God rather than being enabled truly to be itself.

In his paper, 'On the Prometheus of Aeschylus', he offers an immensely valuable threefold typology of world-views. There are, he says, three available cosmologies, not just two. (That is to say, he will not simply oppose 'Greek' and 'Hebrew', monist and dualist.) The first he calls the 'Phoenician'. According to this, 'the cosmogony was their theogony and *vice versa*'. That is to say, the origin of the cosmos and the origin of the divine are one and the same process. What emerges is a conception of the world as a kind of undifferentiated unity. We have an equation containing only two terms: 'a self-organising chaos' and 'nature as the result'.[46] We might see in modern pantheism a typical form of this cosmology. According to Spinoza, for example, the coming to be of God and of the world are one and the same thing, except of course that in Spinoza's timeless system to speak of a cosmogony is perhaps not easy; none the less, his cosmogony is his theogony.

45. Einstein, *The World as I See It*, p. 134.
46. Samuel Taylor Coleridge, 'On the Prometheus of Aeschylus', *Complete Works*, edited by W. G. T. Shedd (New York: Harper and Brothers, 1853), Vol. IV, pp. 344–65 (pp. 353, 354–5).

Coleridge's objection to such cosmologies lies in the absolute necessitarian determinism that results. (Similar are the implications of an effective divinisation of the process of evolution, which makes all that happens a function of some automatic and impersonal process.)

Coleridge's second cosmology, which he names the Greek, differs in
that it does assume a divinity 'antecedent to the matter of the world. But
on the other hand it coincides with the Phoenician in considering this
antecedent ground . . . not so properly the cause of (corporeal matter),
as the occasion and the still continuing substance . . . The corporeal was
supposed co-essential with the antecedent of its corporeity.' There are
important and positive theological implications, of which Coleridge is
aware, particularly in its revealing of the distinction between the human
and the other creation. But that is also the beginning of danger, for a
dualism of this kind, by dividing the world into mind and matter, material and intellectual, and positing a continuity between the human mind
and the divine, militates against a full doctrine of the createdness of all
that is not God. In some respects, therefore, as Coleridge points out 'the
Greek philosopheme does not differ essentially from the identification
of God with the universe . . .'.[47] To posit the essential divinity of the
mind is to risk a collapse back into pantheism by virtue of the mind's
continuity with the divine. (That, as we have seen, is the almost universal tendency in mediaeval thought.)

Coleridge rightly saw that a trinitarian theology generates a different
conception of the relation of God to the world. His chief interest was
in its possibilities for making room for human freedom in a conception
of the relation of God and the world, in contrast to the determinism
implicit in both pantheism and mechanism. Because, however, our primary concern is with the theology of nature, we shall turn for illumi-
nation to a near contemporary, Michael Faraday. His example makes
clear that theology can liberate as often as restrict science, because by it
he was enabled to develop the first steps towards field theory by virtue
of his theological discontent with Newtonianism. It is worth remarking
here that in the view of one historian of modern field theory, Faraday
was nearer to the truth than any of his predecessors and successors,
including Einstein.[48] Could this derive from his view of the relation of
God and the world? It is noteworthy that Faraday was driven to his

47. Coleridge, 'On the Prometheus', pp. 354 and 360. This passage is taken from my *The
Promise of Trinitarian Theology* (Second edition, T. & T. Clark, 1997), pp. 105–7.
48. William Berkson, *Fields of Force. The Development of a World View from Faraday to
Einstein* (London: Routledge, 1974), p. xi.

science by his confidence in the truth of Genesis. In his biography of
Faraday, Geoffrey Cantor claims that:

> Faraday conceived the laws of physics and chemistry as willed by
> God at the Creation. Moreover, the world manifests the aim of its
> designer. Secondly, since God created a perfect system both matter
> and 'force' are conserved and the system is self-sustaining.[49]

But there were more subtle theological influences than that, for
Faraday's conception of the diversity and unity of the world drew on
trinitarian conceptuality:

> [W]ithin this considerable diversity the various powers are interre-
> lated, or, as he expressed the principle . . . in 1849, there is proba-
> bly *'unity in one'*. The clear echo of the Christian tri-unity suggests
> both that the individual powers are mysteriously united and also
> that the different powers are the outward symbols of the invisible
> Godhead . . . [W]hile there is great diversity in nature's appear-
> ances, this diversity is the result of a few simple laws co-operat-
> ing.[50]

Here we have a theology of nature according to which conceptions of
the unity and diversity of nature derive in some way from an understanding of the unity-in-trinity of God.

Conceptions of nature are inextricably bound up with doctrines of
God. In Newton's case, and more especially in the Newtonianism that
developed from his thought, the doctrine that God is related to the universe especially by omnipresence – a spatial presence – encouraged not
only the making of both space and time ultimate in some way, but also
the spatialising of time. That is to say, Newtonianism suggests that time
is rather like space because it is understood on the analogy of space. That
appears problematic for one reason in particular. We are beings whose
temporality is irreversible: it is a fact of our being, taught by the Bible
as well as Heidegger, that we are those who move inexorably to our
death. By contrast, spatial relations are reversible: what moves forward can,
other conditions allowing, move backwards also. The effect of the spatialising of time is to treat it as reversible, like a machine. While Newton's
view of the world is by no means dead – for in recent cosmology, as in
theology, there is little consensus on fundamental matters – it appears to

49. Geoffrey Cantor, *Michael Faraday: Sandemanian and Scientist. A Study of Science and
    Religion in the Nineteenth Century* (London: Macmillan, 1991), p. 168.
50. Cantor, *Michael Faraday*, p. 172.

be one of the implications of the view of nature that has developed from Faraday's beginnings that there is much to be said for the doctrine that space and time are in certain respects different, however much they are equally features of one space-time universe.

The contrast between the classical mechanist and some more recent accounts of the universe is brought out by Prigogine and Stengers, who contrast the classical view of the reversibility of time with a more recent evolutionary view of the whole universe: 'In the classical view (sc. of the physical world) the basic processes of nature were considered to be deterministic and reversible. Processes involving randomness or irreversibility were considered only exceptions.'[51] Determinism and reversibility both imply an essentially static universe, not in the sense that there is no movement, but that all that happens is decided in advance (determinism) and that any process can in theory be taken back the way it came. There can thus in principle be no novelty. This means that as in some forms of the ancient doctrine of creation, the end is not different from the beginning. The Newtonian cosmology thus shared some of the features of the essentially non-trinitarian doctrines of creation that tended to characterise the Western world before modern times. Essentially the same is the case with Einstein, whose Spinozan vision, according to these authors, prevented him from realising some of the implications for time of his discoveries.[52] Einstein's world, for all its relativity, remained finally static in the sense I have been using the word. By contrast, Prigogine and Stengers are able to relate indeterminacy or contingence, relativity and a true dynamism. Theirs is a world whose reality is constituted by the arrow of time. It is a world congruent, though by no means identical, with that of Irenaeus, in the sense that it is consistent with his kind of eschatological dynamic.

The question of whether we can remain free from a spatialising – and ultimately pantheistic – conception of time is in large part a theological one. As we have seen, doctrines of God shape theologies of nature. The ghost of Newton still walks with greater or lesser influence in a number of modern trinitarian theologies, particularly in suggestions that the universe is to be understood as in some way (spatially) within the being of God. Moltmann's panentheistic notion of creation as kenosis is a case in point. According to this doctrine, God in some way contracts into himself in order to make room for creation 'outside'. 'Theologians have made [the] distinction between God's "inward" and his "outward"

---

51. Ilya Prigogine and Isabelle Stengers, *Order Out of Chaos. Man's New Dialogue with Nature* (London: Fontana, 1985), p. xxvii.
52. Prigogine and Stengers, *Order Out of Chaos*, pp. 214–15.

aspect so much a matter of course that no one has even asked the critical question: can the omnipotent God have an "outward" aspect at all? . . . If there were a realm outside God, God would not be omnipresent.' 'In order to create a world "outside" himself, the infinite God must have made room beforehand for a finitude in himself.'[53] 'God makes room for his creation by withdrawing his presence.'[54] '[I]f creation *ad extra* takes place in the space freed by God himself, then . . . the reality outside God still remains in the God who has yielded up that "outwards" in himself.'[55] This is an unconvincing argument because, as we shall see, it is possible to conceive a created world that is external to God and which does not yet exclude interrelationship and omnipresence. Another difficulty for the doctrine espoused by Moltmann is that there is little biblical support. There appears to be no reason why creation should involve a self-emptying of God if the universe is truly to be itself. If God as creator is the one who gives reality to the other, must he do it by making space within rather than without himself? Space, like time, is a function of the created world. Similarly, there is no suggestion in the Bible that the act of creation is anything but a joyful giving of reality to the other, 'when the morning stars sang together, and all the sons of God shouted for joy' (Job 38:7). This suggests that the metaphor of kenosis has been displaced from soteriology, where it belongs, to the doctrine of creation, where it does not, because it is a concept designed to deal with God's bearing in relation to a fallen world, not to be applied promiscuously to any of God's relations to the world.

Even the more trinitarianly orthodox Robert Jenson has a somewhat more nuanced version of the doctrine that creation is within God. It is interesting that Jenson is using the idea of the roominess of God – a spatial image – to generate an alternative to Augustine's view of time. He writes:

> for God to create is for him to open place in his triune life for others than the three whose mutual life he is. John of Damascus again: 'God is . . . his own place'. In that place, he *makes room*, and that act is the event of creation.

53. Jürgen Moltmann, *God in Creation. An Ecological Doctrine of Creation*, translated by Margaret Kohl (London: SCM Press, 1985), p. 86.
54. Moltmann, *God in Creation*, pp. 87–8. He continues: 'What comes into being is a *nihil* . . . which represents the partial negation of the divine Being, inasmuch as God is not yet Creator. This space . . . is a literally God-forsaken space'. This he then describes as hell, absolute death, though he then qualifies this by adding 'Admittedly the *nihil* only acquires this menacing character through the self-isolation of created beings to which we give the name of sin and godlessness.'
55. Moltmann, *God in Creation*, pp. 88–89.

This place in the triune life we call 'time'. That creation is above all the making of time for us, is of course again an ancient insight, most famously exemplified in Book XI of Augustine's *Confessions*, where the passion to understand God's creating turns out to have as its content the one question, 'What is time?' My answer: created time is room in God's own life.[56]

That will not do, because an adequate theology of the spaciousness of the created order will need to make more of the notion of creation as externalising.[57] As Moltmann has observed, some forms of externalising do lead to a doctrine of external relations – as in mechanism – where the doctrine of God's omnipresence is endangered or becomes oppressive.[58] But if the world is truly to be the world, it needs to be 'outside' of God, not in such a relationship according to which it is in some way enclosed within God. For this reason, panentheism cannot finally be distinguished from pantheism, because it does not allow the other space to be itself. There are a number of reasons for this, and they have been set out in detail by Thomas McFarland.[59] Chief among the arguments is that the conception's dependence on a notion of the relation between part and whole to couch the relation between God and the world inevitably introduces some form of ontological continuity. It tends to generate an idea of creation out of God rather than out of nothing. Similarly, those doctrines which in some way make time eternal, or read our temporality and spatiality up into God's eternity and infinity confuse the creature with the creator. Once again, we meet the problem that has followed us from the beginning. If the creation is to be truly creaturely, it requires its own time and space which are given by God but not continuous with his reality. But can this be done without taking God and the world out of relation with one another?

The clue is given in that otherwise perplexing preposition, according to which '*in* him all things were created, in heaven and on earth, visible and invisible . . .' (Colossians 1:16). There is a great deal of difference between saying that all things were created in God, *simpliciter*, and that

---

56. Robert W. Jenson, 'Aspects of a Doctrine of Creation', in *The Doctrine of Creation. Essays in Dogmatics, History and Philosophy*, edited by Colin E. Gunton (Edinburgh: T. & T. Clark, 1997), p. 24, citing John of Damascus, *The Catholic Faith*, 13. 9–11.
57. Athanasius, *Against the Arians*, 1. 29: 'a work is external to the nature, but a son is the proper offspring of the essence.'
58. Moltmann, *God in Creation*, p. 14.
59. Thomas McFarland, *Coleridge and the Pantheist Tradition* (Oxford: Clarendon Press, 1969), pp. 268–71.

it happened and happens in Christ. The reason is, as Pannenberg has pointed out, that the Son is the principle of the distinction between God and the world.[60] It follows that to create in the Son means to create by the mediation of the one who is the way of God out into that which is not himself. As the particular and free presence of God to the world, Jesus Christ is the basis of a doctrine of omnipresence.[61] But that cannot be adequately conceived without the Holy Spirit, the one by whose mediation the Son became incarnate and is made the means of the relating of the creation to God the Father. The Spirit, by thus relating the world to the Father through the Son in whom 'all things hold together' (Colossians 1:17), enables an omnipresence which is not the homogeneous presence of a container but the presence of one enabling the world to be and become truly itself. This is the case because the Holy Spirit, as the one who perfects creation, achieves the creation's true plurality by relating the 'many' to the Father through the Son. When creation is understood as a triune act, that is to say, the coherence and true diversity of the created order and its being enabled to be what it truly is are able to be given due place. They are maintained because the universe is held in personal relation to God, as creature to creator who remains other, rather than by some form of ontological continuity. When God the Son is the (personal) principle of the world's unity and coherence, the Holy Spirit, through that same Son, becomes the focus of the particularity of things; their becoming 'perfect' – complete – as distinctly themselves.

Accordingly, by returning to a more fully trinitarian account we are freed at once from mechanism and pantheism, as well as the latter's near relation, panentheism, because we have a way of establishing the reality of the world as world, while yet it remains in relation to the one who made it. It follows first that the world of space and time is what it is by virtue of its relation-in-otherness with the creator. Space and time are not continuous with God, which means that they are, as created realities, in some way functions of there being a created order. They are real – created – yet relative, relative to there being things which are what they are by virtue of their relation to God and to one another in space and time. It follows, second, that this universe of related things, taking shape in time and space, is constituted in relation to God through his creating Son and perfecting Spirit, and so also remains open to more

---

60. See below, chapter 7, section III.
61. Karl Barth, *Church Dogmatics*, translation edited by G. W. Bromiley and T. F. Torrance (Edinburgh: T. & T. Clark, 1957–75), 2/1, p. 468.

things than reductionist science imagines to be possible, human freedom and both worldly and artistic beauty as *realities* among them. These are real as part of the variously good creation and therefore need not be reduced to the movement of genes (or whatever), because those things can be granted their place and even their centrality without it being necessary to concede that they are mini-divinities. They, too, characterise only one sector of the multiple and varied universe whose dynamism in space and time is the gift of the personal creator. That is the created world's *nature*.

This conception of a world in personal and contingent relation to God has implications for the way in which we can use it as evidence for the existence of its maker. If it is truly itself, and not in necessary relation to God, the validity of all arguments which purport to demonstrate the existence of God from the existence of the world is thrown into question. There is something to be said here for the argument of Kant that there is no necessary way of moving from this world to another. The point, however, should depend not upon the philosophical scepticism that Kant learned from David Hume, but on the theological consideration that the world is the world, of interest simply for itself. Further, as should by now be clear, there are alternative views of understanding the nature of the world; in particular there is an absolute gulf between pantheism, which effectively denies creation, and trinitarian theism. Which deity is derived from an argument simply from the natural world, as we know it? It can be no accident that arguments purely from the world tend to produce polytheism and pantheism, or something near to the latter.[62]

It does not follow, however, that we must deny all contentions that the world in some way speaks the being of the one who made it. Yet if these are not to be arguments which effectively posit a continuity between the mind and the deity, they can be developed only on the basis of prior belief: on the church's confession of the triune creator. After all, there are no arguments without presuppositions, and those shape what we expect to see when we contemplate the glories of the created order. Interestingly, Athanasius takes even Romans 1:20 christologically. 'He who contemplates the creation is contemplating also the Word who framed it.'[63] And even here, there are problems. Is not the evidence, even for belief, ambiguous? Can there be a theology of nature

---

62. Arguments like those of Aquinas are shaped by the Christian tradition within which he worked, and are by no means 'natural' in an absolute sense.

which does not take into account the evil manifestly present in and to the world? We shall come to that question in due time.

But first, a summary of the conclusion of the chapter. It is generally agreed now that theology should not have attempted, in the way it did in the time of Galileo, to lay down the possibilities for natural science, even though we need not, either, share Galileo's other-worldly vision expressed in his oft-quoted view that theology is about how to go to heaven, not how the heavens go. Theology does have an interest in the theology of nature, at least to the extent that it can show, drawing on analyses like that of Coleridge, the hidden assumptions of some scientific positions, as, for example, Keith Ward and Mary Midgley have done in their criticisms of the positions of Dawkins and others.[64] The conclusion to be drawn is that if we see the world outside its relation to God, we do not see it properly. We may indeed see it partially, but may also see it falsely, in the distorting mirror of our own projections and wishes. When God is not confessed as the Lord of creation, either titanic man or deified gene take the floor, with the result that both understanding and the world are distorted. That is not to suggest that there is no nature, no world conceived as having its own proper reality and *Selbständigkeit*: not 'independence' but relative independence, according to the law of its being, which is to be what it is as God makes it. The key to this, as has already been made clear, is the doctrine of the Trinity, which allows us to understand the created world in various ways, according to the richness of God's trinitarian activity. In the two following chapters we shall follow first the historical re-emergence of a trinitarian conception of creation, and after that something of the systematic possibilities this opens up.

63. Athanasius, *Against the Arians*, 1. 12.
64. See, again, Keith Ward, *God, Chance and Necessity* (Oxford: Oneworld, 1996); Mary Midgley, *Evolution as a Religion. Strange Hopes and Stranger Fears* (London: Methuen, 1985); *Science as Salvation* (London: Routledge, 1992); and Richard Lewontin, *The Doctrine of DNA. Biology as Ideology* (London: Penguin Books, 1993).

7

RETURNING TO THE TRINITY:
A TALE OF FIVE CENTURIES

It is not the case that there is no trinitarian dimension to the theology of creation of the Middle Ages. As we have seen, certainly in the later period, there is a return to trinitarian considerations which appears to have had some effect on the wider world. In any case there are always continuities within the discontinuities of history. The first with which we are concerned is that between the later Middle Ages and the Reformation, for although there is a new beginning, it does not come out of the blue. We have seen that there is in Scotus a conception of the christological determination of all reality, and the influence of Scotus and his successors on John Calvin has recently been charted.[1] On the other hand, the shape of the discontinuity – although, again, it is not a complete one, as we shall see when we come to trace the theology of Calvin – is marked by the extreme voluntarism of William of Ockham. We have already seen that his essentially monistic and non-trinitarian conception of the divine willing helped to engender the world of deism with its vanishing creator. Crucial here is the distinction between the absolute and the ordained power of God. At the outset, we must affirm that some distinction between what God could have done and what he actually did in creating the universe is essential, not only for the notion

1. T. F. Torrance, *The Hermeneutics of John Calvin*, (Edinburgh: Scottish Academic Press, 1988).

of the contingency of the world – the world is what it actually is, not what it had necessarily to be – but also for maintaining the distinction between God and the world. But it does not follow that all formulations of the doctrine are adequate.

The weakness of the Ockhamist theology is that it tends to move from the former to the latter: from what God can do to what he has done, rather than the other way round. The tendency of all theology of creation after Augustine is to move from the abstract to the concrete: from abstract omnipotence or absolute power to the economy of creation and redemption. The deficiencies of the theologies we have traced are shown in part by a concentration on the concept of causality at the expense of a more personally conceived relation between God and the world. Instead of action mediated through Jesus Christ we are presented with abstract considerations which effectively by-pass the second and third persons of the Trinity in favour of some immanent continuity between God and the semi-divine ideas, and so between the mind and God. A similar problem returns in the nineteenth century with Schleiermacher, whose conception of the absolute dependence of the world on God, by being conceived for the most part independently of the eternal, let alone the incarnate, Son – in whom that theologian appears not to have believed – is always liable to collapse into pantheism.

With the Reformers two notes are struck which help to generate a renewal of the trinitarian tradition. One is a more strongly biblical note, according to which a more personal relation of God to the world displaces the mediaeval causal conception. The other is a greater stress on the concrete relevance of the doctrine to everyday life in the world. The Reformers are, in one sense but not another, more 'anthropocentric' than their predecessors. They are anthropocentric in the sense that they wish to show that the doctrine of creation is not abstract philosophy but an implication of the gospel and so primarily oriented to human life in the world. But they are not anthropocentric in the sense of later Enlightenment thought, for they do not see the world simply as at arbitrary human disposal. The weakness of much modern secular thought is to be found in its loss of that theocentrism which places human life in its broader cosmic context and so orders human activity to the creator's disposition for all created being, human and non-human alike.

I LUTHER AND CALVIN

In view of what we have just noted about the relatively non-trinitarian treatment of creation in the Middle Ages, Luther's claim that he was the

147

only person to have understood the first chapter of Genesis is only
slightly exaggerated. The change he brings about is remarkable. Unlike
Augustine, in his *Lectures on Genesis* Luther interprets the text in trinitarian fashion,[2] and is right to read it in the way that he does, especially
in the light of a theological understanding of the unity of the
Testaments. Both witness the action of the same God, and if he is indeed
triune, then his Old Testament revelation should also be so understood.
'Luther', says Regin Prenter, 'always speaks about creation in terms of
the Trinity.'[3] This enables Luther, first, to deny Augustine's neoplatonising
view that matter is almost nothing ('I disagree entirely'). To the contrary,
the text teaches us not about 'mystical days of knowledge among the
angels', 'not about allegorical creatures and an allegorical world, but about
real creatures and a visible world apprehended by the senses.'[4] Second,
recognising the forms of mediation in the chapter, Luther reaffirms that
God created heaven and earth out of nothing. He can do this because
he sees it to take place through the work of the Son, who adorns and
separates the crude mass which was brought out of nothing; and the
Spirit, who makes alive.[5] Whatever we are to make of his exegesis, the fact
remains that with Luther doctrines to which little more than lip service
had been paid for centuries come again to life. The result is that Luther's
theology of creation is one not of absolute so much as of personal
dependence: its atmosphere is of grace and gratitude. 'For here we may
see how the Father has given Himself to us, with all that he has created,
and how abundantly he has cared for us in this life . . .'[6]

There are, of course, problems, and it might be said that here too more
might have been done for the substantiality of the created world. There
is to be seen in Luther's treatment of creation in the *Greater Catechism*[7]
a tendency to the reduction of the created world to its instrumental use

2. Martin Luther, *Luther's Works*, 1, *Lectures on Genesis chapters 1–5*, edited by J. Pelikan
   (St Louis: Concordia, 1958), p. 9. Luther is contemptuous of Augustine's mystical
   interpretation of the text, as well of his and Hilary's view that God created instantaneously, pp. 4–5.
3. Regin Prenter, *Spiritus Creator. Luther's Concept of the Holy Spirit* (Philadelphia: Muhlenberg, 1953), p. 192.
4. Luther, *Lectures on Genesis*, pp. 4–5.
5. Luther, *Lectures on Genesis*, p. 9.
6. Luther, *Lectures on Genesis*, p. 98.
7. Martin Luther, *Greater Catechism*, The First Article. Luther's exposition of the creed
   in the second part of *The Greater Catechism* appropriates creation to God the Father,
   following the rather modalistic manner of the Apostles' Creed. He also understands
   creation personally, from the point of view of the believer. Creation means that: 'I
   understand and believe that I am God's creature, that is, that He gave me and preserves

for us. But it is only a tendency, and Oswald Bayer has argued that not only must Luther's view be sharply distinguished from later anthropocentrism, but that his theology of creation is far broader in scope than is often supposed. In the first place, Luther is able to affirm the reality and goodness of the whole created order in a way that was not achieved by representative figures from the ancient and modern worlds. Whereas relation to God is for Augustine very much a direct relation between God and the soul, for Luther it is *'ein wesentlich weltlich vermitteltes Verhältnis.'*[8] Similarly, Luther's stress that God has created me *and all creatures* leads him to a view of things far removed from Descartes' distinction between thinking and extended being (pp. 91–2). Equally important is the distinction of Luther from Schleiermacher. His faith in creation, far from being a taste for the infinite, is on the contrary an affirmation of the finite (p. 95). Thus is Luther able to affirm what is central to a Christian theology of creation, that creation is to be understood not only as God's address *to* but also *through* the creature (p. 93).

Second, this combination of 'to' and 'through' – which Bayer rightly prefers to the parallel pairing of transcendence and immanence – enables Luther to stress the witness of the Psalms to God's present action as creator in such a way as to avoid a deistic reading of the priestly creation narrative. His juxtaposition of perfect ('he has created') and present tenses ('he gives') guards against a 'punctualist' understanding of God's action in the world, and must be understood in relation to Luther's understanding of the Lord's Supper as the paradigmatic mode of God's presence to the world.[9] We shall return to this theme, but before moving to Calvin must note the importance of the reference to the Supper as enabling the maintenance of the christological and pneumatological mediation of the doctrine of creation. It enables in particular a continuing orientation to the doctrine of creation's affirmation of the importance of the material

---

for me continually my body, my soul and life, etc.', pp. 96–7. Luther is not very interested in the non-personal world for its own sake. Creatures are there to 'serve for my use and the necessities of life' (p. 97). But there is no trace of the causal conception of creation which is so dominant in the thought of his predecessors.

8. Oswald Bayer, *Schöpfung als Anrede* (Tübingen: J. C. B. Mohr, Paul Siebeck, 1990, 1st edition 1986), p. 95: 'a relation mediated in an authentically worldly way.'

9. Bayer, *Schöpfung als Anrede*, pp. 97–101. Similarly, Christoph Schwöbel has pointed out that by connecting justification to the notion of creation out of nothing, Luther has shown that for him creation is already an order of righteousness. 'Theologie der Schöpfung im Dialog zwischen Naturwissenschaft und Dogmatik', *Unsere Welt: Gottes Schöpfung. Festschrift für E. Wölfel* (Marburg: N. G. Elwert Verlag, 1992), pp. 199–221.

world. Despite all this, however, there is still some danger that Luther might be understood in too anthropocentric a way. The strong orientation of all his thought to justification does encourage an overweighting of redemptive themes in his theology as a whole, as is the case with many western theologians.

Calvin's legacy is similar, and again somewhat ambiguous. As is well known, his theology of creation has an existential orientation similar to Luther's, articulated as it is in a dialectic of the knowledge of God the creator and of ourselves. The characteristic Reformation polemic against scholastic abstraction can be observed in his claim that these two together constitute almost the sum of wisdom.[10] There is no interest in abstract speculation. But the other side is also apparent, in Calvin's tendency to narrow the scope of a theology of creation to its anthropological relevance, a narrowing similar to Luther's. Although he affirms the doctrine of creation out of nothing in his commentary on Genesis,[11] there is surprisingly little interest in it in the *Institutes*. There is, again in line with Luther, a new interest in the christological mediation of creation. Yet what interests Calvin is not speculation, Augustinian or other, about creation out of nothing, so much as the relevance of conceptions of divine action for the confidence of the believer in God's government of things. It should not be denied that some of the implications of creation out of nothing do appear in Calvin's thought, and are of crucial importance in that process of freeing the created order from the Platonic and Aristotelian intermediate quasi-agencies that was so essential for the development of a satisfactory doctrine of creation.[12] The presentation of the created order as a semiotic system, a system of signs which as a system pointed beyond itself to its maker, helped to assure the relative independence of creation from the creator without which a proper notion of contingency could not develop. But there is an Achilles' heel, which can be inspected through a study of Calvin's writings on the continuing relation of creator with his creation. His real interaction with his predecessors comes in the extended treatment of providence that dominates the latter chapters of Book 1 of the *Institutes*.

In it we meet a theology of the omnipotent will of God containing

---

10. John Calvin, *Institutes*, 1. 1. 1.
11. John Calvin, *Genesis*, translated by John King (Edinburgh: Banner of Truth, 1965), p. 70.
12. The way in which features of a disappearing way of thinking continue to leave their mark is illustrated by Bouwsma's remark that Calvin 'also slipped once into claiming that the heavens are "eternal and exempt from alteration".' William J. Bouwsma, *John Calvin. A Sixteenth Century Portrait* (Oxford University Press, 1988), p. 73.

more than a few echoes of the rather 'monotheistic' treatment which we met in the Schoolmen. Augustine is cited in support of the claim that there is no higher cause of things than God's will (14. 1). Repeatedly it is asserted that there is no such thing as chance. What may appear to be chance faith recognises as a secret impulse from God (16. 2 and 9). In what may be a criticism of a Thomist conception, Calvin refuses to say 'that God is the first agent because he is the beginning and cause of all motion.' Quite the reverse: 'believers comfort themselves with the solace that they suffer nothing except by God's ordinance and command . . .' (16. 3). '[P]rovidence is lodged in the act', not simply the foreknowledge of God (16. 4). Elsewhere he appeals to Augustine in defence of a belief that 'nothing is more absurd than that anything should happen without God's ordaining it, because it would then happen without any cause' (16. 8). What are we to make of all this? There are three main points.

(1) It is sometimes remarked that Calvin is not very interested in the third possible form of knowledge beyond the knowledge of God and of ourselves, that of the world in and for itself, though much is made in treatments of his relation to science of the encouragement given to the development of science by his celebration of the glory of God visible in the created world. But the question must remain of whether the sum of wisdom includes knowledge of the world also. As we have already seen, it was the recovery of the doctrine of creation out of nothing that facilitated the emergence of the belief, so important for the development of modern science, in the contingency of the world. Certainly Calvin's world is contingent in the sense that it does not have to be, because it is freely created by the will of a personal God. But it is not so securely contingent in the respect that what happens in it does not have to happen as it does. Contingency has, it must be remembered, two senses, referring first to the dependence of the world on God, a sense that was undoubtedly present in Aquinas; and also, second, to the world's non-necessity, particularly in relation to its divine source. Calvin in fact, rightly careful as he is to escape any entanglement in the concepts of fortune or chance, appears also, as we have seen, to deny any concept of contingency. On the one hand, he denies a Stoic necessitarianism; but on the other by appearing to equate the concepts of contingency and chance, has rightly or wrongly laid himself open to the same charge. The unqualified assertion of divine willing is not adequate to escape a tendency to necessitarianism.[13]

---

13. Calvin, *Institutes*, 1. 16. 8. After the equation of the two concepts of chance and contingency, the latter disappears from the discussion.

(2) The immense and rather repetitive length in which Calvin wrestles with the problem of divine agency in relation to the world no doubt has something to do with what Bouwsma has called his anxiety.[14] These were times very much imbued with a sense of Heraclitean flux and the uncertainty of things, as that historian also records. But there are also signs that Calvin was himself uneasy about the apparently determinist direction of his thought, as his brief appeals to the concept of secondary causation reveal. He would not rule out secondary causes 'in their proper place',[15] but of the status of these secondary causes nothing is said.[16] In general therefore Calvin is able to give a more satisfying account of the universal providential care of God than of the correlative thesis that human agents are responsible for their actions. The reason for this is to be found in:

(3) In some contrast to the rest of his theology, there is in Calvin's account of the relation of God and the world little substantive part played by Christ and the Holy Spirit. There is in the passages we have reviewed from Calvin only one statement of the christological mediation of divine action in creation (1. 16. 4). Similarly, the splendid characterisation of the Spirit's universal and life-giving work – 'everywhere diffused' he 'sustains all things, causes them to grow, and quickens them in heaven and earth' (1. 13. 14) – is to be found in the chapter on the doctrine of the Trinity, and does not recur with the same weight in the long treatment of providence. It is at least arguable that the return of the category of cause to a more prominent place in the theology of Edwards has something to do with the intimations of omnicausality in Calvin. And

---

14. Bouwsma, *John Calvin. A Sixteenth Century Portrait*, chapter 2.
15. Calvin, *Institutes*, 1. 17. 6 and 9.
16. It is surely significant that the concept of secondary causality was introduced in order to establish some form of limited autonomy in the creature. But it is problematic. Without a satisfactory concept of mediation, it simply replicates the problems we have met. The question that must be asked is whether the concept of secondary causation is an attempt to ensure the relative autonomy of the creature in the absence of an adequate conception of the mediation of creation and of providence or conservation. Creation trinitarianly conceived is thus the necessary condition of a doctrine of creation out of nothing, because without it matter, or some other feature of the universe, becomes the mediator, and thus eternal. Secondary causation is therefore either too strong – producing the redundancy of God in deism – or it is too weak, and the world becomes once again the determined product of divine monocausality, as for example in Spinoza. Here it is instructive to return to the case of Bishop Berkeley. Berkeley rejected the concept of mediation by created substance on various grounds, among them that substance was unknowable and that it effectively replaced God as the real agent of creation. But his solution, lacking a trinitarian concept of mediation, failed to achieve its end.

part of the reason is that we meet here somewhat more of a theology of will than of love, more of an omnipotent monocausal God than of the one who works through his two hands, the Son and the Spirit.

In concluding this section, however, my concern is to summarise the positive developments in both Luther and Calvin. There is in both of these theologians a major shift away from the language of causality to one of personal action. The result is that the doctrine of creation is taken out of the largely philosophical context in which it had tended to be located, where it had become a semi-independent propaedeutic for faith, and returned to the confessed creed. This is the clear outcome equally of Luther's trinitarian reading of Genesis – as well as his close relating of creation with the believer's trust in God – and of Calvin's concern with God's personal and providential oversight of the creation.[17] Thus there is much to be said for the claim that the Reformers contributed to, indeed achieved with little assistance from their Western predecessors, the recovery of the doctrine of creation. The heart of this achievement was, first, that in continuity with Ockham, they did much to re-establish a doctrine of the contingency of the created order on a freely willed act of God, and in this way encouraged the reappropriation of the onto-logical distinction of creator from creation which had been obscured by doctrines of quasi-eternal forms and hierarchies of causes. There are on this account only two realities, creator and creation. Along with this went the reappropriation of the doctrine of the ontological homoge-neity of the created order. Equally important, secondly, the Reformers began a process of replacing a conception of causality, relatively imper-sonally conceived, or, if not, of creation rather monistically construed in terms of will, with conceptions of agency in terms of trinitarian medi-ation, and that means agency far more personally conceived. Here they went far beyond their mediaeval predecessors. It follows that the God who creates the world is distinguished from all causes and emanations by the personal and intentional freedom by which he works.

The chief problem bequeathed by the Reformers derives from the fact that they were less successful in developing an account of the world's continuing relation with God the creator. Tradition, as in the Apostles' Creed, and even in the confessions of the rule of faith that are quoted by Irenaeus, attributes creation to the Father, salvation to the

17. A link between christology and the abandonment of the scholastic idiom of causality has been observed by Ralph Del Colle to take place in Catholic theology, though at a much later date. Ralph Del Colle, *Christ and the Spirit. Spirit-Christology in Trinitarian Perspective* (New York and Oxford: Oxford University Press, 1994), *passim*, though see, for example, p. 132.

Son and life in the church (etc.) to the Spirit. That encourages modalism and draws attention away from the New Testament affirmations of the place of Jesus Christ in the mediation of creation as well as of salvation. That is perhaps the reason why the doctrine of creation is so often merely monotheistically or unitarianly construed. Rather, it should be said that creation, reconciliation and redemption are all to be attributed to the Father, all realised through the work of his two hands, the Son and the Spirit, who are themselves substantially God. There is mediation, but it is through God, not ontological intermediates. This tends to be lost when any other mediator conceived independently of the 'two hands' – Platonic forms, Aristotelian causes, Lockean or Newtonian substance, Berkeleyan archetypes – becomes the central focus of attention.

II AFTER THE REFORMATION

Much of the history of Reformation thought after Luther and Calvin represents a return to mediaeval, indeed Thomist, ways of couching the fundamental relation between God and the world.[18] The Trinity becomes largely irrelevant to the doctrine of creation, which is increasingly understood in a monistic manner. Already with Jonathan Edwards, for all of the strongly trinitarian orientation of much of his thought, there are signs of a return to traditional concepts of God's causal action in the world. For all his greatness, he can be seen to have introduced disturbingly determinist elements into his own Reformed heritage. Edwards appears to understand the concept of cause as an analogical one. Created causality is not determinist or necessitarian. 'CAUSE is that, after or upon the existence of which, or the existence of it after such a manner, the existence of another thing follows.'[19] But the causality exercised by God does appear to be understood in a determinist or even necessitarian manner. Along with Berkeley, Edwards wished to replace the theory that sensations were caused by substance with one that they were caused directly by God:

> The reason why it is so exceedingly natural to men to suppose that there is some latent substance, or something that is altogether hid,

18. See R. N. Frost, 'Richard Sibbes' Theology of Grace and the Division of English Reformed Theology', PhD. London, 1996, for a documenting of the increasing preponderance of Thomist categories in English Puritanism after the Reformation.
19. Jonathan Edwards, *Scientific and Philosophical Writings, The Works of Jonathan Edwards*, volume 6, edited by Wallace E. Anderson (New Haven and London: Yale University Press, 1980), p. 350.

that upholds the properties of bodies, is because all see at first sight that the properties of bodies are such as need some cause that shall every moment have influence to their continuance, as well as a cause of their first existence. All therefore agree that there is something that is there, and upholds these properties; and it is most true, there undoubtedly is. But men are wont to content themselves in saying merely that it is something; but that 'something' is he by whom all things consist.[20]

This led Edwards to what a recent commentator has called his doctrine of omnicausality. Michael Jinkins says that 'he wanted to demonstrate that it is reasonable to enlightened people, not only to believe that all things are causally determined, but that all things are causally determined *by God.*'[21] And he notes the reason: there is otherwise no way of ascending by a chain of causation to prove the existence of God.[22]

The attempt to use the doctrine of creation evidentially or as the basis of a proof of the existence of God is one of the signs of a return to an abstract conception of the absolute power of God. In what is sometimes called Protestant scholasticism we witness another symptom, a return to the platonic notion of the ideas in the mind of God which, as we have seen, tend to displace the christological mediation of creation. In his compendium of Reformed dogmatics Heinrich Heppe cites the seventeenth-century dogmatician Polanus, to the effect that:

> Let it stand fixed and sure that in the divine mind there had been and were ideas of everything that was created . . . as is admitted since *Augustine.* – The divine ideas of the things created are forms existing in the divine mind from eternity, not really distinct from the divine essence, but which are actually the same as the divine essence.[23]

---

20. Edwards, *Scientific and Philosophical Writings*, p. 380, cf p. 339: 'Our perceptions, or ideas that we passively receive by our bodies, are communicated to us immediately by God while our minds are united with our bodies.'
21. Michael Jinkins, '"The Being of Beings". Jonathan Edwards' Understanding of God as Reflected in his final Treatises', *Scottish Journal of Theology* 46 (1993), pp. 161–90 (p.164).
22. Jinkins, "The Being of Beings", p. 172–3, citing *The Freedom of the Will, The works of Jonathan Edwards*, volume 1, edited by Paul Ramsey (New Haven and London: Yale University Press, 1957), p. 182.
23. Heinrich Heppe, *Reformed Dogmatics. Set out and Illustrated from the Sources*, edited by E. Bizer (Grand Rapids, Michigan: Baker, 1978 edition), p. 192. Compare Chapter 5, above, especially note 1.

Whether or not Barth is right, therefore, in all the details of his understanding of the Thomist analogy, there can be little doubt that in so far as patterns of causality intrinsic to the created order displace the christological mediation of creation, the analogy of being is resistant to a fully trinitarian construal of the relation of God and the world.

Darkness tends to return in the nineteenth century, with theology's two leading German exponents, Hegel and Schleiermacher, sailing too close to the wind blowing from Romanticism, whose natural movement was to a form of pantheism or near pantheism.[24] On the liberal side of Protestantism, a renewed abstractness is to be seen in Schleiermacher's conception of creation as absolute dependence, which is essentially non-christological, and generates a fusion of creation and providence, as Schleiermacher himself acknowledges.[25] The young Schleiermacher has to defend himself in long and unconvincing footnotes against the charges of pantheism which the first edition of the *On Religion* had evoked. His later work is saved from a straight pantheism by its more robust christology but, despite this, it does not have much effect on the doctrine of creation, which, as we shall see in the next chapter, has difficulty in preventing divine action from being assimilated to the timeless action of a platonic form. Suffice it to say that the self-confessedly Sabellian nature of Schleiermacher's theology excludes the Son and the Spirit from playing any constitutive part in the mediation of creation.

Hegel's thought is similarly modalist, although it takes a more temporal and ultimately pantheist form. The world is for him the outcome of God's self-externalisation in time. As a form of history, it represents God's going out from himself and final return to himself *as Spirit*. It is clearly not an unrelieved pantheism, because it seeks a genuine externalisation of God *in* the other, but eschatologically it tends to pantheism because of the world's ultimate return to God as God. Its eschatological roots are in Plotinus rather than Irenaeus, a difference which brings into relief what is being attempted in this book: not an account of God's self-externalisation, but as the mediation, through Son and Spirit, of a world that is genuinely other than God while yet remaining in relation with him. History is thus not the realisation of divinity as it is for Hegel, but the realm of the perfecting of that which God creates and redeems in order to be the object of his love.

24. We have already seen that Coleridge's conception was more robustly trinitarian.
25. See F. D. E. Schleiermacher, *The Christian Faith*, translated by H. R. Mackintosh and J. S. Stewart (Edinburgh: T. & T. Clark, 1928), pp. 142–6; and below, Chapter 8, section II.

III TWO TWENTIETH-CENTURY THEOLOGIES: KARL BARTH AND WOLFHART PANNENBERG

To Karl Barth (1886–1968) must go much credit for the restoration of a trinitarian mediation of creation, to be witnessed both in his determinedly credal construing of the doctrine and in his attempt to integrate creation and salvation christologically. Barth's fundamental affirmation is a repetition of that of Irenaeus. The doctrine of creation is not a piece of natural theology, but the first article of the church's confession of faith. Moreover, it belongs within the structure of the *Church Dogmatics* as a work of the whole Trinity, though one which is, on the basis of revelation, attributed particularly to the Father. It is thus not the work of an unknown god, or a god of reason, but of the one made known as the God and Father of our Lord Jesus Christ. Barth's doctrine of creation as an act of God the Father is rooted in his christological determination of the meaning of that term. God the Father is not a projection of fatherhood on to eternity, but the one who is known as Lord of all specifically with reference to the death and resurrection of Jesus Christ. This implies that God is Father 'in the strict sense and to the degree that He is Lord over the life and death of man' (1/1, p. 388). The christological determination of this is clear: 'God our Father means God our Creator . . . And it should be clear . . . that it is specifically in Christ, as the Father of our Lord Jesus Christ, that God is called our Creator' (p. 398).

While in the first volume of the *Church Dogmatics*, in the section devoted to the three persons of the Trinity, attention is directed to the character of the God who is known as Father, in the third volume it is turned to the implications of this theology for the doctrine of creation itself. Because God is defined as the God and Father of our Lord Jesus Christ, it follows that the doctrine of creation is an article of faith, dependent upon the gift of God himself: 'an article . . . which no man has procured for himself, or ever will . . .' (3/1, p. 3). The reason is that apart from revelation there is no way of deciding from the ambiguous evidence of the world that the world is divine creation. 'It is not self-evident that the reality which surrounds man . . . is a reflection of the benevolence of the One to whom it owes its reality . . . Menacing evil, or a polluted source of no less evil than good . . . might equally well underlie it . . .' (p. 38). That explains one reason for the reference to cross and resurrection. It is only where the threat to creation's goodness is faced and overcome that its intrinsic goodness can be understood; apart from that, its meaning is ambiguous.

157

The content of the doctrine of creation is threefold. First, 'that another exists before, near and with God, having its own differentiated being quite distinct from God' (p. 5). Second, God being the one he is, he is free in relation to what is not himself, and therefore could be alone. Creation is the result of the free will of God. 'God is before the world in the strictest sense that He is its absolute origin, its purpose, the power which rules it, its Lord' (p. 7). Third, the doctrine is of biblical origin, in that only from scripture do we learn that God is not to be equated with a world cause and that creation is a completed and contingent act, as the result of which there exists the sum of reality which is distinct from God, what the Bible calls 'heaven and earth' (pp. 11–22). As usual, Barth goes right to the heart of the matter. The doctrine of creation is a faith-affirmation, rationally supported indeed, but not the result of a philosophical inference of some kind. If there is a weakness, it is in replicating – at least so far as the opening summary of the teaching is concerned – the weaknesses of the Western tradition. It is indeed the act of the triune God, knowledge of whom is christologically determined. But Barth does not at this stage in any way stress the christological determination or mediation of the doctrine itself.

This does begin to appear in the second section, on creation and covenant, but even there the stress is on christology as a focus of a promised salvation, rather than as the basis of the act of creating (pp. 50–1). We shall realise the force of this point if we compare it with Pannenberg's more explicitly trinitarian conception of the mediation of creation, where we shall find some echoes of Barth, particularly in a stress on the freedom and contingency of creation. The differences between the two are to be seen in Pannenberg's stronger stress on the agency of the Son and the Spirit in the triune act of creating. The christology is particularly strong and distinctive. Barth does not have so much a conception of the christological mediation of creation as a stress on the analogy between the Son's and the world's distinction from the Father. 'The eternal fellowship between Father and Son . . . finds a correspondence (*Entsprechung*) in the very different but not dissimilar fellowship between God and His creature' (p. 50). By contrast, in his treatise on the doctrine of creation in the second volume of his *Systematic Theology*,[26] Pannenberg (1928–) makes the personal distinction the basis of the ontological. 'The Son is the primary object of the Father's love. In all the creatures to which he addresses his love he loves the Son' (p. 21).

---

26. Wolfhart Pannenberg, *Systematic Theology* 2, translated by G. W. Bromiley, (Edinburgh: T. & T. Clark, 1994).

But, more than this, '[i]n the Son is the origin of all that differs from the Father, and therefore of the creatures' independence vis-à-vis the Father' (p. 22). 'The creation of creatures distinct from God rests on the self-distinction of the eternal Son' (p. 63). Further, the Son is also the link between God and the distinct created reality in its distinctness (p. 31). Christology thus both distinguishes and relates God and the world.

What, however, is at once Pannenberg's most original and questionable contribution is that this difference is based in the Son's *self-distinction* from the Father, rather than the traditional notion of his eternal begottenness as the basis of a distinction between God's being and his act of creation.

> Decisive in this regard is the self-distinction of Jesus from the Father, by which he lets God be God as Father over against himself, differentiating himself as a mere creature from the Father, subjecting himself to the one true God . . . This event of the self-distinction of Jesus from the Father constitutes the revelation of the eternal Son in the earthly existence of Jesus . . . Hence we have first a noetic basis for his eternal sonship in this distinction from the Father. But are we not also to seek in the self-distinction of the eternal Son from the Father an *ontic* basis for the existence of the creature in its distinction from the Creator? The self-distinction of the Son . . . forms a starting point for the otherness and independence of creaturely existence. (p. 22)

The chief question to be asked of this is whether it attributes too great a role to God the Son in initiating creation, rather than as the one through whom God creates the world. (Is there a trace of tritheism?) There is a danger that the idea of Jesus' self-distinction from the Father will override the more central notion of his being sent by the Father and being what he is in free obedience to his Father's will.[27] In the latter case, Jesus Christ remains the mediator of the Father's act, but as the one who is the eternal object of the Father's love, and so *other* than the Father, and accordingly the one who enables the created order, too, to be genuinely other, though also other in inextricable relation. Nevertheless, that aspect apart, Pannenberg's central claim about the function of christology in the construction of the doctrine of creation is precisely right: 'the Son is the origin of creaturely existence not only as the principle of distinction and self-distinction but also as the link with that which is thus distinct' (p. 31).

27. I know from conversation with him that Pannenberg would not accept that this is the implication of his position.

Pannenberg's pneumatology stands also in marked contrast with Barth's. The latter tends to minimise the part played by the Holy Spirit in the act of creation, refusing an explicitly pneumatological reading of Genesis 1:2 because of his concern to see in the verse the promise of eschatological defeat of *das Nichtige* (3/1, pp. 108–10). Pannenberg, however, in another contribution at once interesting and questionable, couches the creating act of the Spirit in language borrowed from cosmological theory. The notion of the Spirit as the divine 'field of force' enables Pannenberg to show that, just as some modern field theory enables us to see created reality not as impermeable atoms but of interacting fields of force, so the divine Spirit is the field of force through which the world becomes and is upheld as what it essentially is. This enables him to say, in summary of what he holds to be the biblical teaching of the place of the Spirit in creation, that 'On the one side the Spirit is the principle of the creative presence of the transcendent God with his creatures; on the other side he is the medium of participation of the creatures in the divine life and therefore in life as such' (p. 32).

There are two objections to the latter of those two varying conceptions of the place of the Holy Spirit in relation to creation. The first is not the connection with life, for the affirmation that the Spirit is Lord and giver of life is surely one of the great legacies we receive from the tradition. But must life be understood as participation in the life of God? The danger here is that something will be taken away from the creature's enjoyment of life in itself, as other than God. We must beware, having made the Son the basis of the distinction-in-relation of God and the world, of taking away with the left hand what is given with the right. The fact that Pannenberg may be conceding too much to the Neoplatonist tradition is indicated also by the second difficulty with his position, and that is the relative failure to give an eschatological role to the Spirit, who becomes more nearly the mediator of a timeless relationship. That is, to be sure, not quite fair. Pannenberg retains from his earlier work the stress on the future: the Spirit's 'field operations are temporally structured, so that each new event proceeds from the future of God' (p. 109). Yet here too there is a tendency for the left hand to undo the work of the right. 'Eternity is the undivided presence of life in its totality . . . Unlike our human experience of time, it is a present that comprehends all time, that has no future outside itself' (p. 92). Can this Plotinian view of eternity really be compatible with a pneumatology which conceives the Spirit as the one who, through the Son, achieves the perfecting of the creature *through time*? It is not that the redemptive and transformative office of the Spirit receives no emphasis in Pannenberg's treatment, but that it sits uncomfortably with the Plotinian/Augustinian view of eternity as a timeless embracing of time.

The real weakness of Pannenberg's conception of the Spirit is his identification the third Person of the Trinity *as* a divine field of force. Here it must be conceded that it is not improper to use physical or material analogies to characterise the operations of the Holy Spirit. The suggestions of mysterious and unpredictable power, the freedom of the Spirit in relation to the created order, make it quite understandable that his work should be described in metaphors suggesting materiality. The Spirit is the Father's agent enabling the created order in all its material concreteness to be and do that for which it was created. Yet if we are to understand the Spirit as the third 'person' of the Trinity, the one whose personal agency perfects the created order through the Son, we must understand all the material analogies, from both Old and New Testaments, in the light both of the Fourth Gospel's conception of the Spirit and of the Spirit's paradigmatic eschatological act of resurrection. Here the personal, the material and the eschatological come together. As the Spirit's recreating power transforms the body of the crucified, so it is the Spirit's office to enable the world to be transfigured into that which it is created to be.[28]

One must not, however, here stress what might be called the trans-formative–redemptive dimensions of the Spirit's action at the expense of the ordinary and everyday. It is that with which we are particularly concerned in this chapter. When in the ancient creeds the Spirit is cel-ebrated as the Lord and giver of life, he is seen as the one who enables created things, and particularly living created beings, to be what they truly and variously are in their manifoldness. The world does indeed cohere in the Son, but is diversified and particularised as the second hand of the Father enables things to be what they are created to be in the Son, even before the end and even despite the chaos and disorder inserted into the good order of things by sin and evil. The perfecting of the creation sometimes involves the maintaining of the order of things in its regularity, sometimes the restoration of a lost order; and sometimes the eschatological transformation of the world into anticipation of that which it will become. It is a function of the diversity of the creation that

28. I am not suggesting that Pannenberg does not, in both of the first volumes of his *Systematic Theology*, attribute to the Spirit a range of activities, some of them con-strued in terms of personal agency. It is rather that he allows the notion of the field of force to dominate his conception of the Spirit's action in relation to the created order and to preclude the kind of personal eschatological agency that is so important in this connection.

its perfection is realised in a diversity of ways through the work of the particularising Spirit. If the Son is the one through whom and in whom God the Father creates, upholds and redeems, the action of the one who brings the created order, perfected, to the Father through the Son will necessarily do so in harmony with the real diversity and variety of the creator's work. It follows that the way in which the relation between creation and redemption is conceived is crucial, so that we cannot complete a chapter on the dogmatic renewal of the doctrine of creation without some attention to it. Once again, we shall find that the way in which the work of the 'two hands' of God the Father is related makes all the difference.

IV CREATION AND REDEMPTION: (1) KARL BARTH

The second of the merits of Barth's attempt in the twentieth century to restore the doctrine of creation is his renewed attention to the relation between creation and redemption or salvation. As is well known, he is a theologian whose attention to christology necessarily suggests a strong emphasis on salvation, or reconciliation (*Versöhnung*) to use his preferred term. We shall see that his treatment of the relation of creation and redemption does bear this mark, but is also significant for its attempt to relate the two positively. In fact, the interest of his teaching lies in the fact that it attempts to subordinate creation and redemption alike to a higher principle which will serve to relate them. That principle, perhaps better simply called a doctrine, is the covenant, according to which God's eternal purpose in Christ is to elect the human race into reconciled relation with him. The historical, temporal, covenant is the outcome of God's eternal choice to elect Jesus Christ and in him the whole human race. On this account salvation means the working out of the divine purpose, which precedes the creation in the divine intention, to come into reconciled relation with humankind. Given the way things are, this must necessarily take the form of an overcoming of human sin through the incarnation, death and resurrection of Jesus Christ. Because sin is the irrational human refusal of God's covenant love, reconciliation is the restoration of the original covenantal intention. But it is a reconciliation purposed from the beginning rather than a second attempt after a first failed enterprise.

What, then, is the place of the creation? The created order is the stage on which God's covenant purposes are brought to pass, the field, to change the metaphor, on which reconciliation takes place. What we find is a combination of Irenaean and more recent Western themes. Reconciliation is for Barth a kind of recapitulation. It is a completion of the original intention, and also an enrichment of it rather than simply being a return to a perfect beginning. 'What He effects and does and reveals by becoming man – for us – is much more than the restoration of the status quo ante – the obviating of the loss caused by our own transgression . . .' (4/1, p. 13).[29] Another interesting feature is provided by the characteristically Barthian stress on the freedom of God in creation and reconciliation. We have seen how in Ockham this can lead to an arbitrary creating, as an absolutely undetermined act. In Barth, the trinitarian links with election in the beginning and reconciliation in the centre mean that creating is a free act, but free as the outcome of God's determining to have a world with which to share his love:

> He wills and posits the creature neither out of caprice nor necessity, but because He has loved it from eternity, because He wills to demonstrate His love for it, and because He wills not to limit His glory by its existence and being, but to reveal and manifest in it his own coexistence with it. (3/1, p. 95)

Notice the movement of thought: he loves the creature from eternity, *and so* creates it freely.

The second half of the quoted statement is not problematic, and is typically Barthian: the glory of God is revealed in God's co-existence with the creature. But there is a difficulty with the logic of eternity. There appears to be a sense in which Barth's God, because he is eternally the God of Jesus Christ, has freely committed himself to the human race for eternity. We are on the verge of the Origenist-Augustinian doctrine of an eternal creation here; and although it is only the verge, there is a way in which Barth's Christ is dangerously close to becoming a near equivalent to the platonic forms, as Robert Jenson has argued.[30] If God loves the creature from eternity, is he not in effect bound to create it? According to Barth, that is not the case. Whatever we make of the matter of the details of interpretation, however, the doctrine as a whole is Barth's way of showing that salvation is bound up systematically with creation, and is not a late intervention to make the best of a bad job.

Central to Barth's way of linking creation and covenant is a twofold and complementary way of conceiving the relation. First, creation is the

---

29. Parenthetical references in this section are to Karl Barth, *Church Dogmatics*, translation edited by G. W. Bromiley and T. F. Torrance (Edinburgh: T. & T. Clark, 1957–75).
30. Robert Jenson, *Alpha and Omega. A Study in the Theology of Karl Barth* (New York: Nelson, 1963).

external basis of the covenant. There has to be a place on which God's love for his people can be worked out. Creation is external in the sense of being a presupposition 'of the realisation of the divine purpose of love in relation to the creature.' In fact, it is an implication of the nature of God's love. 'Here the one who is loved has its existence and being independent of the one who loves' (3/1, p. 96). To be love, there must be a distinct being to love. Creation is the bringing to be of that object of love. God creates that which he may love; and a world on which he may love it. That is the point, according to Barth, of the creation account in Genesis 1. Second, it follows that the covenant is the *internal* basis of the creation. It is that which gives creation its meaning. The creature does not merely exist, but its existence has a point, and that is to 'realise a purpose and plan and order' (p. 229). The covenant is the goal of the creation. Thus Genesis 2, the account of the creation of Adam and Eve, is to be taken as a sign and anticipation of creation's goal: God's covenant with the whole human race. It is thus 'in some sense . . . a history of creation from inside' (p. 232). '[H]erein lies the peculiar dignity of the creation, that as the external beginning of all things it stands in certain respects in direct confrontation with its inner beginning, its eternal source in God's decision and plan' (p. 43).

Before we come to a discussion of where Barth appears to have fallen short in his account of the relation of creation and redemption, something must be said of its strengths. It is a magnificent piece of work, like all of Barth's theology, christologically driven, and, both here and in his celebrations of the music of Mozart, Barth shows that he can appreciate the created order as the good gift of God, good in itself as well as for us. It has other strengths, too. Contrary to what is sometimes alleged, what Barth says in relation to Mozart is not in essential contradiction of what he says dogmatically. In his section on creation as justification, Barth says quite explicitly that:

> the creature does not 'merely' exist . . . Its being is not neutral; it is not bad but good . . . Because it is affirmed and not denied, elected and not rejected, it is the object of God's good-pleasure. Because it may be by God, it may also be very good . . . This is valid without reservation and qualification.

There is also in the same paragraph an eschatological note: 'The only thing which can be better than what is by God (apart from God Himself) is what is to develop out of what is in its communion and encounter with God' (p. 366). Like Irenaeus, Barth understands creation as project, a project to be completed eschatologically. Whatever else may have to be said about the limitations of the way in which this is developed, we must not deny its dogmatic importance. By affirming the doctrine of creation not as a piece of natural theology but as part of Christian credal confession, Barth is able to begin a move towards the integration of that which the tradition tended to hold apart, the spheres of creation and redemption, of divine action in the beginning and in the middle, and to do it by means of christology. All that Barth's God does is mediated by Jesus Christ, and so there can be no question of a gnosticising abstraction of the one from the other.

Yet that christology is not enough – or, rather, that the *shape* of a christology must also come into consideration – is shown by the fact that Barth, too, fails finally to integrate our two themes adequately. There, is, undoubtedly, a measure of integration, and Barth's concern to distinguish between creation in the beginning and God's continuing providential activity is here of major importance, as we shall see in the next chapter. But the chief weakness of this way of relating creation and redemption is the way in which Barth conceives 'God's decision and plan.' The covenant is oriented to the election of the human race. Now, there is no objection to this as such; the eternal Son is incarnate in Jesus of Nazareth, signalling the fact that it is human beings who, as the image of God, are his particular delight. But there are ways of conceiving the matter which effectively place the non-human creation lower in the scheme of things than it ought to be. There is no doubt that Barth affirms, and affirms gladly the whole of the created order: as we have seen, 'Creation as justification' bespeaks God's rejoicing in the whole of his works (3/1, pp. 366–414), while the fact that wood, metal and catgut can be used, particularly through the pen of W. A. Mozart, to produce music of transcendent beauty, is a sign of this theologian's contribution to the development of our doctrine (3/3, pp. 297–9). And yet there is, as there was in Origen, a tendency to treat the created order instrumentally, as a means to an end in which it shares, indeed, but not as fully as it should. The weakness of Barth's theology of creation is not found in the fact that he did not have the time to go into the complications of the question of science, but in his repetition, albeit in improved form, of the Western tendency so to subordinate creation to redemption that the status of the material world as a whole is endangered. In this case, as the field on which election takes place, the created order is treated rather too externally to that which takes place on it. We must continue to ask what status the field of redemption has as good in itself, in distinction from, though to be sure in company with, those who are the chief objects of the love of him whose Son was given up for them.

V CREATION AND REDEMPTION:
(2) 'THE TWO HANDS OF GOD'

Systematically, the chief question arising here is that concerning the place of the Son and the Holy Spirit in the mediation of creation. The lesson to be learned from the developments we have followed is that – as we shall see in further detail in the next chapter – the way they are construed has much to do with our estimation of what the created order, human and non-human, essentially is. The traditional weakness of the Western tradition is put in exaggerated form by the atheist critic of Christianity, Ludwig Feuerbach. 'Nature, the world, has no value, no interest, for Christians. The Christian thinks only of himself and the salvation of his soul.'[31] This means that, according to this critic, for the Christian redemption only, and not creation, is important. About this, one thing has to be made plain at the outset. However distorted the tradition may have become, though it was never so distorted as Feuerbach makes it, the salvation and flourishing of human people is, and should remain, at the heart of Christian teaching. This is clearly demonstrated by the centrality of the mission of Jesus to his fellow humans, and by the fact that the cross is at once caused by human sin and is the means by which our alienation from God, each other and the world is set right. Moreover, even if we see in the distorted relation of man and nature that is causing so much anxiety the heart of that which needs to be put right in our world, as some do, it is clear that the disruption is caused by human behaviour towards the natural world, so that even there we are faced with the same problem: of the world's most problematic inhabitant.

What is causing the misapprehension of the Christian gospel is not then whether something needs to be done about the human presence in the world, but about how it relates to the rest of the created order. The problem thrown up by Feuerbach and other more recent critics of the Christian tradition is the anthropocentrism of the tradition: the stress on the human at the expense of the wider creation. This, it is claimed, produces an excessive stress on sin and salvation, as well as an attitude of domination of the created order which has been the cause of so many of the problems we face today. Why this analysis is at best only half right we shall see if we a look at the narrative of Adam and Eve in the second chapter of Genesis. They are there to tend a garden. They do

31. Ludwig Feuerbach, *The Essence of Christianity*, translated by George Eliot (New York: Harper and Brothers, 1957), p. 287.

not live in paradise, as is often suggested. That understanding entered the Christian tradition as a contamination from Greek mythology. They are called to work – it is the character of the work that changes after the Fall – and in particular to garden, an activity which involves a form of dominion over nature. Some form of dominion is inescapable: if we do not use chemicals, we must still pull weeds by hand, or we shall starve. Yet those made in the image of God on earth – and we shall examine that doctrine in detail in Chapter 9 below – are, as Genesis 2 re-emphasises, yet made of the dust of the earth, not of some divine stuff, as other doctrines, and particularly the Greek, suggest. However little lower than the gods we are made, the fundamental ontological divide between the creator and the creation is never violated.

What, then, is the relation between the gardeners and the garden? Our engagement in Chapter 2 with Schmid's interpretation of the creation documents showed him arguing that creation is in all the texts he is considering a framework for social order.[32] None the less, because, as we have seen, it must not be completely subordinated to the human order, and is of importance in its own right, two questions remain. The first is that concerning the relative weighting of the two dimensions of creation and redemption. In what way is the created order to be valued for itself, in what way considered a framework for the development of human life? That this is complicated beyond measure is, of course, shown by the fact that human life is itself part of the created order. And so our question arises again: which part? The second is like it, and is the problem of sin and evil. Things are not as they should be, and if we think that anything useful can be achieved simply by putting a theology of creation in place of one of salvation or redemption, we are making the greatest possible mistake. To be sure, attempts have been made to redress what was thought to be the imbalance of the tradition, in what is known as 'creation spirituality' – sometimes even called creation theology – and various forms of green theology, but they tend to be a kind of reaction to an opposite position rather than an integrating. It does not follow from the fact – if it is a fact – that Christians have stressed original sin and the anthropocentric side of Christian belief too strongly that those doctrines have no truth or value; or that the most important sins are against the eco-system, or that the created order can save us if only we let it have its head. All that is to place trust in the creation rather than in creation's Lord. Once again, the matter of weighting and emphasis comes in; there must be redemption if creation is to be itself.

32. See above, p. 5.

For Christian theology, all the questions come to a centre in christology. As a human being, God become man, Jesus of Nazareth shares in the structures, and that includes the fallen structures, of the created order. He is tempted to turn stones into bread, and indeed does multiply loaves and fishes, in the one miracle recorded in all four gospels. He stills the wind and the waves, and cures sickness. Yet to what end? Human salvation alone? It has been argued that when the New Testament speaks of 'new creation' – and that includes the apparently cosmic language of Romans 8 – it is speaking only of the remaking of human life.[33] But that begs the question of what is involved in human salvation. Here we reach one necessary complication in our approach to a resolution of the problem, if such can be expected. For 'salvation' may appear to centre on the human – and why should it not, for we are the problem? – but we still have to ask the questions of, first, what is the nature of that salvation, and, second, how it involves us in the material world. After all, war, sex and abortion all concern action towards the created world, and specifically towards the image of God embodied in that world; and Christian conversion has always involved a change of attitude and bearing towards these realities.

The real weakness of the Western tradition is that neglect of the trinitarian mediation of the doctrine of creation enabled gnostic elements to enter the bloodstream of theology. After the achievement of Irenaeus, no mainstream Christian theologian has entirely succumbed to the heresy he repudiated in so splendid and thoroughgoing a manner. The creator of the whole world, material and spiritual alike, is the one God and Father of the Lord Jesus Christ. Jesus' recapitulation, in the flesh, of the human story is also a recapitulation of the cosmic story, and at once reverses the fall and re-inaugurates the project of creation. However, since that time Irenaeus' affirmation of the goodness of the material world has come to be qualified in a number of ways inimical to his wholeheartedness. Origen's teaching that the material world is essentially a secondary purpose of God, produced in order to provide a place of education for the fallen spirits, was succeeded by Augustine's less damaging but none the less problematic teaching that the material world was less real and important than the spiritual. The rather gnosticising outcome is to be found in the tendency Feuerbach exaggerates: to see salvation as being out of this world rather than in and with it.

33. John Reumann, *Creation and New Creation. The Past, Present and Future of God's Creative Activity* (Minneapolis: Augsburg Publishing House, 1973), pp. 98 and 102.

In his study of *The Travail of Nature* Paul Santmire spoke of an *ambivalence*: that there are in many theologians of the tradition competing pulls, so that even those mediaeval theologies most affirmative of the glories of nature cannot in the end avoid using it as a ladder, to be kicked away when the summit is reached, of human ascent to the spiritual realm. Only one real exception is found in Santmire's review of the Middle Ages, and it is St Francis. As he says, there is much romanticising of St Francis, and it is important to see whence the heart of his difference from his age derived. It is, according to this author, to be found in his christology:

> Francis . . . became the Christ-like servant of nature. He impoverished himself in order that he might give himself to others, both to human and to natural creatures. So in his life and thought . . . he, in effect, united two grand theological schemes: on the one hand, the vision of the descending goodness of God, which makes all things good and worthy of respect, in their own right . . . on the other hand, the vision of the descending love of God in Christ, the self-giving . . . Savior, who, in turn, mandated sacrificial love for the world.[34]

Christology, then, is our first key, because it is Jesus Christ, the incarnate, crucified, risen and ascended Lord, who must be at the centre of any satisfactory construing of the relation of creation and redemption. According to the New Testament he is, after all, the agent of both creation and redemption, the one through whom, in the text that was one of Irenaeus' great inspirations, God proposes to reconcile all things, things in heaven and things on earth: not merely, that is to say, the human species (Ephesians 1:10). Here, if we are to take seriously the radical nature of the evil that impedes the end of creation, the centre of the story in the crucifixion of Jesus must never be underplayed.

This means in turn that the shape of a christology depends upon what can be called its trinitarian placing: how do we understand the work of Christ in the world in relation to the work of the Father and the Spirit? As the history of the tradition shows, an apparently orthodox christology can co-exist with a view of the creation, according to which it exists mainly to provide a place for a spatial ascent of the human spirit beyond and outside the material order to a higher spiritual realm. We meet again the crucial question of how we construe the work of the Spirit.

---

34. Paul Santmire, *The Travail of Nature. The Ambiguous Ecological Promise of Christian Theology* (Philadelphia: Fortress Press, 1985), p. 111.

In so far as modernity has a conception of the Spirit, it is a secularised version of the Christian. Spirit becomes, as in Hegel's definitive execution of the modern project, an inner force propelling human culture to its eschatological perfection. Ultimately, this is the most thoroughgoing spiritualising of all, and certainly leaves far behind the human, fleshly, Jesus. But although its centre is completely wrong, for there is no divine Spirit who is not the Spirit of Jesus of Nazareth, it is looking in the right place, and in two respects.

First, it stresses the time dimension rather than the merely spatial, recalling us to our theology of creation as project and the eschatological dimensions of the doctrine. We are created not to ascend through the material to the spiritual, but to be perfected in time, through Christ and the Spirit, in and with the created order as a whole. Second, there is throughout the Bible, and nowhere more than in characterisations of the resurrection, a clear relation between the Holy Spirit and God's presence to the creation in perfecting power. Hegel's mistake was thus to secularise the Spirit, bringing him out of eternity and out of perichoretic relation with the Son and Father into what is in effect a complete or unqualified and immanent involvement in time. The divine Spirit becomes almost a function of the created order, not its lord. But if the Spirit is first of all the eternal Spirit of the one triune God, his relation to the created order can only be from 'outside', however much he works towards and within the structures of created reality. Here, the resurrection serves as the model for an understanding of the action of the Spirit, the eschatological action *par excellence*. Like the wind in Ezekiel's vision of the bones, the Spirit blows upon the crucified Jesus – as 'the coming God' of Moltmann's characterisation.[35] And that 'outsideness' must not be understood merely spatially, because as eternal the Spirit transcends both our space and our time: indeed, the whole space-time universe which it is his function to perfect by relating it to the Father through the Son, the one through whom it came to be and in whom it holds together.

The introduction of a theology of the Spirit, as the one who brings the creation to God through the Son who became incarnate, also makes possible a more integrated account of the place of human action in relation to the natural world. It is sometimes taken as an implication of Irenaeus' theology that the human creature is the one through whom the remainder of the created world is enabled to become articulate. He

---

35. Jürgen Moltmann, *The Coming of God*, translated by Margaret Kohl (London: SCM Press, 1996).

centred his account of this human calling in the church's use of the bread and wine of the Lord's Supper, thus reminding us that the project of creation, as both creation and providence, is not finally complete without the rescue, through Christ and the Spirit, of all things from their bondage to decay and dissolution. This produces the apparently anthropocentric conclusion that the perfection of the creation comes about only by means of what some New Testament writers call the new creation, the recreating action of God realised through the Spirit's formation in the womb of Mary of a body for the Son, through the same Spirit's enablement of the incarnate Son's obedience until the cross, his raising him from the tomb on the third day, and his calling of a people to embody that redemption in the world. But it is only anthropocentric in a limited sense, and certainly far from Feuerbach's charge that the Christian is interested only in the salvation of the soul. For the birth, ministry, death, resurrection and ascension of Jesus are all functions of his full humanity, just as the water, bread and wine are material. The Christian gospel bears upon the whole embodied person, and along with that the whole created world which is the context of that embodied life. The Spirit's redemptive action is similarly eschatological in that it brings about the perfection of this particular sector of the created order – the humanity of Jesus Christ – as the guarantee and first fruits of the reconciliation of all things. This is the work of the Lord who is the Spirit. Redemption means the completion of the whole project of creation, not the saving of a few souls from hell. But it also means its completion in the face of that which would subvert its end. And so we come to the question of evil.

VI REDEMPTION AND EVIL

The theology of redemption sketched in the previous paragraphs raises the question that hovers around any treatment of creation. The confession, in face of much of the apparent evidence, that the world was created good entails that Christian theology may not, along with the traditions of Hellenism which we have frequently met upon the way to this point, attribute the origin of evil either to the material world, or, along with some pantheist theologies, to the weakness or incapacity of God, in implicit denial of the resurrection. The only position consistent with the doctrine of creation is to derive evil from something external to the creation, almost certainly personal wills or a personal will, but in any case in some inexplicable rebellion against the creator. Irenaeus refused to speculate about the origin of evil, and perhaps that is in any case the best course. But whatever we are to make of the biblical account of the Fall – and there are many biblical characterisations of sin and evil that are different in form from that – we cannot escape its implications that in some way or other the created order suffered a primal catastrophe of cosmic proportions, and that human sin – a disrupted relation with the creator – is in some way constitutive of it. Even the no doubt distorted notion of salvation as the saving of souls from hell has its basis in a proper concern with the radical evil, amounting to a slavery to forces beyond its control, that is centred upon human rejection of grace and that breaks in upon the created order.

Being personal at its heart, evil afflicts the human race more radically than the non-personal creation, which more nearly than the human world maintains its relatively good order through the providence of God. Theologically, the notion of the demonic serves to give some account of the shared slavery of man and cosmos. In some way or other, the evil that is transmitted to the cosmos like some universal infection returns to enslave the human creature.[36] But the character of evil can be understood, in so far as so irrational a force can be understood – and it is the offence of many 'theodicies' that they attempt to explain the inexplicable, and so seek to tame it – only through its overcoming in the life, death, resurrection and ascension of Jesus of Nazareth, who by bearing the effects of that evil in the flesh in order to destroy it, made manifest its character as the enemy of the whole created order. Karl Barth attempted an account, not entirely successfully, with his conception of Nothingness (*das Nichtige*), which he conceived as a kind of negative force resisting the good purposes of the creator. This cannot be dismissed as another version of the so-called privative conception of evil, which sees it as in some way the absence of good. As an attempt to destroy the creation, it has an active – one could almost say 'positive', if that were not to suggest something protologically positive – force, and is more than mere negation. In any case, privative concepts of evil, as suggesting something actively parasitic upon, and so destructive of, the good, are rarely merely privative. *Corruptio optimi pessima!* It is at least possible in this way to understand evil as that which corrupts the good creation and, if not 'unreal', it is at least real only in being parasitic upon the good. What should give us pause is, rather, that Barth's conception of evil shares some of the characteristics of the Manichaean interpretation of the darkness in Genesis 1:2, as, in Grosseteste's citation of Basil, 'an evil power, or rather evil itself, having its own principle of origin in itself,

36. Colin E. Gunton, *The Actuality of Atonement* (Edinburgh: T. & T. Clark, 1989), chapter 3.

opposed to the goodness of God.'[37] To be sure, there is no Manichaeism about Barth, whose conception of evil as an 'impossible possibility', as the utterly irrational, is meant to suggest that eschatologically it has no reality. But the conception is perhaps guilty by association, and it is one of Barth's theologoumena which has widely failed to convince.

Yet the notion of *das Nichtige* does give him the space to distinguish between two distinct forms which we tend to equate. On the one hand, there is what he calls the shadow side of the creation, 'that in creaturely existence, and especially in the existence of man, there are hours, days and years both bright and dark, success and failure, laughter and tears, youth and age, gain and loss, birth and sooner or later its inevitable corollary, death.' Even though it serves as a reminder of it, this is not to be equated with nothingness, that which in no way belongs to God's good creation.[38] There is therefore a distinction to be drawn between death as the proper limit of our days on earth, and the death that breaks in to make them deadly; that which is the creator's gift of limits to our days on earth, and that which turns that finitude into a threat of nothingness. Sin is that which causes the one to be the other, so that without Christ's bearing of death upon the cross and the promise of resurrection, death as the cessation of all relationships, above all that with God, would be the final fact to be narrated of us, and so the final nullifying of God's purposes in creation. That is why much of the tradition has held with Athanasius that it was in some way unfitting for God's goodness that he should have allowed the creation to go to ruin.[39]

Can we then say no more than that evil has no other explanation than that it is the corruption of the creation, diverting it from its proper end, that is overcome on the cross in promise of its final defeat? That brings another problem into view. As great a mystery as the origin of evil is the time taken to destroy it. In face of this, all we can say is that the nature of its overcoming by the patient obedience of the incarnate Son makes it clear that evil is finally to be destroyed only eschatologically (1 Corinthians 15). The means of the overcoming of evil on the cross gives a hint: it is to be overcome eschatologically, in God's good time, just as God 'takes time' to enable the created order to achieve its perfecting. That overcoming is, to be sure, anticipated in the resurrection of Jesus and in our times by the works of the Spirit, who enables particular

37. Robert Grosseteste, *On the Six Days of Creation*, translated by C. F. J. Martin (Oxford: Oxford University Press for The British Academy, 1996), p. 82.
38. Barth, *Church Dogmatics*, 3/3, pp. 295–99 (p. 297).
39. Athanasius, *On the Incarnation*, 6.

beings and events to become what they are created to be in the Son. But until then it is only partial and by anticipation.

We then lead into the discussion of providence by saying that the narrative which follows that of the Fall in Genesis demonstrates something of the character of God's response to evil. His providence is such that at each stage the aim is to limit the force of evil, to keep it within bounds so that it may not reap its full harvest. The mark of Cain, the murderer, is paradigmatic, for it is to provide him with immunity from further punishment (Genesis 4:15). Similarly, the flood, for all its catastrophic nature, is not universal in effect, and becomes the basis for a renewal of the covenant of creation. These stories form a matrix for the overcoming of evil on the cross, which at once fulfils and transcends them. But they also serve to show how the cross is not to be understood apart from God's providential action in general, but rather as its climax.

8

CREATION AND PROVIDENCE:
GOD'S INTERACTION WITH
THE WORLD

—◦—

I SOME PRELIMINARY DEFINITIONS

While Pannenberg may not be right in characterising the Holy Spirit's economic activity in terms of fields of force, it is without doubt the case that the notion of physical reality, owed first of all to Michael Faraday, as interacting fields of force rather than billiard–ball–like entities bumping into one another, is of extreme importance in showing that the world is open to God's continuing interaction with it. Whereas mechanism suggests a world impervious to anything but the laws of its own being, except in terms of miracles which 'violate' supposed 'laws' of nature, field theory at least enables it to be conceivable that nature may be generally law-abiding, but contingently rather than rigidly so. For Faraday, as Berkson has observed, forces themselves are the sole physical substance.[1] If everything created is to be understood as energy taking various shapes, energy, indeed, deriving from the God who is triune personal energy, we can understand the world variously, as containing a variety of forms of being: sometimes the things we call material because

1. William Berkson, *Fields of Force. The Development of a World View from Faraday to Einstein* (London: Routledge, 1974), p. 50.

175

we can see and touch them, but also sometimes those equally real and concrete things like music. Such a vision will prevent us from falling into the trap of being perplexed at how a 'spiritual' being – God – can interact with 'material' beings which are apparently resistant to his action. Rather, we have to understand the world as energy taking all kinds of different shapes as it comes from the hand of that energetic dynamism of persons in relation, the eternal triune God.[2]

Thus the creator's love – his energy at work through the mediating action of the Son and the Spirit – not only made the universe, consisting of diverse and interacting fields of force organised in different ways, but also shows itself in the day to day upholding and directing of what has been made. In this chapter, we shall be concerned generally with all those forms of action I shall summarise under the concept of providence: conservation, governance, perfecting, and the rest. It is important to stress that according to such a conception no distinction in principle is to be drawn between the ordinary and the extraordinary. God's action, as energy giving rise to energy variously organised, may be conceived to shape the day to day life of the world, even sometimes miraculously – in anticipation of its eschatological destiny – without violating that which is 'natural', because what is natural is that which enables the creation to achieve its promised destiny.

General providence is a name for that activity by which God is conceived to hold in being the order of creation: maintaining the order and teleology of the human and non-human realms. By contrast, particular and special providence are ways of speaking of saving or redemptive acts directed to restoring the right order, or, better, directedness, of creation. The incarnation of the Son of God in Jesus of Nazareth provides a way of showing that the distinction of forms of providence is yet embraced within a unity of activity. God's historical action in Christ is, as we have seen, the means by which the order of creation is redirected to its original end. 'General' providence is maintained by a new and unique – 'special' – form of divine interaction with the world, effecting the eschatological destiny of things as a whole by means of particular outcomes involved with and anticipating it: healings, the driving out of

---

2. If I may quote from a related writing: 'We return to the concept of energies, and possibly to the Spirit as in some sense the energy of the Godhead. In such a way, we may understand the Holy Spirit as the divine energy releasing the energies of the world, enabling the world to realise its dynamic interrelatedness. Thus is God the Spirit conceived as the perfecting cause, the true source of the dynamic of the forward movement of the cosmos'. Colin Gunton, *The Promise of Trinitarian Theology* (Edinburgh: T. & T. Clark, second enlarged edition), 1997, p. 153.

demons, the enabling of truth to be spoken and done. Eschatologically conceived, those activities that are sometimes called 'general' as distinct from 'special' or 'particular' providence are both aspects of the same divine activity bringing the world to its intended destiny.

We must here take account of a distinction between providential activity directed respectively to the human and the non-human creation. There is no absolute distinction, because both are equally part of the created order. As we have seen, there is no theological justification for excepting any part of the creation from this fundamental characterisation. But that there is a distinction is shown by the fact that while the human is called to a form of freedom under God, it is more appropriate to speak of the contingency of the remainder of the creation. In a study of the doctrine of creation we shall not be concerned primarily with the fact that human freedom is lost at the fall, and can be restored only through redemption, because our chief focus in approaching providence will be to say something about created freedom, admittedly relatively abstractly, because there is no human freedom apart from its redemption from slavery to sin and evil. Similarly, if it is the case, as we have seen, that it is the function of science to discern the contingent rationalities of the world – the rationality of what actually happens, not of what must take place – then we shall, again relatively abstractly, be directing our attention to created contingency. But it is also true that here, too, there can be no adequate account which does not also bear in mind that divine providence may take extraordinary and even miraculous forms in restoring the direction of the creation from its bondage to vanity.

We shall understand something of the lineaments of God's providential activity as both general and particular if we distinguish two ways in which the work of the Spirit is sometimes characterised. As the lord and giver of life, the Spirit is the upholder of the everyday. It is, as Stanley Hauerwas said recently, the work of the Spirit to uphold the routine: routines of life and worship without which life would be intolerable. That applies to the non-human realm also. While the earth remains, there is summer and winter, seedtime and harvest, and that is a function of the continuing providence of God's Holy Spirit, holding the world within the one in whom all things were and are created. On the other hand, apart from redemption the world, and particularly the human world, is not what it is created to be. The Spirit is both the one who upholds the human Jesus in the truth of his being and calling and the one who, by mediating the Father's action in raising him from the dead, transforms his body to the life of the world to come. All particular acts of providence derive from and take something of the shape of that paradigmatic redemptive act. But the point is: both of these forms of providence serve the same divine project of enabling the created order to be that which it is called to be. The Spirit thus both shapes the interacting fields of force that are the universe and is the one who realises those particular surges of divine activity which call created beings back from destruction and on to their course to perfection. It is in the light of some such definitions as these that we shall now examine features of the relation between creation and providence.

In the light of such a theology of providence we should not be reluctant to make some supporting use of current scientific theories which encourage belief in both the essentially limited and partial scope of scientific knowledge and the openness of the structures of the universe. The 'anthropic principle', and all variations on the theme of the fine-tuning of the initial conditions of the universe; the combination of determination and contingency suggested by some versions of chaos theory; the apparent implications of quantum theory for the openness of the universe and the structures of human rationality; all these factors are much discussed in recent treatment of the relation of science and theology and may encourage us in hoping for a greater measure of conversation between the two realms. In many of the writings of biologists, to be sure, things are rather different, and suggest that we should not hang our hearts on any particular scientific development, for things may change. What we must acknowledge, and we shall have reason to engage with aspects of evolutionary theory later, is that when we come to the doctrine of providence there is more need to be aware of interactions with natural science than in discussion of creation out of nothing. But in this book the main intention is to set out the theology of the matter.

II DOGMATIC DISTINCTIONS

The dogmatic differences between creation and providence have been well summarised by Karl Barth in the third part volume of his treatment of the doctrine of creation.[3] For Barth, as for the classical tradition of creation theology, the creation has an absolute beginning. But, as we have also seen, there are different ways of conceiving that beginning, and they bear upon our understanding of providence. To stress the timelessness of the act of creation is to risk evacuating the world of time of its proper significance and *Selbständigkeit*. Therefore Barth stresses that creation as a specific act of God taking place in relation to the creation cannot be

---

3. Karl Barth, *Church Dogmatics*, translation edited by G. W. Bromiley and T. F. Torrance (Edinburgh: T. & T. Clark, 1957–75), 3/3.

understood in terms of timelessness. 'Creation is not a timeless truth, even though time begins with it, and it extends to all times, and God is the Creator at every point of time' (3/1, p. 60). That is to say, creation is not timeless absolute dependence. Barth is not saying that God is limited by time, but that the doctrine of creation posits an absolute rather than timeless beginning, in the sense that once the universe was not, and now it is. By contrast, providence – which Barth prefers to 'conservation', as suggesting a more dynamic, forward-looking form of activity – is to do with what God makes of the creation: 'the superior dealings of the Creator with His creation, the wisdom, omnipotence and goodness with which He maintains and governs in time this distinct reality according to the counsel of His own will' (3/3, p. 3). The chief difference between the concepts of creation and providence is, then, first that providence presupposes creation, presupposes that there is something to provide for; while, second, creation presupposes providence, for although it is a finished act, it is not the finished act of the deist machine maker, but of one who has in view the care for and governing of the creation. There are thus different forms of divine relationship to the creation: one which, because it is concerned with origination, distinguishes the creator from the creation; and the other which brings them together in an active co-existence (p. 13). Providence is what God makes of the created world which has been given its own being distinct from him. There is a different form of relationship: interaction as distinct from origination.

Barth's way of expressing divine providential action leads us to our next phase of discussion. 'He co-exists with it actively, in an action which never ceases and does not leave any loopholes' (p. 13). Is this a form of absolute dependence? If it is, can Barth evade the charge that, like Schleiermacher, he has produced a form of absolute dependence that 'opens the door to every kind of caprice and tyranny. . .'? (2/2, p. 553). While there may be difficulties for Barth, he does not entirely fall into the trap, for the following reasons. First, there is a clearer conception of God in Barth, and so more of a capacity to distinguish clearly between God and the world. Second, there is a more explicit notion of divine agency. Schleiermacher's shying away from miracle is a sign of two things: he rightly rejects deistic 'proofs' of God from miracles, but wrongly has no room for specific and particular divine acts in and towards the world.[4] Third, there is in Schleiermacher no adequate concept of active providence either, but a platonising tendency to see the whole relation

4. See F. D. E. Schleiermacher, *The Christian Faith*, translated by H. R. Mackintosh and J. S. Stewart (Edinburgh: T. & T. Clark, 1928), p. 179, for a reference to nature's 'original immutable course.'

between God and the world timelessly. The weakness of Barth comes in what he shares with his great predecessor, the traditional Western tendency to relegate creation to second place to human salvation. There is, as we have seen, relatively little conception of the world as a whole as the object of the covenant, and, what perhaps is the same thing, a deficiency in the pneumatological couching of the relation between God and the world. But let us for now build upon the positive achievement of Barth's christological focus for the distinction and relation between God and the world.

Barth's opposition to Schleiermacher's reduction of creation to providence might equally have been an opposition to mediaeval tendencies to stress the present dependence of things on God at the expense of their being made, in the beginning, with a relative independence. To see what is at stake, let us pause to look at two representative treatments by Barth's predecessors. Schleiermacher's is typically modern, and represents a serious attempt to engage with the dominating Newtonian world of his time through a general conception that God acts by means of the laws of nature. The drawback is that by couching the relation between God and the world in essentially platonic categories of the dependence of the temporal upon the timeless, Schleiermacher at once deprives the world of its relative independence and God of his freedom of action within it. He is really only interested in creation as a function of our present experience of absolute dependence, and therefore tends to make the doctrine of creation secondary to a doctrine of what he calls preservation. '[T]he proposition, "God has created"... appears to belong to Dogmatics only so far as creation is complementary to the idea of preservation, with a view of reaching again the idea of unconditional all-inclusive dependence' (pp. 142–3). In fact, it is not so much secondary as reduced to it: there is, 'nothing the origin of which cannot be brought under the concept of Preservation, so that the doctrine of Creation is completely absorbed in the doctrine of Preservation' (p. 146).[5] This is not to deny that Schleiermacher is right to couch the discussion in terms of divine action, as he does in much of his discussion, even though his near pantheism – about the appearance of which he is a little defensive (p. 174) – makes it impossible for him to do all that ought to be done. Here he clearly belongs in the line of John Calvin. As we have seen, Calvin's position is developed in opposition to the

---

5. It is to be noted that E. L. Mascall understands Aquinas to be saying in *Summa Theologiae* 1. 9. 2 that creation and preservation are identical. *Christian Theology and Natural Science. Some Questions on their Relations* (London: Longmans, Green and Co., 1956), p. 134.

mediaeval tendency to understand providence in terms of divine fore-knowledge rather than action. While all doctrines of divine agency may be conceived to threaten human freedom unless very carefully delimited – for if the creator does everything, it appears that the creature does nothing – images of divine foreknowledge that, in Aquinas' famous analogy, make God like an observer on a mountainside seeing the whole of a road laid out below, appear impossible to free from charges of deter-minism.[6] Let us pause to review Aquinas' conception of providence.

Noteworthy is that despite his earlier use of the image of the observer, when it comes to his explicit treatment of providence, Aquinas is dom-inated by the concept of causality rather than vision, with providence being understood largely in terms of the relation between God as first cause and the created order as a hierarchically structured set of secondary causes. In his treatment of government (*gubernatio*) and sustaining (*con-servatio*) in Questions 103 and 104 of the first book of the *Summa*, Aquinas draws many useful conceptual distinctions, indicating that although in a government of the universe by God everything cannot happen by chance – by which he means 'unintentional occurrence' (103. 5) – it does not follow that there is no room for chance in a prov-identially ordered world. Similarly, he argues that God's sustaining activity means that creatures would fall into nothingness if they were not sus-tained by God's providence (104. 1), and distinguishes between normal and miraculous forms of divine action (104. 4, 105. 6). But there are two symptoms which suggest that Aquinas is in thrall to an inadequately trinitarian conception of mediation, and both are allowed room in his theology by the fact that there is no direct christological reference in the whole of the two Questions, despite the quotation of Hebrews 1:3. The first symptom is the persistence of pagan ideas of the eternity of matter, 'which is not subject to corruption in that it stands as the substrate of (creatures') coming to be and passing away' (104. 4). And the second is that a hierarchy of causes usurps the place of the hands of God as the mediators of divine action: 'the intermediate causes are secondary sus-tainers and to a degree that is greater as the cause is higher in the sequence and nearer to the first cause' (104. 3). Similarly, the immense time and attention given in succeeding Questions to the mediating activities of the angels is another sign of the displacement of trinitarian categories from the tradition.[7]

6. Thomas Aquinas, *Summa Theologiae*, 1. 14. 13 and ad 3.
7. The displacement by the angels goes back at least as far as Augustine. For references in *The City of God*, see Colin E. Gunton, *The Promise of Trinitarian Theology* (Edin-burgh: T. & T. Clark, second edition, 1997), chapter 9.

As Aquinas' conception of divine action in terms of rational causes was replaced in course of time by a more voluntarist view, there developed in later mediaeval thought discussions about the apparently determinist implications of divine omniscience, and it will profit us to pause to consider aspects of these, because they bring us to the heart of the doctrine of providence. If God knows everything, can there be human freedom and cosmic contingency? Alexander Broadie shows that the Scottish philosopher, John Ireland (c. 1440–95) opened the way to a less problematic account of God's relationship to the world by likening it to that of a poet to his poetry, or a composer's to a piece of music. Despite the difficulties that remain:

> I do think that this model is more helpful than Boethius' watchman in a high tower or Aquinas's mountaineer in providing us with some conception of how God can simultaneously perceive things that are temporally successive - He does so in somewhat the same way that the poet holds in his mind simultaneously the temporally structured poem with which he has suddenly been presented by the muse.
>
> Here, then, we have a means to understanding John Ireland's claim that the world throughout its history is simultaneously present to God.[8]

The outcome is the beginnings of a distinction between divine intellect and divine act. 'Distinguishing between divine intellect and divine will, [Ireland] argues that God wills into existence creatures with a will, and then leaves us to do what we will to do. He knows our acts, but does not will that we perform them' (p. 98). Whether this is a satisfactory distinction will always, it can confidently be predicted, be a subject of debate. The issues at stake can at least be clarified if we return once again to the problem of mediation.

III THE MEDIATION OF PROVIDENTIAL ACTION

The problem bequeathed by the Reformers derives from the fact that despite their part in the recovery of the doctrine of creation out of nothing they were less successful in developing an account of the world's continuing relation with God the creator. What was lacking was

---

8. Alexander Broadie, *The Shadow of Scotus. Philosophy and Faith in Pre-Reformation Scotland* (Edinburgh: T. & T. Clark, 1995), p. 66.

a satisfactory conception of mediation, by which is intended, as will by now be evident, a trinitarian one. The clearest lesson to be learned from Barth's, as distinct from Calvin's and Schleiermacher's, understanding of divine providential action is that a stronger christology forms the basis for a more satisfactory account of mediation. If Jesus Christ is a model of God's determination of the creature, then clearly it is a determination that realises rather than stunts freedom. When Barth speaks, as we have seen him do, of 'the superior dealings of the Creator with His creation, the wisdom, omnipotence and goodness with which he governs in time this distinct reality according to the counsel of His own will',[9] we will recall that his conception of omnipotent divine action is provided by the cross of Jesus Christ.[10]

But a problem remains. As was commented in Chapter 7, tradition, as in the Apostles' Creed, and even in the versions of the rule of faith that are quoted by Irenaeus, attributes creation to the Father, salvation to the Son and life in the church to the Spirit. Barth's attribution of creation to the Father, reconciliation to the Son and eschatological redemption to the Spirit only begins to solve the problem. Dogmatically the structuring not only encourages modalism, but also draws attention away from the New Testament affirmations of the place of Jesus Christ in the mediation of creation as well as of salvation, and also from the conception of mediation of the work of the Father through his two hands. The incarnation – the act of free divine interrelation with the created world – provides the model of mediation that we need. Christology, not the ontologically intermediate being represented by some (Origenistic) conceptions of the Logos, but the Son of God in free personal relation to the world, indeed identification with part of that world, is the basis for an understanding of God the Father's relations with his creation.

But that is only a beginning, for something must also be said about the work of the 'second hand'. How might a more strongly pneumatological orientation be able to take up the possibilities inherent in the model of the artist suggested in Broadie's appeal to John Ireland's thought? It has already been suggested from time to time in this book that we should understand creation dynamically as project. The perfection of beginning is not the perfection of the completed, but of that which is to be perfected. The advantage of a conception of providence centring on act rather than knowledge is that an action can be understood to leave room for the free 'space' between one thing and another. There are

9. Karl Barth, *Church Dogmatics*, 3/3, p. 3.
10. Karl Barth, *Church Dogmatics*, 2/1, p. 607.

many ways of making something happen without forcing it to do so. This is less deterministic if handled pneumatologically because it suggests divine action which enables something to move from an uncompleted or unsatisfactory present to a completion that is destined, but not fully determined, in advance. This is the strength of recent theologies like that of Pannenberg which speak of things being created from the future. To be sure, the future *simpliciter* can be as deterministically conceived as the past. The key is in who or what determines the future, and how. The Spirit, by relating the world – or worldly particulars – to God through Christ releases them to be what they have been created to be. As a form of enabling personal action, providential action, the Spirit's action is that which liberates things and people to be themselves, as, paradigmatically, the Spirit's leading enabled the human Jesus to be truly himself in relation to God the Father and the world. We shall see something more of this eschatological action when we move, in Chapter 10, to eschatology proper. But at this stage, the conception of mediation which is involved requires further discussion.

IV PROVIDENCE AND
THE PROBLEM OF 'DARWINISM'

During the last two centuries, immanentist forms of providential action have tended to replace traditional Christian ones. That is to say, concepts implying automatic or self-sustaining internal development like progress, evolution or dialectical materialism have served as models – in some cases remarkably unsuccessful ones – to account for the way in which the world in some way or other attains its ends by forces intrinsic to it rather than by the action of a God who is other than the world. This need cause no intrinsic problems for a theology of nature which accepts the relative independence of the created world: enabled to be itself by the mediating action of God the Son and God the Holy Spirit. That there have been problems is in part due to the way in which theories like evolution have been understood, in part to the foolishness of some theologians whose negative contributions to the debate have been exaggerated beyond all measure by what James R. Moore shows to be proponents of a false view of history, and in part to secularising forces typical of the modern period. That the problems are not chiefly dogmatic has been shown by a number of recent studies. Moore's study of the Protestant response to Darwin shows that at the time it should not have been difficult for orthodox believers to accept the theory of evolution. It was other things which motivated Christian Anti-Darwinism. 'The anti-Darwinian element in Christian Anti-Darwinism may thus in fact have had little to do with Christian doctrines. Perhaps, after all, what conflicted with Darwinism were the philosophical assumptions with which the Christian faith had been allied.'[11] The philosophical beliefs Moore cites were those whose contamination of the doctrine of creation we have had cause to describe at length in previous chapters: the belief in the fixity of forms and a naive view of scripture.

That is not to deny that there are problems even on a non-literalistic interpretation of Genesis. The first cultural problem, exacerbated, as Moore shows, by a journalistic and combative tendency to turn the whole debate into a war, was the turning of evolution from a scientific theory to what would now by postmodernists be called a totalising theory of reality: a theory claiming to encompass all of life and reality. Evolution, from being a relatively neutral description of the way in which more complex forms of life are seen to emerge from the less complex becomes an all-embracing ideology to account for an 'upwards' movement of the world, and of human society in particular. Just as Newtonianism represents the turning of Newton's physics into an all-embracing philosophy, so it was and is with those who would use Darwin's and others' discoveries for effectively developing a doctrine of merely 'worldly' providence.

The historical basis for the development of such enterprises is interestingly parallel to the forces which employed Galileo's fate for propagandist purposes. Just as above we saw that the Galileo affair reveals a deficiency in the church's theology of nature, so it is with the Darwinian controversy. Galileo raised the question of the kind of world we inhabit, and so implicitly the question of the relation of God to the world. As we have seen, alongside this question was that of the interpretation of scripture, but that was relatively peripheral to the central question at stake in the controversy. The same can be said about evolution, where the dispute was both similar to that over Galileo, but in some ways more wide-ranging. Both concerned the kind of world that God has created, in the first case whether part of the creation is nearer to God than the lower, sublunary sphere; in the second, whether Genesis implies that there is a limited number of fixed forms created in the beginning (effectively,

---

11. James R. Moore, *The Post-Darwinian Controversies. A Study of the Protestant Struggle to come to terms with Darwin in Great Britain and America 1870–1900* (Cambridge: Cambridge University Press, 1979), p. 215. For the early debates about Darwinism, see also David N. Livingstone, 'The Idea of Design: The Vicissitudes of a Key Response in the Princeton Response to Darwin', *Scottish Journal of Theology* 37 (1984), pp. 329–57; James R. Moore, 'Evangelicals and Evolution. Henry Drummond, Herbert Spencer and the Naturalisation of the Spiritual World', *Scottish Journal of Theology* 38 1985), pp. 383–417.

the platonic ideas in the mind of God.) In the fourth century, Basil, as we have seen, wrote as if he believed that this was not the case. In the case of Darwin, however, the entrenched status of the mechanist metaphor for the creation meant that people tended to think deistically, so that on this occasion what is at stake is also the doctrine of providence and its implied belief in God's continuing involvement with the world.

Prominent in early worries about evolution was its apparent relegation of the human species to a similar level to that of the animals, undermining teaching of its uniqueness. But that is by no means an achievement peculiar to theories of evolution. The real threat to human uniqueness – and so to such personal realities as love and artistic endeavour, as well as rationality and science – arose long before Darwin was born, and is to be found in that philosophy, over which we have already spent much time, known as Newtonianism. As Hume had long ago realised, a mechanistic view of the world puts in question any concept of a particular providence: of God being understood to bring about this rather than that in process of time.[12] In one respect, Darwinism represented but a modification of Newtonianism, its impersonal categories applied to the way in which life emerged from that which was not alive. That is the real threat of Darwinism also: as an all-encompassing dogma rather than a theory of how things happen to work in the world, it is an alternative to the doctrine of providence. It is, that is to say, a catapulting of the God of deism into time. Previously understood to make a mechanism and leave it to itself, the shadowy God of modern rationalism disappears further into the background as attention is called away from his action in the beginning not to his providential activity in the present, but to worldly happenings which displace or replace that activity. Evolution as a religion – to allude once again to the title of Mary Midgley's book[13] – is in that respect secularised providence. Evolution becomes capitalised, almost hypostatised – just as Richard Dawkins and others hypostatise genes as agents determining the way things are – and displaces divine providence.[14]

But there are gains even there, as John Zizioulas has pointed out. Dualistic views of the human person, dividing the soul or mind from

12. David Hume, *An Enquiry concerning Human Understanding*, section 11.
13. Mary Midgley, *Evolution as a Religion. Strange Hopes and Stranger Fears* (London: Methuen, 1985).
14. R. C. Lewontin, 'The Dream of the Human Genome', *New York Review of Books*, 39 (28 May, 1992), p. 31, attacks the tendency to ascribe agency to inert chemicals. In *The Doctrine of DNA. Biology as Ideology* (London: Penguin Books, 1993) he develops a sustained attack on some of the more absurd claims being made, distinguishing

the body, had tended to isolate the human race from the remainder of the creation.[15] We have seen already that Genesis presumes a continuity: a difference indeed, but a continuity. Being reminded of our essential createdness is salutary, although in the light of the way Christian anthropology had sometimes been taught, Darwinism clearly represented a threat. It remains a threat under two conditions. The first is if it can somehow demonstrate that the sole reason for the emergence of the human is impersonal evolution. It is clear that this cannot be done on merely scientific grounds. How could it be demonstrated that something happens only by virtue of natural forces rather than by those as directed by God's providential guidance? It is clear that matters of world-view are also at work in the making of a decision about which interpretation is the more reasonable. The second condition is that there should be no way of showing how it can be that the distinctness of the human species remains despite the demonstration of our earthly origins. The Bible can do it: Adam and Eve are made from the dust of the ground, and, as we shall see in the chapter devoted to anthropology, it is the uniqueness of the human relation to God that is crucial, rather than philosophical dualism. The human species emerges into the history of the creation. What is made of that remains an open question, whatever biological determinists may claim.

It is time, however, to inject a little more theology into the discussion. We have already seen that, on a trinitarian view of the created order, the Holy Spirit can be understood to move the creation forwards, towards its eschatological perfection, rather than simply upwards. If the movement is understood to be merely forwards, this alteration tends to mean, as is well known, a theological imprimatur on the modern doctrine of progress, reminding us again of Darwinism's displacement of the doctrine of providence. But that does not take away the proper concern of the doctrine of providence to see the creation as having a forward direction, as God's project. The question is: who or what moves the created order 'forward', to its destiny, God, or a surrogate? On a theology which

---

them from the implications of Darwin's actual heritage, pp. 108–9. His observation of the displacement is explicitly theological. According to the ideology he is attacking, 'Our genes and the DNA molecules that make them up are the modern form of grace, and in this view we will understand what we are when we know what our genes are made of . . . In the words of Richard Dawkins, one of the leading proponents of this biological view, we are "lumbering robots" whose genes "created us bodies and mind".' (p. 13). Plentiful evidence of the higher absurdity is provided in Lewontin's book.

15. John D. Zizioulas, 'Preserving God's Creation. Three Lectures on Theology and Ecology. I., *King's Theological Review* 12 (1989), pp. 1–5 (p. 4).

takes into account both the 'horizontal' and the 'vertical' structuring of relations, we are free to treat evolution with a little more detachment. Evolution may be the way by which the Spirit perfects the creation by relating it to God the Father through the Son; but equally, it may not. It is well known that, as Basil Willey said, deism represents a kind of cosmic toryism: what is, is right; and in that respect, Darwinism as represented by such triumphalists as Richard Dawkins and Peter Atkins is a form of modern rationalist deism. But if the Spirit is the Spirit of God the Son who was crucified, creation may move towards its perfection as much through the enablement of, or merely acts of love for, the severely handicapped – to take one example – as by the evolution of so-called higher forms of being. It must be remembered here that those who have turned Darwinism into an ideology – the ideology of the escalator – have far departed from the work of Darwin himself, who saw evolution more in terms of a tree, with branches going out in many directions, rather than an ascending series. If the Spirit is the Spirit of him who raised Jesus Christ from the dead, then the question of what represents 'progress' – the movement of creation to its true destiny – becomes a far more open one. Further, if the end of creation is the reconciliation of all things with their creator, any particular evolutionary 'advance' may or may not bring about that end.

Unfortunately that is not the way the matter is often treated. Many attempted theological encounters with the theory of evolution have put their eggs in the basket of a theology of immanence: of conceding to religious evolutionism the fact that God works within the natural order, and then trying to show, often christologically, that evolution is a means of the advancement of God's purposes. Like most modern natural theologies, this falls into the trap of the God of the gaps, inviting committal both to a tomb of irrelevance by developing scientific theories and to cosmic toryism, specifically the justification of using 'lower' creatures as steps to 'higher', often understood as more intelligent, beings.[16] A doctrine of a free and transcendent Spirit, who belongs to God's eternity but by virtue of his relation to the immanent event of the incarnation can also be seen to operate in and with the created order, leaves open the possibility for a conception of divine involvement in the world which is not constricted by the scientific theories of the moment. Against any predetermining of the question by cultural factors, we must hold that it is God the Spirit, and not the automatic forward movement of the universe, who enables the world to become what it is projected to be. That

16. Is this far, or even distinguishable, from the position of Teilhard de Chardin?

is why the theory of evolution is irrelevant to Christian belief, at least with the possible exception that, like all observations of the nature of the world and life within it, it raises in its own distinctive way the question of the nature and overcoming of evil – in a word, of redemption.[17]

Let us then summarise the position by saying that theories of evolution are not as such so serious a problem for a theology which holds to the relative rather than absolute perfection of creation 'in the beginning'. Such a doctrine modifies the problem of evil that is presented by evolutionary theory in a number of ways. The process appears to be long and wasteful, and indeed there is a great deal of suffering involved. But is it necessarily wasteful that dinosaurs once had their day and now cease to be, or that we ourselves shall eventually disappear from the universe? If things have their due times and intrinsic value, it is not necessarily a problem, any more than it is necessarily wasteful that a species of fungus produces millions of spores only a few of which, if any, germinate. Much depends on what is conceived as waste, what as the liberality and overflowing generosity and creativity of God. This brings us to a more direct encounter with the problem of evil. Again, we must consider what scripture actually claims. There is at the very least a struggle to be waged from the beginning on behalf of the perfecting of creation. The earth needs to be subdued, which should not be understood merely technologically or as an encouragement for a consumer society, but as a call to endow it with that which it yet lacks. The second chapter of Genesis here supports the first: Eden is a garden, an enclosed area within the wider (untamed?) creation, so that it is not supposed that the whole earth is yet prepared for human life and its proper work. Furthermore – and here we reach complications – the serpent is already present in the garden. Does this mean that there is evil already, deriving from a premundane fall of angels? The evidence for this is doubtful, to say the least, yet it does attempt to give some account of the fact that the evil that breaks into the world largely through human disobedience is not merely that. Here again it should be repeated that we do not base a theology on Genesis alone, but on that interpreted through the way in which Jesus overcame evil in his ministry and on the cross. Here that which has to be overcome in order that the project of creation may be complete is a fallenness of the human realm which involves relations with a created world which is not yet that which it was created to be,

17. Michael B. Roberts, 'Darwin's Doubts about Design – The Darwin-Gray Correspondence of 1860', *Science and Christian Belief,* 9 (1997), pp. 113–27, has suggested that it was not evolution that troubled Darwin's religious faith, but evil. In that light, what is new about evolution?

and indeed at some profound level participates in the human fall. The death which, according to 1 Corinthians 15, is the last enemy to be overcome is not the death that derives from finitude – our being limited in time – but the death under the curse which afflicts all created being apart from redemption in Christ – death, rather than mere mortality. Divine providential action takes place in a world which can be perfected only through the death of the mediator of creation on the cross of Calvary. In sum, the death and resurrection of Jesus is the model for all providential action, as those acts which enable the world to become itself by action within, and over against, its fallen structures. And so we return to the theology of nature.

V THE THEOLOGY OF NATURE AGAIN

It is evident that many recent developments in the sciences, particularly the critique of the Newtonian closed universe, appear to be more sympathetic than some of their predecessors to the doctrine of providence. There are exceptions, particularly in the biological sciences, but it could reasonably be contended that some of the most vigorous remaining anti-theologians are still operating with at least latently mechanistic models of the way in which the universe moves.[18] However, before we indulge in unqualified rejoicing, two warnings must be given. The first is that the history of science gives no confidence that things may not move into reverse. Put not your trust in the latest theories must be the warning, along with a confidence that theology has always been at its best when it has put its trust in divine revelation as saying the last – or at least the penultimate! – word. It must surely stand as a warning that the strongest opposition to Darwinism from theologians came from their indignation on behalf of Baconian and Newtonian philosophies of science, not on behalf of orthodox belief.[19] A large part of theological wisdom consists in knowing which barriers are worthy of fortification.

The second warning note to be sounded concerns the status of culture in general. The interpretation of the history of ideas offered in this book suggests that, while theology has made grievous mistakes in her treatment of some of her relations with science, the overall intellectual situation is that science owes some of its originating impulses from the doctrine of creation and may still implicitly depend upon assumptions that only such a theology can give. Yet we must not assume that this

18. And other problems: see again Keith Ward's assault on some of Dawkins' assumptions, *God, Chance and Necessity* (Oxford: One World, 1996).
19. Moore, *The Post-Darwinian Controversies*, chapter 9.

culturally successful form of life will be in future as dominant as it is now or dominant in the same respects. If pollution is as serious as some of the prophets of doom protest, there may be a revulsion against science which changes the whole balance of our culture. In view of the fact that such a change would be likely to be more in the direction of a pagan pantheism, Christian theology should know that, whatever the number of its atheist critics among the scientists, it is better off with those who accept the created world as a secular fact than with a recrudescence of a religion which denies the free and personal creator in favour of a necessarily impersonal and oppressive self-creating universe.

It is for this reason that theology should stick to its dogmatic last, and not look over its shoulder all the time at the fashions of popular or ideological science. And its dogmatic last in this area is its responsibility to develop a view of the providential activity of God which allows for both the orderedness and even determination of things 'from above' and their granting of a proper reality which enables them to be truly themselves. For this to happen, there must be a proper relationship between the way in which we understand creation in the beginning and the continuing upholding and directing activity of God. Too strong an emphasis on creation in the beginning, particularly if that is understood as an eternal act, and the contingency of the order of time and space is endangered. That might be said to be the danger of Calvin's sometimes rather non-trinitarian account of the matter. But the reverse can also be the case, and an over-strong emphasis on providence in terms of the present upholding of things – an effective assimilation of creation in the beginning to creation as present ontological dependence – can lead equally to a form of unmediated and therefore oppressive dependence.

To achieve the proper weighting of the doctrines, we should avoid too great a stress on providence in terms of knowledge and emphasise more creation as action. That is to say, we should consider providence not in its meaning as *seeing in advance* but as *providing for*. The reason is that a stress on foreknowledge is difficult to disentangle from suggestions of determinism. The picture evoked is necessarily that of the all seeing unitary eye, looking from above at the whole panorama of things, rather than that of mediation by the two hands of God. Now, if God is eternal and the world temporal, some such conception is inescapable, because without it we are likely to develop some notion of God's temporality – God's being in some way limited to time – which effectively deprives time of its true being as created time. By mythologising time, we take away its status as creature. None the less, as has already been suggested, we would be better advised here to use analogies of making – as of the composer or poet – than of seeing, not chiefly because the philosophical problems become easier to solve – as they do – but simply because that makes better sense of the trinitarian mediation of things which scripture suggests. It is often suggested that a great playwright will 'create' characters which then to an extent create themselves. They take on their own life within the imagination of the author. That is something of what is meant by a theology of nature: a conception of the world which is enabled to be and become that which it is made to be by forms of divine action which respect and enable that which it is.

What has been developed of that in this book suggests that we conceive providence chiefly in terms of two models: the Son as the giver of structure, and the Holy Spirit as the one who gives the world space to become within but not apart from that structuring. The hinge on which all turns, so often neglected in theologies of creation, is the incarnation. A christological structuring of divine providential action understands it in the light of the one who became human, identifying with the world's structures in order to reshape them to their eschatological destiny. Incarnationally conceived action – action understood through the focus provided by the true humanity and self-giving to death of Jesus – indicates contingency but not 'pure' chance as the heart of the matter. There is nothing outside God's ordering activity. But that divine determining is not deterministic, because the action of the Spirit defines the kind of order that there is, or can be. The Spirit's action is eschatological action, enabling things to be themselves. The future is 'open' because the Holy Spirit is the one who enables things to become what they are made to be by relating them to the Father through the one who became incarnate. Providential action is thus that which enables particular human actions and worldly events to become what they will be. In that sense, all providence is particular.

As we have seen, the facts of human sin and cosmological evil mean that much of this ordering can take place only by an overcoming of disorder. But the doctrine of creation teaches that order is not absolutely taken away by sin, however disrupted it may sometimes be. Nothing is outside the providential activity of God. The enduring glory of the book of Genesis is that it shows the covenant love of God to be such that he continues graciously to overrule the worst that the human race can do to subvert his order. And so we come to a closing definition of providence as that activity, mediated by the two hands of God, which at once upholds the creation against its utter dissolution and provides for its redemption by the election of Israel and the incarnation of the one through whom all things were made and are upheld, and to whom, as the head of the church (Colossians 1:18), in the Spirit all things move.

9

CREATION AND NEW CREATION:
IN THE IMAGE
AND LIKENESS OF GOD

—·····ᴬᴬᴬᴬᴬᴼᴬᴬᴬᴬᴬ·····—

I THE POINT OF THE IMAGE

The doctrine of the image of God shares with the other topics we have encountered intrinsic difficulties which are complicated by the history of their articulation. The literature on the doctrine of the image of God is immense, and, like other immensities of discussion, comes to no agreed conclusion.[1] If there is something approaching a consensus in recent theology, it is that the belief, going at least as far back as Philo of Alexandria, that the image of God consists in human rationality, requires, at the very least, to be radically qualified. Asking what differentiated the human from the non-human creation, many early theologians drew on aspects of philosophical thought to say that it was reason, and then drew the further conclusion that this difference was that in which the image consisted. That might be part of the truth, but none the less derives from asking the wrong question: about the way in which the human is different from the non-human – the secondary question – not the primary one of the distinctive human being-in-relation to God.

---

1. I am already guilty of adding to it: *The Promise of Trinitarian Theology* (Edinburgh: T. & T. Clark, second edition, 1997), chapter 6; and *Christ and Creation* (Carlisle: Paternoster Press and Grand Rapids: Eerdmans, 1992), chapter 4.

Moreover, to argue in such a way appears to presuppose that God's primary characteristic is reason – again, after the Aristotelian view that deity is reason thinking itself – rather than, say, love or relationality. Other candidates for characterising the image have been freedom, or, more recently, creativity,[2] or a combination, as in John of Damascus: 'being after God's image signifies his capacity for understanding, and for making free decisions, and his mastery of himself.'[3] That is to say, while there may be a case for saying that possession of rationality and the rest is part of what it means to be created in the image of God, that must not be at the expense of other characteristics, and particularly not at the expense of the body. Once again, we meet a similar opposition between the two fathers of the doctrine of creation. Origen belongs in the tradition of Philo. In the *Contra Celsum* there is clear evidence for the rationalising of image: 'the part which is "in the image of God" is to be preserved in the rational soul, which has the capacity for virtue' (7. 66). Similarly, he argues philosophically for the necessity that the soul, like God, must be simple or uncompounded: if the expression 'in the image of God' applies to body and soul together, 'God must be composite and, as it were, must consist of body and soul Himself' (6. 63).

Irenaeus is in some contrast, though he does show signs of influence by Greek rationalism. However, in so far as he does appeal to rationality as a mark of human distinctiveness, it is not on philosophical grounds. Rationality is concerned with right human living, so that even when Irenaeus refers to 'man, being endowed with reason, and in this respect like to God . . .', he attributes the loss of human likeness to God to the misuse of free will which opposes the righteousness of God.[4] Elsewhere, he is explicit:

> Now the soul and the spirit are certainly a *part* of the man, but certainly not *the* man; for the perfect man consists in the commingling and the union of the soul receiving the spirit of the Father, and the admixture of that fleshly nature which was moulded after the image of God. (5. 6. 1)

2. The inadequacy of this interpretation of the doctrine derives from the fact that creation is but *one* of the modes of divine activity towards the world, and to choose this one to characterise the image appears both arbitrary and to detract from the freedom of God's creative activity. Rather, God is *essentially* the love-in-relation of Father, Son and Spirit, but only contingently creator. Otherwise, creation is necessary to God, and it becomes difficult to avoid the conclusion that it is also continuous with him.
3. Cited by Aquinas, *Summa Theologiae*, 1a. 93. 5.
4. Irenaeus, *Against the Heresies*, 4. 4. 3.

It is interesting that Calvin, as so often, is the witness for both sides of the tradition. At times he sounds very platonist;[5] while when he is considering matters which operate anti-platonically, and above all the resurrection, he is enabled to say that the whole human person, body and soul, is made in the image of God.[6] Recent Old Testament commentators have stressed this latter side of things. According to von Rad, 'one will do well to split the physical from the spiritual as little as possible.'[7] Querying this, Westermann has argued that the text is speaking more about divine action than the nature of humankind, so that 'humans are created in such a way that their existence is intended to be their relationship with God',[8] but whether this marks a real difference from his great predecessor must be doubtful. It is unlikely that this relational view of the image, which Westermann shares with Barth, can be construed without involving some physical embodiment; we shall return to the question of 'essentialism' raised by this claim.

A second problem is that the doctrine of the image appears but rarely in scripture, so that any theological use of the concept must serve as the conceptual means of saying something about human being according to the whole of the teaching of scripture. As with the doctrine of creation as a whole, we are concerned primarily not with the texts which refer to the image explicitly – though we must do justice to them – but with whether or not the concept enables us to articulate something of what it is to be a human creature in relation to God. For historical reasons, we cannot articulate a doctrine of the human creature without putting this concept somewhere near the centre, because it is the vehicle of so much discussion of the topic. Yet, as we have seen, the history is in many ways so problematic that much care is necessary if misunderstanding is not to result.

Third, and complicating the matter systematically, is the fact that in speaking of the image we are not speaking of the order of creation alone. We have seen already that the doctrine of creation cannot be adequately treated without due reference to redemption, both in the present and in eschatological perspective. That is doubly the case here,

<hr />

5. John Calvin, *Institutes*, 1. 15. 3, where he says that the proper seat of the image is the soul.
6. Calvin, *Institutes*, 1. 15. 3: the outward form joins us to God; 3. 25. 4: we are temples of the Spirit. 1. 15. 4: the true nature of the image is made known from what scripture says of its renewal in Christ.
7. Gerhard von Rad, *Genesis. A Commentary*, translated by J. S. Marks (London: SCM Press, 1963), p. 56.
8. Claus Westermann, *Genesis 1–11. A Commentary*, translated by J. J. Scullion (London: SPCK, 1984), pp. 148–58.

for not only is man in some way at the heart of the problem of evil, in some way or other involving the created order in the fall, but also in the New Testament the assimilation of image language almost exclusively to Jesus Christ means that the doctrine is now concerned as much with new creation as with creation: with the redemption of the distorted image as much as with its status as creation. We cannot, as has been argued above, begin to understand the creation apart from the mediation of the Son and the Spirit. In relation to the image of God, this becomes, if that is possible, even more crucial a consideration, for while the non-human creation retains a measure of good order, albeit an often disrupted order, the fallen human creature is characterised by an active creativity in evil, as the history of our century only too well testifies. Just as, therefore, we cannot understand the creation apart from Christ, so we fail even more completely to understand human being apart from Christ, and particularly apart from Christ crucified.

II BIBLICAL CONSIDERATIONS

Genesis 1:26–7 is the locus classicus, at least historically speaking, for the teaching of the image of God. In the first place, it is stating a universal claim. It is not merely the ruler who shares this characteristic, as tended to be the doctrine of the nations surrounding Israel. All, male and female alike, are made in the image of God.[9] In the second place, it is the fountainhead of a distinction between image and likeness which has muddied the waters for many centuries. Sometimes the drawing of a distinction between likeness to God, which has been lost at the Fall, and the image, which has not, has been attributed to Irenaeus.[10] While there may be some evidence that Irenaeus sometimes speaks like that, for example, in 5. 6. 1, that is not generally his view, which is to treat the two as synonymous (for example, 3. 23. 2 and 4. 38. 3). However that may be, the distinction, as it did develop, goes in harness with the rationalising we have already met, often being supposed to teach that although there is a fall, there is a sense in which human rational capacities remain relatively – in different degree in different theologians – untouched by human sin. Thus it is sometimes suggested that while the will is fallen,

9. We can, then, set aside without more ado, one distortion. If it was ever taught by the church that only men, or men more than women, are truly in the image of God, then that was wrong, and should be rejected, as should any doctrines made in that image.
10. For example, by Emil Brunner, *Man in Revolt. A Christian Anthropology*, translated by Olive Wyon (London: Lutterworth, 1939), pp. 504–5.

the reason is not, or not so completely. At least as early as Calvin the essential, although not absolute, equivalence of the two words in the Hebrew had been recognised, a distinction remaining only in the respect that the author is enriching the meaning of the first term by linking with it a second, almost synonymous, which emphasises its importance. Calvin also emphasises rightly that sin effects the fall of will and reason alike.[11]

The teaching of the verses is that some likeness or similarity to God characterises the being of the whole human race. If, however, they are to be understood theologically in the context of the canon of scripture as a whole, the following must also be taken into account.

(1) In Genesis 2 and 3 the teaching of human dominion over the creation is expressed narratively in the story of the garden and the naming of the animals. Neither the care of a garden nor the naming of the creatures represent a form of absolute domination. To garden is to tend, while to name is a way of entering into a relation, containing elements of reciprocity, though not necessarily symmetrical reciprocity, with the other. Just as God names Jacob as Israel, and so brings him into a covenant of promise, so it is when the creatures are named in the garden.

(2) Eden is a garden, and not a paradise. This is an important distinction. In paradise, the fruits simply fall off the trees on to our tables; in a garden, trees have to be tended. Further, tending the garden would appear, certainly if it is eschatologically understood, to be a beginning of a task which will be completed only at the end of the world. Outside the boundaries of Eden, the world is not yet fit for habitation. That there is a task to complete is shown by the command to 'subdue': things are not yet as they should be. To use an image from sculpture, the block of stone which in some mysterious sense contains the statue has to be so shaped that the final work of art can emerge from it. This is not, as is sometimes charged, in all respects an anthropocentric doctrine. It is theocentric: all derives from the divine creating and providing action. In charging the human race with responsibility for the tending and perfecting of the created order, it does have an anthropocentric aspect, but it is as calling, not as an encouragement to do with the earth what we want. As Irenaeus is sometimes understood to imply, and it is certainly consistent with the drift of his teaching, the bread and the wine of the Lord's Supper show that the human creature is the one through whom the whole of the created order becomes articulate: is enabled to speak. This does not mean that the world does not, in its own way, speak: though it has no voice,

11. John Calvin, *Institutes*, 2. 1. 9.

it yet speaks volumes as some translations of Psalm 19:3–4 suggest. Yet without Psalms like this, we should not know it.

(3) Just as naming is primarily a relation to the animals, so the doctrine of the image of God represents a relation, primarily to God the creator and secondarily to the other creatures, animate and inanimate alike. It is not, as has so often been held in the past, a capacity to know or not to know God, or at least not primarily that, especially if that is taken in the sense of intellectual knowledge. This means that the discussion about how much of this capacity is maintained or lost at the fall is an arid one. The point rather is that the relationship continues – how can the creature possibly not be in some form of relation to its creator? – but in a distorted form. It is significant that the doctrine of the image is re-affirmed after the fall, indeed, in connection with the flood, when the waters of judgement and destruction threaten to break in upon the creation and destroy it (Genesis 9:8–16). And it is also significant that the image has an ethical centre, returning us to the notion that it is centrally to do with relations with the other. It is the reason why we should not kill, and, as the letter of James adds, slander our neighbour (Genesis 9:6, James 3:9).

(4) The ethical dimension provides part of the reason why in the New Testament there is very little reference to the general doctrine of the image – James, again, and the less than judicious use of the idea in 1 Corinthians 11 – but its assimilation to christology. Jesus is the true image of God and the means of the restoration of its true form in others – those who are 'conformed' to his image (Romans 8:29). We shall pursue this aspect further below. Additional confirmation that Irenaeus is not guilty of a dualistic interpretation of the image is found in his view that for him both image and likeness are lost in Adam, both restored in Christ (3. 18. 1; 4. 38. 4; cf. 5. 16. 2). And that is the point. As the last and eschatological Adam, the first born from the dead, Jesus inaugurates the redemption of all things, particularly by calling into community those to be conformed to him. In this respect, the resurrection is central in establishing that here is the one in and through whom the human project will be completed.

III CHRISTOLOGICAL CONSIDERATIONS

As has already been much stressed, Genesis 1:26–7 forms part of a chapter devoted to an account of the creation of the world by God, and shows the creation of men and women to be part, a climactic part, indeed, of that process. Human creatures, that is to say, have their being in continuity with the remainder of the created order, though in some sense they are also its crown. Theologically this characterisation raises the question of created human being: with what kind of being are we concerned when we speak of man as male and female together being created by God in his own image? What are we essaying in such a theology? To capture an essence? A first approach to this question is best attempted in the light of Barth's determined attempt to avoid any sug-gestion of a timeless essence or centre. All of Barth's theology is con-cerned with reality, both divine and created, as event, and in particular human reality as history. Can there be an essence of one who is ever-lastingly in movement? Well, yes: we can describe man as one who is essentially in movement, or condemned to be free, or whatever. All of these are attempts to identify the kind of being with which we are concerned, and to suggest anything else is obfuscation.

And yet, as Kenneth Paul Wesche has recently argued, essentialism of a certain kind is a real enemy, for it derives from the Greek quest to understand the human in terms of soul. Speaking of Plato, though much of his description could also be of the currently fashionable, essentially gnostic, ideology of gender, he writes that, 'The real "self" of a man or woman is therefore the genderless *psychic* particle dwelling *within* and *distinct from* the body; the self is the universal Soul divided into many essential particles and distributed throughout different bodies; the self is the *inner man*, the inner *essence* or *real man* dwelling within a body.'[12] Similar things could be said of Aristotle, so that the only way to evade the abolition of particularity – essentialism in that sense – inherent in the Greek approach is to derive anthropology from christology.[13]

That is the heart, as is well known, of Barth's approach, but also of Francis Watson's recent contention in *Text and Truth*[14] that the Old Testament teaching cannot stand on its own, but must be interpreted, as the New Testament interprets the doctrine of image, christologically. Such an approach, rather than distorting, enables him to give due weight to the form of the Old Testament texts, far better, indeed, than the old Hellenising attempt to construe the image in terms of reason, a tradition that effectively takes it out of the realm of exegesis altogether. What is

12. That is why many of the things said in the modern world about 'sexual preference', sex change and homosexuality are essentially gnostic in evading the respect in which we *are* our bodies.

13. Kenneth Paul Wesche, 'The Soul and Personality: Tracing the Roots of the Christo-logical Problem', *Pro Ecclesia* 5 (1996), pp. 23–42 (p. 34).

14. Francis Watson, *Text and Truth. Redefining Biblical Theology* (Edinburgh: T. & T. Clark, 1997).

noteworthy here is that 'the relationship is one of physical resemblance' (p. 289), a point made, as we have seen, a generation or so ago by von Rad. The christological reading enables Watson, in a kind of returning movement, to throw light also on other relevant texts. Ezekiel's vision of God whose 'likeness [was] as it were of a human appearance'(Ezekiel 1:26) 'corresponds to that of Genesis: if humans are made in the likeness of God, then God will resemble the human form if and when he makes himself visible' (p. 289). Such is the irreducible link between the human and the divine.

The implications of this teaching, Watson continues, were drawn by Irenaeus: 'The prophet sees God in human likeness not because God is human in form . . . but because, without abandoning his holiness and his spirituality, God purposes to become human, in the incarnation of his Word, and to be seen as such' (p. 290). Watson concludes: 'The Son's person and action are therefore the one true *homoioma* of the Father's person and action; this particular human person is the image and likeness of God in the strictest possible sense.' Therefore, 'All humans may be said to be like God in the sense that they are like Jesus' (p. 291). This point is related to that made by Irenaeus, when he says that the Word of God himself is a pattern in the creation of human beings (5. 1. 1. and 6. 1; and not, we might repeat, some platonic form of humanity). Watson rightly concludes that, as a result, questions about the ethics of the image, such as that concerning human dominion over the remainder of the creation, are secondary and consequent, rather than constitutive of the image.

IV THE NATURE OF THE IMAGE: CREATION AND REDEMPTION AGAIN

We have, then, the first, tentative, answer to our question as to what kind of a thing is man, created male and female. We are not seeking a timeless essence, but attempting to characterise what kind of reality it is that has a beginning, a middle and an end of the kind which Jesus of Nazareth makes known by making real. Human creatures are those whose being is constituted, along with the rest of the created order, by the action of God the Father in Jesus Christ and the Spirit, but constituted in a distinctive way: they are like God, while the remainder of creation reflects and reveals his glory. The contention made on historical and exegetical grounds that one cannot understand the image of God apart from the person of Christ has the double consequence that the question of createdness is bound up with teleological – or, better, eschatological – and soteriological questions. They are those raised by the author to the

Hebrews. Citing the second Psalm's celebration of the human dominion over the creation, he comments, 'As it is, we do not yet see everything in subjection to him (man)' (Hebrews 2:8). Let us examine the two concerns this raises one at a time.

The question of eschatology concerns the end to which human life is directed, and in particular that it is more than simply a moral end, but in some sense ontological: that is to say, it is ontologically constitutive of being human that there is a process of perfecting or completing which involves something that is not already inherent in, or achieved by, the beginning. If there is an essence, it cannot then be construed as a 'static' one, simply in terms of characteristics and capacities. There must also be an element of directedness. Those who rather patronisingly described certain patristic theologies of salvation as 'physical' at least had this in their favour: they realised that for some of the Fathers redemption, the completion of the human story, is ontological as well as moral. It is not simply the final removal of the sin that clings so closely, but that understood in a wide sense as the rounding off of the whole person. Irenaeus famously spoke of Adam and Eve as being in some way childlike, as called to growth and maturity, and this is helpful so long as it is not interpreted in the light of a metaphor of evolution or in terms of a (Hegelian) 'fall upwards', as is too often suggested. More on that when we come to soteriology. The real eschatological question, rather, concerns what one recent writer has called 'The necessary imperfection of creation.' 'In his protracted rebuttal of Gnostic sects, Irenaeus repeatedly emphasises the unqualified goodness of the creation. But in iv. 38 he springs upon the reader the surprising contention that Adam, as first created by God, was imperfect.'[15] Brown's conclusion is that there are two conflicting doctrines in Irenaeus, the one taken up by such as Hick,[16] and making Irenaeus a proto-liberal or moral evolutionist, and that which became the orthodox view in the West, of a fall only reversed by redemption. Douglas Farrow has pointed out that this is to misunderstand:

> The 'imperfection' is this: The love for God which is the life of man cannot emerge *ex nihilo* in full bloom; it requires to grow with experience. But that in turn is what makes the fall, however unsurprising, such a devastating affair. In the fall, man is 'turned backwards.' He does not grow up in love of God as he is intended to.

---

15. Robert F. Brown, 'On the Necessary Imperfection of Creation: Irenaeus' *Adversus Haereses* iv, 38', *Scottish Journal of Theology* 28 (1975), pp. 17–25 (p. 18).

16. John Hick, *Evil and the God of Love* (London: Collins, 1968. 1st edition 1966).

> The course of his time, his so-called progress, is set in the wrong direction.[17]

The solution to the problem of the relation of what can be called absolute and relative perfection is eschatological. Creation is a project. As created, it is perfect, because it is God's project: what he purposes for that which is not God but creation, and therefore intrinsically finite and temporal. But it is not perfect in the sense of complete. It has somewhere to go, and that is one of the points of the doctrine of recapitulation. Jesus Christ recapitulates our human story in order that the project of the perfection of all things may be achieved. The doctrine of Christ as the Second Adam has therefore this function, to show that the destiny of the created human being – the first Adam – is in some sense bound up with him. 'Just as we have borne the image of the man of dust, we shall also bear the image of the man of heaven' (1 Corinthians 15:49). Here we find a reinforcement of the doctrine of the irreducible link between the human and the divine rendered christologically.

However, given those things reported in Genesis 3, and given the treatment of the second Adam in Paul, eschatological teleology is inextricably bound up with soteriology. Not only is it the case that apart from Christ there is no perfection; the end is furthermore not attained without redemption of both man and nature, for from the beginning the human creation refused to be that which it was created to become, and so became the means – possibly, as we have seen, not the only means – of subjecting to futility that which had quite another teleology. That redemption is set in train from within space and time by the work of the second Adam, who thus achieves, in his person through the Spirit, what the first Adam failed to do: the right direction which, through that same Spirit, then becomes available universally. The recapitulation of the human story by Jesus is then the means of perfection in the senses both of restoration and of completion. God re-inaugurates the project of creation by means of the life, death, resurrection and ascension of Jesus.

That brings us to the most pressing problem of the doctrine of the image of God. It has to do with the status of our createdness given not only its incompleteness, but its corruption. We may be in the image of God in so far as we are like the human Jesus, but in what sense and how far do those who can be called the ordinarily sinful, let alone the most depraved, remain like him? The situation is similar to, but more difficult, than, that of the general problem of the doctrine of creation. In affirming

17. Douglas Farrow, 'St Irenaeus of Lyons. The Church and the World', *Pro Ecclesia* 4 (1995), pp. 333–55 (p. 348).

that the creation, because it is the work and gift of God, is good, it is necessary to conclude that evil – in so far as we are sure that we know what that is – is not intrinsic to the creation, but some corruption of, or invasion into, that which is essentially good. In the case of the human creature, we have the case of one not only capable, but also guilty, of offences against others made in the image of God which too often confound the imagination. A doctrine like that of the image of God, which claims universality, must be able to deal with the hardest cases. They are of two kinds.

The first concerns, as we have seen, moral corruption: the manifest unfreedom of much of our existence, enslaved as we are, apart from redemption, to sin and 'the powers'. The question is whether those so enslaved to evil as to be virtually deprived of the capacity to love are thus far deprived of personhood, which, as I shall later claim, is the heart of the matter of the image. What are we to make of those who, it appears, can no longer love in freedom: those daemonic persons, in Dorothy Emmet's description,[18] who are so enslaved to the lie that they call evil their good, consigning millions of those made in the image of God to gas chambers or death by war, poisoning or starvation? What are we to make of those who so violate the order of being that their likeness to the human Jesus is discernible only by their physical shape? One cannot locate the image of God in freedom or creativity, if there are those whose creativity is only, or largely, in evil; or even in love when there are those so alienated from their creator that love is overridden by hatred, destructiveness and violence. What God has created, he has created; or, to adapt a saying of Ockham, what God has created stays created unless he chooses to annihilate it, so that we cannot deny even to the perpetrators of monstrous evils the fact that they are made and, in some respects remain, in the image of their creator, uniquely of the whole created order. Similarly, the second and less difficult case theologically, but problem enough in modern culture, there are the physically and mentally handicapped. Again, if we take the worst cases, in what sense are we to regard as in the image of God those so incapacitated as to be incapable of any 'human' response, let alone the rationality or consciousness traditionally ascribed to those in the image: the senile, the victims of brain damage, or, at the other end of the scale of life, the foetus? We must say at least that those whose physical shape is deformed or not yet fully formed retain the intrinsic dignity conferred by virtue of their inextinguishable relation to God the Father through Christ and the Spirit.

18. Dorothy Emmet, *the Moral Prism* (London: Macmillan, 1979), p. 151.

More trinitarianly, we should say that even the apparently irremediably lost remain in the likeness of God because he continues, in Christ, to be creator, whether freedom to love is exercised or rejected for slavery. This means that however horrible the deformity, however great the need for redemption in its broadest sense, those created in God's image remain so, and hence Genesis' prohibition on killing one so created. (Here, of course, is the heart of the objection to capital punishment and 'euthanasia'.) At the very least, the human being, simply as created, is of the kind of *being* that a certain radical moral respect is due to every human person, however sunk in villainy and depravity. This entails at the very least the ascription of a certain unique *status*, though what it is can surely not be understood without some form of ontology – because status, certainly status before God, is a mode of being. It would seem to follow, then, that, as created, the image of God is in a sense something given, even though it can finally be perfected only eschatologically, and through redemption. That something given cannot be taken away, except by God, because it is part of what it is to be a created human being.

Against this, it might be contended that, if Jesus is the one truly in the image of God, and if it is a requirement of redeemed humanity to be conformed to his image, then to speak of some intrinsic image, some essence of created humanity, remains a mistake or irrelevance. Quite apart, however, from the dangers of Gnosticism in its Marcionite form, that would seem to be a mistake. What God has made, he has made, and made through the mediator of his creation, the one, as we have seen, intrinsically oriented to human being, so that redemption is not a creation out of nothing but a perfecting of that which has been made. (The risen Jesus remains Jesus of Nazareth.) It is not that Genesis 1 is overcome, either by Genesis 3 or the resurrection of Jesus from the dead, but rather that it is in some way fulfilled by, and so can be understood only on the basis of, that eschatological event. Whatever we make of the traditional distinction between image and likeness which implies that the latter only was lost by sin – and I do not want to make anything – it can at least be seen that it is attempting something quite proper: to show that whatever happened at the Fall, human likeness to God remained. If evil is corruption of the good, then we have to continue to ask: what exactly is it that is corrupted and enslaved? What remains to be the basis of the moral respect with which, at the very least, we are concerned?

For an approach to an answer, let us return to the text of Genesis 1. Here we must note that whatever the human likeness to God is, it does not appear to license the positing of any continuity between the human and the divine. The text's maintaining of a clear distinction between the creator and his creation, a distinction continued and reinforced by orthodox christology's ascription of divinity to Jesus Christ uniquely of the human race, rules out any intrinsic endowment or capacity which makes man in some sense inherently divine, whether by virtue of reason or any other similar character. Although in maintaining the indestructibility of the image some doctrine of the divine spark might appear to be a help, it will not do, not only because of its apparent Hellenic presumption of continuity between the human and the divine, but also – the converse of the same syndrome – it calls attention away from the *christologically guaranteed* physical likeness which must in some way be maintained.

In any case, the one continuity which the text posits for humankind is with the remainder of the created order. Nothing about being in the image of God abolishes the fundamental distinction between the creator and the created. This is the hinge on which turns the difference between Christianity and Hellenism, as well as the Gnosticism which is its debased counterpart. The continuity is made clear by the way in which the creation story is told. We belong with and alongside the creatures, whatever our in other ways special relationship with the creator. In that respect, there is more in common between us and the 'lowest' of the creatures than between God and ourselves. We referred in the previous chapter to John Zizioulas' contention that, whatever else Darwin has done, he has at least performed us the service of reminding us of our continuity with the beasts. We are material, bodily beings, and are so essentially. Idealism both ancient and modern has ignored that lesson, and always tended in the direction of a Gnosticism which at the very least belittles the materiality both our own and that of the world in general. Any notion of the image of God which spiritualises it, in the sense of dematerialising it, misses its meaning.

This is particularly important with respect to human sexuality. We do not have to go as far as Barth in suggesting – if he does – that in some sense our being created as male and female is that in which the image of God consists. Yet to be true to our text we must realise that our *particular* embodiment – the sense that in certain respects, however much that has to be qualified, we are our bodies – is inseparable from our being in the image of God. To deprive the text of that is to refuse to allow it to say what it says. Thus, among other things – and I think that it cannot be limited to this, as we shall see – our text is drawing an analogy, pointing a likeness, between man as male and female – as what might be called with due care an embodied spirit – and God. To be in the image of God is to be structured in a manner in some way similar

205

to that in which the divine being is ordered. To the taxis of God there corresponds a human taxis, a human way of being in and with the world.

Here it is worth mentioning the notion, sometimes encountered today, of the image of God as address. To be human is to be addressed by God, to be called to be in particular forms of relationship with him, with one another and with the rest of the created world. The advantages of this are several: it maintains the distinction between God and the world while supposing a personal relation. It has the further advantage of underwriting what can be called a dialogical relation of human beings one with another, of the kind developed by Alistair McFadyen.[19] There are, however, a number of limitations. The first is the perennial danger of minimising the materiality of human created existence. To be sure, address requires ears, or eyes if the word comes through reading, but taken by itself the notion is surely only a part of what we need to say. The second limitation is that such a conception inadequately characterises the human likeness to God implied in the Genesis text, except, again, so far as verbal communication is concerned, a conception dangerously near to the idea of the image as reason. That is to say, the notion that we are in the image in so far as we are the recipients of and responders to God's address understates the range of forms of relationality involved in imaging. But it is an improvement on some of its predecessors.

V THE MATTER OF THE IMAGE

The next stage of the argument becomes possible when we recall that relation is an ontological category: relation constitutes who and what we are. Many of the difficulties facing the image doctrine derive from a failure to see this, and to construe the image as something characterising us as individuals, rather than as persons in relation. This is where Barth and Bonhoeffer are right: we are concerned with an analogy of relation rather than one of being.[20] (In point of fact, perhaps we must, if the argument of the previous section is right, move towards an analogy of relation that generates a kind of analogy of being, for we are concerned with ontology.) But we begin with something that is not an analogy – that is, not something indicating a form of comparison – but a fairly

19. Alistair I. McFadyen, *The Call to Personhood. A Christian Theory of the Individual in Social Relationships* (Cambridge: Cambridge University Press, 1990). See also Kevin Vanhoozer, 'Human being, individual and social', in *The Cambridge Companion to Christian Doctrine*, edited by Colin E. Gunton (Cambridge: Cambridge University Press, 1997), pp. 158–88.

20. Dietrich Bonhoeffer, *Creation and Fall. A Theological Interpretation of Genesis 1–3*, translated by J. C. Fletcher (London: SCM Press, 1959), pp. 36–7.

straightforward statement of fact deriving from the doctrine of creation. To be a creature is to be in a particular kind of relation to the creator. That is what createdness means. If the creator's upholding is withdrawn, then the creature perishes: 'when thou takest away their breath, they die, and return to the dust' (Psalm 104. 29). This holds for human and non-human creature alike, even though the form of the relation is different. It follows that we are free from any need to couch the doctrine of the image in terms of – 'static' – characteristics or endowments, etc., even though they may eventually be part of the overall picture, because what is crucial are the actual relations in which the human creature, as distinct from other creatures, exists.

As we have seen, part of that relation is unrealised, or distorted, so that it can be restored only through redemption. But not the whole: the covenant promise, repeated in different forms throughout saving history, is that something is irremovable, and that is God's commitment to those made in his image. If God upholds all the creation, and *a fortiori* the human creation, in and through Jesus Christ, then that is the primary ontology of the continuing subsistence of the image of God in human-kind. To be created in the image of God is not simply to be made and upheld by the triune God; it is, more specifically, to be upheld by him through the Son, that is, through Jesus Christ, who is the true image of God. Even those moving in the wrong direction are upheld by the Son and drawn to their perfection by the Spirit, even if in their recalcitrance they seek to escape the hands of God. This is reinforced if we recall that it is often remarked that the doctrine of creation, and the doctrine of the image of God would even more importantly be included, has its primary reference to God, and only secondarily to the world. To say that man is created in the image of God refers to the fact that God constitutes a particular being among all the other created beings to subsist in a particular and unique kind of relation with him. In that respect at least the image is indelible.

But is it also indelible at the horizontal level, in terms of our relations with one another and the rest of the created order? In the matter of horizontal relations, we must repeat the point made in the previous discussion: here, too, we cannot understand our likeness to God apart from our continuing relation with God, through Christ and the perfecting Spirit. But if we are created like the triune God, and if the doctrine of creation is concerned not only with the triune God, but also with the kind of beings he has created and holds in being, then we must take the risk of drawing conclusions also about human being in its creaturehood. This is where we encounter the analogy proper. What likeness is there between the creator and those created to be the crown of creation? What is the likeness to God that subsists in and through the relationship mediated through Son and Spirit? In what sense are we like the triune God, while being ontologically totally other than he?

Likeness to God consists in the fact that human beings are persons, while the remainder of the created world is not. We are in certain ways analogous to the persons of the Trinity, in particular in being in mutually constitutive relations to other persons. Who and what we are derives not only from our relations to God, our creator, but to those others who have made and continue to make us what we are. Just as Father, Son and Holy Spirit constitute the being of God, so created persons are those who, insofar as they are authentically personal – and we shall return to that matter – are characterised by subsisting in mutually constitutive relations with one another. That means that we must reject a primarily individualistic way of construing the image. That is where Barth is right to link the image with co-humanity, and Augustine wrong to say that: 'man by himself alone is the image of God, just as fully as when he and the woman are joined together in one'.[21] Augustine is right to the extent that to kill or slander one human being is to violate the image, but not in so far as it might imply that being in the image can be understood without some intrinsic reference to other human beings. Just as to be God is not to be an individual but three persons inextricably interrelated as being in communion, so to be man, as male and female, is to be created for life in community. And that perhaps gives us a clue to what we are looking for: however deformed the image, an element of co-humanity remains constitutive of our being, though some adults attempt, by reclusive behaviour, for example, to reverse the necessarily inter-relational aspects of their formation. To be in the image of God is therefore to be in necessary relation to others so made.

There is a further element of being in the image of God which derives from our being created persons, and this is our continuity with the remainder of creation and our necessary embodiment. We take our distinct personal character from the world of which we are a part: genes, dispositions, nourishment, culture – by which I mean all human activity in making use of the creation – and the rest. Central to this is our being made male and female, because that is in a distinctive way constitutive of our co-humanity, as Barth has argued. This is not merely the fact that we are dependent on the relations of being male and female if we are to be born at all, but that more broadly our being created with the particular bodies that we have – male and female bodies, constituted for

21. Augustine, *On the Trinity*, 12. 7. 10.

certain kinds of physical and non-physical relations to one another – is part of what it means to be made in the image of God. This is reinforced by the fact that redeemed relations of men and women are in some way central to the meaning of the gospel, as Paul in particular has made clear (Galatians 3:28), and that fallenness takes the form of disorderly sexual relations, among other things (Romans 1:24–7). It is surely the case that some such theology of the mutually constitutive character of relations underlies Paul's contention that 'he who joins himself to a prostitute becomes one body with her' (1 Corinthians 6:16). A further consequence of our embodiedness, as is clear from the Genesis text, is a necessary relation between being in the image of God and a calling to dominion of the remainder of the created order. This, too, is a form of relation, and, like the sexual relation, subject to disorder – as we have seen the writer to the Hebrews contending – but that does not detract from the teaching that our relation to the world is, if not constitutive of our being in the image of God, then certainly in some way the consequence of it.

At this place, we are returned to the inextricable connection between creation and redemption. In even the best, the image is perfected only through redemption, and in that sense the demonic and the depraved are in the same boat as the rest of us. As John Zizioulas has pointed out, 'person' is an eschatological concept 'in that true personhood will be realised only in the final Kingdom of God.'[22] This means that because creation is a project, that is to say, something to be perfected, being in the image of God is also being in movement to an end. Again, as Irenaeus makes clear, by attempting to move away from the hands of God, we attempt to nullify the project, but the directedness remains, even when we are kicking against the pricks. The Spirit's perfecting activity may be rejected, but it remains a form of divine relation even to those apparently seeking to destroy themselves, indeed, those also who apparently succeed in the attempt.

But there is also a respect in which there is a difference between those who have accepted the call to be in redeemed relation to God in Jesus Christ and those who have not. We have already made much of the christological determination of the image of God. One of the places where it is expounded is the letter to the Colossians, where the writer draws a direct link between Christ the mediator of creation and the church. 'He is before all things, and in him all things hold together. He is the head of the body, the church; he is the beginning, the first-born

---

22. This is a contribution of his incorporated in British Council of Churches, *The Forgotten Trinity, Volume 1, The Report of the BCC Study Commission on Trinitarian Doctrine Today* (London: British Council of Churches, 1989), p. 22.

from the dead, that in everything he might be pre-eminent' (Colossians
1:17–18). Modern commentators, finding the reference to the church
to break the logic of the passage, have sometimes held that the words
are a later addition to a primitive Christian hymn to Christ. But they
miss the point. If Jesus is indeed, as we have seen, the one truly in the
image of God among other things because he is the one in whom the
right human dominion of the creation is re-established – in the speaking of the truth, the healing of the sick and the lifting up of the
oppressed – it follows that as the body of Christ, the community
ordered to Christ by word and sacrament, the church places itself where
the image is to be formed. It is no accident that the two sacraments of
baptism and the Lord's Supper make intrinsic use of the physical creation, as we shall see in Chapter 10.[23]

We conclude this treatment of the anthropology of the creation by
saying that to be in the image of God is to be a created, as distinct from
an uncreated, person. That is where the likeness-in-relation that is the
heart of this matter consists. To be a created person is, first, to be in
inescapable relation to God the Father through his two hands, the Son
and the Spirit, who will not, this side of eternity, cease to hold and direct
those created in hope; and it is to be in such a relation as, second, a
project, according to which it is the purpose of God to perfect to his glory
those he created out of free love to live as a people to his praise, to offer
themselves – their souls and bodies – as a living sacrifice of thanksgiving.
Third, the project is a personal one in the further sense that human
beings are created to be with and for God in Jesus Christ and so for one
another, in likeness to the triune communion, as male and female and
in responsibility under God for the good ordering of the creation. It is
at this place that we locate the characteristics and callings that we
believe to be in some way intrinsic to personality: freedom, responsibility,
creativity[24] and the rest. Finally, being in the image of God implies, therefore, an ethic, according to which human life is ordered appropriately to
both the personal and the non-personal creation. All are called to relations
of love-in-freedom with others so imaged; all are called to represent
God to the creation. This ethic is a consequence of being in the image,
and, like the image itself, takes its orientation from the 'vertical' relation
of humankind to God.

This means that we must set our face against a dualism of body and

23. I am grateful to Jeremy Thomson for his observation of the need for an ecclesio-
logical dimension in this chapter.
24. See Brian Horne, 'Creation and Creativity', in *The Doctrine of Creation*, edited by
Colin E. Gunton (Edinburgh, T. & T. Clark, 1997), pp. 135–47.

soul. There is clearly a place for some such distinction, for scripture is clear that the body is a subordinate part of the person, to be subjected to control of the spirit. But it is not an ontological dualism: body and spirit alike are created. But that raises a question. If there is no continuity between some human characteristic or endowment and God, how is it possible for us to know God? (This is, of course, the famous 'point of contact.') More important, how do we come to be in relation to God? Now, if what the doctrine of creation says is true, the latter is an unnecessary question, for the doctrine holds that it is an indelible mark of createdness, and not simply of human createdness, to be in relation to God, because to be created is to be made and continuously upheld by God through his Son and Spirit. One cannot cease to be a creature, unless the one who created us should will also to annihilate that which he has made. The knowledge of God is secondary to that, but also mediated by the Spirit through the Son, and is also realised in various ways, as people accept or reject the knowledge of God which is made available to them according to their particular setting in life.

If there is no absolute dualism of soul and body, it follows that we are ontologically continuous with the remainder of the created order. The dispute about whether the biblical doctrine of the image of God is responsible for the ecological crisis finds part of its solution here. The ecological crisis is in large measure caused by human selfishness and greed. It is undoubtedly exacerbated by doctrines which teach a dualistic doctrine according to which the created order is ontologically so different from us, for example related as a machine is to its makers, that its treatment becomes a matter of moral indifference. There is therefore a sense in which modern science can be understood in different respects as obedience and – in its more 'Faustian' side – as sin. The same question can be asked of different aspects of all our attempts at dominion. In place of the damaging dualism of much of our intellectual inheritance, the doctrine of the image thus places us in a layered network of relationships, first to God the creator, then to one another, and then to the world in its diversity. Our continuity with the rest of the world maintains a due measure of our finite and limited state, but our difference from it a witness to our high calling under God to exercise a right dominion over the rest of the created world. Pre-eminent among all human responsibilities, but by no means excluding others, is that to the human world, for other human beings, created in the image of God, are those in relation with whom we first of all learn to be like God, which means to love.

10

ESCHATOLOGY AND ETHICS

—————

We move now from human created reality to consider more directly the human relation to the created world. We were, according to the letter to the Ephesians, 'created for good works' (Ephesians 2:10), and we shall here consider some aspects of these, albeit in a particular perspective. Much reference has been made during the book to the necessity for attention being given to the eschatological orientation of the doctrine of creation. While in one sense the heart of the doctrine is concerned with the 'past' in the sense of the once for all establishment of what God has created, both the nature of the eternal God's relation to time and the fact that creation is 'project', a reality projected for perfection, require attention to the 'present' (as in the doctrine of providence) and 'future' (the point of the quotation marks will appear later). As we have seen, eschatology had a part to play in the development of early doctrines of creation, though it virtually disappeared as a constitutive element of the doctrine after Augustine. Before then the doctrine of the beginning of the universe was frequently defended by appeal to eschatological judgement. The final judgement of the living and the dead, because it came at the end of time, implied the beginning and the directedness of the temporal order. It also implies an ethic of creation, by which is meant a broad conspectus of the human habitation of the world; what Christoph Schwöbel has called an ethic of createdness.[1]

1. Christoph Schwöbel, 'God, Creation and the Christian Community: The Dogmatic Basis of an Ethic of Createdness', *The Doctrine of Creation. Essays in Dogmatics, History and Philosophy* (Edinburgh: T. & T. Clark, 1997), pp. 149–76.

I THE PROBLEM OF AN ESCHATOLOGY OF CREATION

When we seek to speak of the eschatological dimension of creation theology, we should be careful to define what it is that we mean theologically. There are in currency a number of what can be called secular eschatologies, often scientific theories of the end of things in the observable universe, taking the form of the disappearance of everything in an immense black hole, a heat death of everything or the equivalent death by extreme cold. In response, some scientists have attempted to salvage from the wreckage some form of secular salvation, supposing that a kind of immortality might be attainable for the human race if something could be projected into eternity in computerised form. It must be said of all these that they are not truly eschatological, in the sense we shall explore, because they are simply or largely projections on the universe of forms of this-worldly experience. It is possible that some of them may signal the end of all things in a more radical sense, but it remains the case that the end of things as we know them is not necessarily identical with the End, just as speculation about the 'big bang', or whatever, is not the same as the doctrine of creation out of nothing.[2]

We shall begin our study with reference to one recent scientific eschatology, which not so much by its content as by its parallels with a theological eschatology of creation proper will bring many of the questions into focus. As we have seen, problems with the relation of time and eternity underlie some of the modern difficulties with the doctrine of creation. In particular, a failure to understand the fact that the creator God is not restricted to time, and the difficulty of thinking of any other relation, lead to inabilities to give adequate accounts of creation as a beginning and creation as a continuing project. It is, however, of the essence of projects that they have an end in view. And it is of the essence of the modern era that it is an era of projects. Indeed, we hasten, mindlessly and relentlessly, from one project to another, straining to bring in the 'future', a future, which, of course, never comes. That, however, does not in any way limit the volume of projects, to the extent that some scientists have even devoted themselves to the realm of eschatology. Notable among recent secular eschatologies is Frank J. Tipler's *The Physics of Immortality*. In it, he puts forward what he calls the 'Omega Point

---

2. We should consider here the reported remark of Jüngel that the nuclear holocaust has no eschatological relevance. It implies that there is, eschatologically speaking, no qualitative difference between the death of an old man or of a child, and a nuclear holocaust.

Theory, which is a testable physical theory for an omniscient, omni-present God who will one day in the far future resurrect every single one of us to live forever in an abode which is in all essentials the Judeo-Christian Heaven'.[3]

Tipler's dream is at the opposite end of the spectrum to the anti-technological drive of many programmes of ecological conservation. It shares with some of them the desire to make things last for ever, but it is a technological version of the modern desire to conquer death by human action. Part of the programme is, in order to prevent the earth from being vaporised by the sun several million years hence, to take 'the entire planet apart in order to use the material to expand the biosphere. (Dyson has shown that taking a planet apart is technically feasible, if you are willing to take a few million years to do it)' (p. 57). What might be called the penultimate end he has in view is the colonisation of the Milky Way Galaxy, but the long-term aim is greater: 'a claim that *progress* will continue indefinitely, literally to infinity in all standard measures' (p. 66). '"Eternal" progress means that progress will continue literally without limit. Knowledge will grow without bound, per capita wealth will increase to infinity.'[4] This, of course, is in the interests of avoiding the end of the universe in a heat death, or whatever fate awaits it. The means by which this colonisation is to be achieved – the Omega Point – is intelligent robots, self-reproducing machines. This is manifestly a secularised, but not entirely secular, eschatology. Realising that the (sec-ular) alternative is the doctrine of the eternal return – a cyclical universe – Tipler obtains the assistance of Augustine in his account of Christian opposition to Greek notions of a cyclical universe, and he chooses well: 'God forbid that we should believe in [the Eternal Return]. For Christ died once for our sins, and rising again, dies no more.'[5] Tipler's own objections to eternal return are partly moral – the connections between this philosophy and racism – and partly derived from objections to its anti-scientific character.

However, the anti-human, indeed gnostic, character of his own position is brought out in his replies to objections to his project. 'A "person" is

---

3. Frank J. Tipler, *The Physics of Immortality. Modern Cosmology, God and the Resurrection of the Dead* (London: Macmillan, 1995), p. 1.
4. Tipler, *The Physics of Immortality*, p. 104. Some of Tipler's judgements beggar belief. 'Bernal was the first to suggest that the stars – and in particular the Sun – were from the point of view of life, very wasteful of energy. He argued that this waste should stop . . . "The stars cannot be allowed to continue in their own way, but will be turned into efficient heat engines"', p. 108.
5. Tipler, *The Physics of Immortality*, p. 76, citing Augustine, *City of God*, 12. 14.

defined by qualities of mind and soul, not by a particular bodily form'
(p. 87). Although his argument is anti-Nazi, for he claims that Hitler
defined people by bodily form – wrongly, in point of fact, for the Nazi
view, if based on bodily differences at all, is based on imagined ones – it
is gnostic in the sense that it values the mental – informational – over the
more obviously embodied personal qualities which an adequate theology
would hold to be (at least) as central to life. In any case, Tipler is more
concerned with the survival of intelligence than of persons, or rather of
persons heavily understood in terms of intelligence, and this must be the
chief objection to his proposals. 'Ultimately, intelligent machines will
become more intelligent than members of the species *Homo sapiens*, and
will thus dominate civilisation' (p. 87). Other definitions betray the same
weakness. 'I claim that a "living being" is any entity which codes information . . .'.[6] Sad to relate, Tipler does gain some assistance from theology,
and what he says reinforces the point made in previous chapters that
Christian theology has allowed gnostic elements to enter its doctrine of
creation. 'There is actually an astonishing similarity', Tipler writes,
'between the mind-as-computer programme idea and the medieval
Christian idea of the "soul". Both are fundamentally "immaterial" . . .'
(p. 127).

When Tipler comes to theology, he again produces echoes of traditional doctrines, for it is clear that his Omega Point is his deity, which
will eventually, like the God of 1 Corinthians 15, be all in all:

> It is natural to say that the Omega Point is "both transcendent to
> and yet immanent in" every point of spacetime. When life has
> completely engulfed the entire universe . . . the distinction
> between living and nonliving matter will lose its meaning . . .
> "[D]uration" for the Omega Point can be regarded as equivalent
> to the collection of all experiences of life that did, does, and will
> exist for the whole of universal history . . . This "duration" is very
> close to the idea of *aeternitas* of Thomistic philosophy. (pp. 154–5)

There is also a parallel for doctrines of the resurrection of the body, for
the computer simulations which he predicts will be simulations of *all* the
functions he reckons to be human, including sex, which will however,

6. Tipler, *The Physics of Immortality*, p. 124. There is more evidence of the higher lunacy
   in another of Tipler's authorities, Dawkins, for example: 'computers and cars . . . in
   this book will be firmly treated as biological objects. The reader's reaction to this
   may be to ask, "Yes, but are they *really* biological objects?" Words are our servants, not
   our masters.' Who was it who was recorded as saying that words mean what I want
   them to?

be untroubled in the afterlife, because the Omega Point will choose for all persons more appropriate partners than they can often find, with long and tiresome effort, for themselves – in a kind of electronic version of Plato's *Republic*, it seems (p. 256). But it is only a parallel. Tipler attempts to refute objections to the view that his computer simulations will be identical with what we are now, but seems to me to fail. The resurrection is not a doctrine of replication, but of transformation; but of transformation within bodily continuity, so that the risen Christ is Jesus of Nazareth, the transfigured but still human Jesus.

In pursuing his theory, Tipler interrelates with the theology of Wolfhart Pannenberg, again in a way that shows his relations to the theological tradition. What he calls the Universal Wave Function is a means of showing that the Omega Point bears from the future on the direction of evolution. This eschatological function he claims, with the help of Pannenberg, to be the Holy Spirit:

> In the biblical traditions, this life-giving power is the Holy Spirit. I am thus in effect proposing that we identify the universal wave function constrained by the Omega Point Boundary Condition with the Holy Spirit . . . [This] is an omnipresent invisible field, guiding and creating all being, and ultimately Personal – these are the traditional defining properties of the Holy Spirit . . .
>
> The ultimate future guides all presents into itself. But this guidance is *not* determinism. (p. 185)

Like all heresy, this theory parallels orthodox Christian theology while managing to say the opposite. That is to say in this case: by apparently affirming the personal, it effectively divinises the impersonal forces of the universe, because we, embodied human beings, are destined to be displaced by machines which will carry information but not love.[7] Yet as an attempt to relate time and eternity, pneumatologically, indeed, Tipler's work does share one of the concerns of the doctrine of creation.

II AN ALTERNATIVE ESCHATOLOGY

We shall explore the theme of cosmic eschatology with Wolfhart Pannenberg, who has recently treated the relation between time and

---

7. That is not perhaps quite fair, but insofar as Tipler saves himself from the charge, he contradicts his general position. That is to say, he wishes both to devise a future in which we shall be immune from the extremes of temperature that would destroy our bodies, and to maintain the reality of those same bodies in simulations.

eternity in a way with which Tipler has tried to relate. Pannenberg is particularly interesting in that from the beginning of his career he has attempted an eschatological ontology, based upon his affirmation of the historical truth and systematic implications of the resurrection of Jesus. In his earlier work he used this orientation to suggest that the world is created from the future, so that in some sense the future is ontologically prior to – more real than – the present. Although in temporal terms it comes after the present, in some way it precedes it in the order of being. On this account, the present is not yet fully real because not yet fully created. God, then, as the one who brings about the creation of things, should be understood as 'the power of the future': the one who stands in 'contradiction to the present and releases forces to overcome it.'[8] This theology has at least the advantage of standing in stark contrast to some modern tendencies to see in evolution the determining force of the creation, so that the present in some way emerges out of the past. In the case of process theology, the past and present set the direction of creation, which eternally builds up what has gone before. The outcome is that the future is an ever-improving version of the present. Pannenberg's doctrine of God as the power of the future, influenced as it may be by Marxist theories, at least takes into account the fact that the creation is in some way in thraldom to evil, and needs to be released from it.[9]

The converse of the teaching of the ontological priority of the future is that the present is not truly real because it must be transcended by the future. It is not yet created, but will be as the future breaks in. 'Thus, reflection upon the power of the future over the present leads to a new idea of creation, oriented not toward a primeval event in the past but toward the eschatological future'.[10] Similarly, in a characteristic but not in every way transparent expression, Pannenberg says in *Theology and the Kingdom of God*, that 'The future lets go of itself to bring into being our present.'[11] Again, he says: 'Even our past is the creation of the coming God' (p. 61). Pannenberg recognises that the idea of the past creation functioned to preserve causal regularities, for we do need to be able to

---

8. Wolfhart Pannenberg, 'The God of Hope', in *Basic Questions in Theology* 2, translated by G. H. Kehm (London: SCM Press, 1971), pp. 234–49 (p. 243).

9. As is well known, the Marxist philosopher Ernst Bloch was very influential on the early theology of Jürgen Moltmann, which took a similar direction. Jürgen Moltmann, *Theology of Hope. On the Grounds and the Implications of a Christian Eschatology*, translated by J. W. Leitch (London: SCM Press, 1967).

10. Pannenberg, 'The God of Hope', p. 243.

11. Wolfhart Pannenberg, *Theology and the Kingdom of God*, edited by R. J. Neuhaus (Philadelphia: Westminster Press, 1969), p. 59.

rely on settled patterns of experience. But that is not enough. They must be subordinated to those forces which draw them to completion. 'The laws of causation have their own overwhelming significance, but do not plumb the depths of reality's foundation . . . the continuity of nature is no longer understood as the irresistible dynamic of the already existing pushing forward, but as the building of bridges to save the past from getting lost.' The result is that, 'we can understand even our past as the creation of the coming God' (p. 67).

Pannenberg's proper concern here is to establish human freedom and the openness of reality to change. He is right in holding that if our emphasis is solely on past creation, there is a danger that everything will appear to have been determined in advance by God. The idea that in some sense the past emerges out of the future is attractive in the sense that because the future is not yet, it cannot be said to operate deterministically. But there are doubts about whether it will do what is required of it. First, it is doubtful whether the notion is coherent. Can one speak in the way that Pannenberg has? It is certainly a counter-intuitive notion, in the sense that by the future we tend to mean that which has not happened, and is not therefore concretely real. The chief objection would appear to be that the more concretely real we make the future, and therefore the more able to perform the creative function desired of it, the more it approximates to something that is as deterministic in its outworking as the past. Second, the doctrine appears to involve a rather problematic hypostatisation of the future, and, and not only that, to pander unnecessarily to the modern obsession with bringing the future about. If that is too harsh, at least it can be suggested that it appears unnecessarily to play the future against the past. A view of a past creation which in some way contained within itself an openness to novelty has been a feature of many Christian conceptions of providence, continuous creation, secondary causality and the like. It is not quite demonstrated that such a reversal of categories has to take place to maintain that. We shall look later at the positive aspects of Pannenberg's theology, and in particular the insight that eschatology is that which makes possible the very openness of creation.

III THE POINT OF ESCHATOLOGY

But first, some general remarks on eschatology. Eschatology is not a matter of reading from the present of creation to its future. That is the weakness of all views of a processive or evolutionary kind. As many of the efforts of this type, Tipler's included, show, there is always the risk of simply producing a general and worthy philosophical optimism which is then projected on to the universe. Mary Midgley is a particularly trenchant critic of the vague and unsubstantiated 'jam tomorrow' promises of modern scientific projections to the future:

> They are quite simply exaltations of particular ideals within human life at their own epoch, projected on to the screen of a vague and vast 'future' – a term which, since Nietzsche and Wells, is not a name for what is particularly likely to happen, but for a fantasy realm devoted to the staging of visionary dramas.[12]

We might instance here again Tipler's proposal to take the planet apart over a million years in the interests of eternal information.

This is not to deny that doctrines of creation must take seriously the future of the created order. If the reader has reached this far, that, if nothing else, should be by now evident. Eastern and Western Christian traditions alike understand the final redemption in Christ as achieving the divine purpose in creation, however inadequate may be some of the ways in which that purpose is conceived. But although the doctrine of creation must indeed take into account some of the concerns revealed in the scientific eschatologies, it is also the case that the concerns of theological eschatology are in principle different from the business of making the kind of projections that science may sometimes make about the end of the world. Many modern 'apocalypses' are not truly apocalyptic because they do not envisage some form of divine action that is ontologically final. Here we can draw parallels with points made in previous chapters. The doctrine of creation 'in the beginning' is primarily about the originating and establishing action of God, and only secondarily about time as we understand it. The doctrine of providence is primarily a way of speaking of God's free action over against and within the world, and is not to be tied to scientific theories like that of evolution. Similarly, there is a difference to be drawn between God's final perfecting action towards our space-time world and what we may project about its ending.

The point of this has been well made by Jürgen Moltmann in the title of his recent study of eschatology, *The Coming of God*.[13] Alluding to Revelation 1:4, 'who was, and is and is to come', he points out that the

12. Mary Midgley, *Evolution as a Religion. Strange Hopes and Stranger Fears* (London: Methuen, 1985), p. 71.
13. Jürgen Moltmann, *The Coming of God*, translated by Margaret Kohl (London: SCM Press, 1996), p. 23.

words are not 'who was, and is and *will be*', but *is to come*, suggesting a God on the move and coming towards the world. God comes to the world in eschatological action rather than being a static present. Moltmann is insistent that the loss of a true eschatology is not to be attributed primarily to secular culture, but to inadequately understood eschatology in theology and the churches. Something has often been lost, and we can see that it is similar to that to which Pannenberg is also calling attention. For Moltmann, there is a double mistake: the end is, on the one hand, projected *merely* to the future – to a heaven distinct from this world – or, on the other, improperly claimed to be realised already in this one – as in all attempts to identify the rule of a Christian emperor or church with the final kingdom of God.

The key to eschatology is then the way by which we consider the divine 'future' to come down to earth in the here and now of our world. What weight do we give to those biblical expressions employing verbs in the future tense? How, if at all, does the 'future' impinge upon the present? We might call this the realised eschatological dimension of the event of redemption: the fact that although eschatology is to do with the end of the creation, just as creation is to do with its beginning; yet because God is not limited to our tenses in his relations with the world; that is, because the tenses of our verbs do not apply to the free and eternal God, then eschatology is not only to do with the end – though it is – but also with the way the end bears upon the beginning and the middle.

Pannenberg's allusion to Jesus' proclamation of the Kingdom of God reminds the modern reader that, according to much recent interpretation, the eschatological kingdom is in some way already being realised in what Jesus does and says. (Note the pointed complaints of the demons in Matthew's account of the healing at Gadara: 'Have you come here to torment us *before the time*?' Matthew 8:29. Here part of the creation is healed of its alienation from its creator in advance of its universal and final healing.) Something both new and final is being realised, as the saying about new wine and old bottles and the parables of judgement and crisis reveal. Moreover, the kingdom is not merely moral and inter-personal, as much nineteenth-century interpretation supposed, but universal. The kingdom language in the gospels is concerned with the realisation of God's final rule over the whole of the created order, as the healing of demoniacs and the feeding of the 5,000 in different ways suggest. But it is being realised only in anticipation of its completion in God's due time. This is the clear implication of Paul's eschatology of the kingdom in 1 Corinthians 15, according to which it is the end of the Son's economic work to submit everything to God the Father. The realisation of the end is anticipated in the present as the rule of Christ, inaugurated in his ministry, continues in the present, moving forward the project of creation. The notion of the Spirit as the first fruits (Romans 8:23) and down-payment (2 Corinthians 1:22 and 5:5), which represent the final completion of the whole, support Pannenberg's interpretation. Eschatological reality does bear upon the present of creation, although it is not creation that is achieved so much as the creation's redemption and perfection.

Pannenberg has made two important contributions. First is his stress on the eschatological establishing of the openness of the creation. The creation is established with respect to its regularities but not absolutely fixed from the beginning, but must be understood in the light of its end to be open to change. That does not necessarily mean salutary change, but can mean also openness to corruption, misuse and, indeed, demonic infestation. The changes, however, presuppose underlying regularities. The second contribution is Pannenberg's realisation, more manifest in the theology of *Systematic Theology 2*, of the necessity of understanding what might be called the openness of the times to one another. When we see them in the light of the realised eschatology of the Bible, and particularly of the resurrection of Jesus from the dead in anticipation of the general resurrection, we can no longer hold past, present and future apart as, so to speak, realms impermeable to one another:

> On the level of its own creaturely reality, that which is present to God belongs to different times. But before God it is present. In this regard, God's eternity needs no recollection or expectation, for it is itself simultaneous with all events in the strict sense . . .
> Eternity is the undivided present of life in its totality.[14]

In all this, Pannenberg has returned to a surprisingly traditional view of God's eternity, even drawing on the neoplatonist tradition which lay behind Augustine's conception.[15] Whether or not this is an adequate conception of God's eternity, he has realised that much hangs on the distinguishing of the realms of eternity and time. The eternal God's relation to the world is not the same as ours, limited as that is by our past, present and future, and by the fact that we live in fallen time.

And so we return to the way in which christology and pneumatology

14. Wolfhart Pannenberg, *Systematic Theology Volume 2*, translated by Geoffrey W. Bromiley (Edinburgh: T. & T. Clark, 1994), pp. 91–2.
15. Indeed, Neoplatonism is the central cause of that syndrome we met earlier on, of treating the material universe as a ladder to a higher world, a ladder to be kicked away when the climb is complete.

operate in shaping the doctrine of creation. Pannenberg's mature account of creation has place for them both. So far as christology is concerned, according to his account, creation is to be understood as an undetermined act of God the Father, while the independent existence of the created order and its distinction from God are both based upon the self-distinction of the Son from the Father. As we have already seen (p. 159 above), for Pannenberg christology both distinguishes and relates God and the world (p. 31). But, as we have already seen in another connection, there are questions to be asked about his conception of the work of the Spirit, where he is in danger of returning to the view of creation that has been so problematic in the past. According to his account, the work of the Spirit is to establish the 'life of creatures as participation in God that transcends their own finitude.' 'For God alone has unrestricted duration' (p. 33). The odd feature of this is that Pannenberg's perhaps excessively eschatological approach to creation in the earlier writings has not only been modified, but is in danger of disappearing altogether. The question now is whether the theology is eschatological enough. The symptom of the inadequacy is to see the Spirit as the means of participation in God rather than the agent according to whose work the created order is, through the Son, directed to its destiny. (Perhaps it might be fairer to say that there are competing conceptions of the work of the Spirit in Pannenberg, for in a later discussion he speaks of 'a dynamic of the divine Spirit working creatively in all events as the power of the future . . .' p. 101.)

The general point is that it is when we look at the nature of what God achieves through the Son and the Spirit that we are better able to develop an eschatology which is concerned with the completing of that which was once established in the beginning. We should be centrally concerned with the economy of creation, salvation and redemption, and remain agnostic about the precise character of God's eternity. The importance of this for life and ethics will become apparent if we contrast the two types of eschatology which have always warred for ascendancy in the tradition and come to the surface even in the different scientific eschatologies which are emerging. It is significant that Frank Tipler has chosen, as he himself observes, an Origenist orientation in his theology of creation.[16] Eschatology is Origen's weakest hand, not because he believed in universal salvation but because he believed that the end consisted in a return to the original immaterial beginning of

16. Tipler, *The Physics of Immortality*, p. 254.

things. He speculated about the possibility of a succession of worlds in such a way as to reinforce the devaluation of this one implicit in his teaching that it is a secondary creation, serving for the education of the eternal spirits, and consequent only upon their sin.

In contrast to this is the second and more adequate eschatology of creation, represented by Irenaeus, whose stronger affirmation of the goodness of this present world we have already met. That affirmation is based upon the doctrine of the incarnation, as the taking by the Son of God of this actual human flesh. On such an understanding, the eschatological newness of what takes place in the life, death and resurrection of Jesus derives from its character as the means of the transformation of the old world, which it therefore presupposes. As Athanasius was later to summarise, the creating Word comes to his creation to recreate it through his incarnation and atoning death. The new takes place upon the basis of the old, as its perfection by redemption. The shape of the matter becomes clear if we return to some of the themes we have met before, and examine the relation to the created order of certain crucial episodes and dimensions of the life of Jesus. At their heart is the fact that Jesus of Nazareth is the incarnation of the eternal Son of God, through whom the word was made and is upheld, within the structures of the old, which it therefore presupposes. It is thus that there is a continuity of creation and redemption, according to which the latter can be understood as a new act of creation – perhaps better, recreation – on the basis of the old, which is thus renewed and redirected to its true end. That is the contribution of christology to our topic.

Similarly, and in parallel, the conception of Jesus must be understood as an eschatological act, and that is why the Spirit is involved. The Spirit, as the perfecting cause of the creation, is the agent of the perfecting of Jesus' humanity, through the renewal of the fallen flesh which is taken from Mary. It is extremely important not to speak of the conception of Jesus as a creation out of nothing, though that is often done. Any suggestion that his body is not formed of the matter of this fallen world both breaks the links between creation and redemption and renders the saviour irrelevant to this world. It is better to understand the incarnation of the eternal Son in the flesh as the beginning of an eschatological act of renewal, in which the true *telos*, direction, of the creation is restored from within. Thus the conception and life of Jesus is a triune act: as Irving put it, the Father sends the Spirit to form a body for his Son out of the only material available to hand: the soiled flesh of the created order which he comes to redeem; so that this human life, as a perfect sacrifice of and to God the Father becomes the means of the sacrifice of praise of the whole world.[17]

At the other end of Jesus' life, the resurrection is also to be understood as an eschatological act, new because it is the creation of the form of being which belongs to the end time. Again, it is a triune act: the Father raising the Son through the mediating action of the Spirit, and transforming his body to the life of the age to come. The resurrection is thus the anticipatory realisation of the eschatological destiny of the whole creation. 'What is sown is perishable, what is raised is imperishable' (1 Corinthians 15:42). When Paul says that flesh and blood cannot inherit the kingdom of God (v. 50), he is saying, I think, that the final kingdom, when God is to be all in all, can be realised only by the transformation of this world. It is not simply an extension of it. This means not a radically discontinuous world, but one in some way perfected to be a new form of life by and before God. The doctrine of creation asserts strongly that nothing is eternal and infinite but God. The distinction between God and the world is, as I have argued, an absolute qualitative distinction. There is therefore no natural or automatic immortality, as has sometimes been taught. But it does not follow that God cannot freely bestow a share in his eternity on the creatures of his love; rather that eternal life means the end of this present era of time and space – 'flesh and blood'. There can, then, be no endless increase of intelligence and consumer prosperity, as in Tipler's vision. If not moth and rust, then some other forces will end this universe of ours. But that does not take away the point of time and space, any more than death necessarily takes away the point of a life. The one who raised Jesus from the dead is the one who will transform and so perfect this whole order of space and time. To repeat, here we meet not evolution, not development, but transformation. The resurrection completes the perfecting of Jesus' humanity which was inaugurated in his conception in the womb of his mother, the first fruits of the recapitulation of all things. We should take issue here with Moltmann's contention that 'Christ's resurrection is therefore not a historical event; it is an eschatological happening to the crucified Christ and took place "once for all" (Romans 6:10).'[18] All depends upon what is meant by 'historical'. If God is not limited by our times, an act can be at once historical and eschatological. By virtue of the free and sovereign interrelation of the eternal creator with his world, historical events may also be eschatological.

17. G. Carlyle, editor, *The Collected Writings of Edward Irving in Five Volumes*, Vol. V (London: Alexander Strachan, 1865), pp. 115–16.
18. Moltmann, *The Coming of God*, p. 69.

But although the resurrection may signal the perfection of Jesus' story, and end in that sense, it is not its end in the sense of the abolition of his humanity. The much neglected doctrine of the ascension has a crucial bearing on our understanding of the place of our humanity in the world. The one who rules until all his enemies have been defeated – and the last enemy to be defeated is death – is the crucified and risen Jesus, who in his continuing humanity pours out the transforming Spirit on all flesh. The moral importance of this Irenaeus makes clear in his argument against those Gnostics who believed that God is not interested in the body. Drawing upon 1 Corinthians 15 in particular, but not only that, he moves in the final book of *Against Heresies* from an insistence that Jesus received from Mary true human flesh to a demonstration that the body is part of the handiwork of God – 'a man, and not [merely] a part of man was made in the likeness of God' (5. 6. 1) – and from there to an argument that the final resurrection and transformation of the flesh is anticipated by the work of the Spirit now. For him, the Spirit is the one who is both the agent of the raising of Jesus from the dead and the one who enables Christians to live truly 'in the flesh'. Irenaeus' insistence upon the resurrection of the whole person is the key. While redemption is primarily the redemption of the fallen human creature, it is of that in and along with the whole of creation. In some mysterious fashion, human salvation brings with it the redemption, not obsolescence, of its environment, just as human sin incorporates the world in the process of destruction and dissolution. It follows that the restoral of human life to its true end through the sacrifice of the cross involves in some measure a restoration of its material setting to its proper direction. And that brings us to some aspects of what can be called an ethic of creation, if by ethic is meant generally our whole habitation of God's world rather than human moral behaviour narrowly conceived.

IV ESCHATOLOGY AND ETHICS

The acid test of any cosmological theory, in the broad sense of theory about the meaning of the world, or theology, is the ethic it generates. I do not mean by that its detailed prescriptions for behaviour, although some will follow, but its stance over against reality. It is easy to illustrate. Frank Tipler's ethic is one of technological domination, even to the extent of taking the planet apart in order to catapult information into eternity. Stephen Weinberg represents the pessimistic – Manichaean – reading of the same scientific eschatology, a kind of stoic ethic of knowledge in face of the meaninglessness of existence revealed by the fact that we shall die. 'The effort to understand the universe is one of the very few things that lifts human life a little above the level of farce, and gives it some of the grace of tragedy.'[19] The one promotes an ethic of pure domination; the other one of stoic resignation.

But, as we have seen, there is an alternative eschatology, and it generates a different ethic, which, again, can be illustrated simply. The eschatology of the gospels makes clear that there is a close relation between it and living in the present, and it has to do neither with resignation nor domination but with readiness and obedience. The parables of the end – of the return of the landlord and the bridegroom – signal not slackness but seriousness in the performance of daily responsibilities, as does the similar ethic taught by Paul in his letters to the Thessalonians and the Romans. Luther famously said that the right course of action if we knew that the end of the world was imminent would be to plant an apple tree. Eschatology and preparedness are correlatives. No doubt there is truth in the much repeated claim, very much at the heart of the polemics of Moltmann, that the eschatology of the period we know as Christendom was so concerned with going to heaven that this earth was neglected. But that boot is now on the feet of the very scientists who have taken responsibility for the future of our world. We met earlier the claim of Mary Midgley that modern scientific eschatologies are dominated by 'jam tomorrow', and neglect completely the things that are at the door. A colonisation of the galaxy in millions of years pales into insignificance before an atomic winter or ecological desolation; indeed, it increases the likelihood of a confidence in the infinite exploitability of nature – worse than the much berated pie in the sky allegedly taught by Christianity.

All of these considerations converge in the question of what we shall do with those immediate sectors of the world with which we are in closest contact. Modern Christianity is so strongly inclined to lecture the world on the merits of justice, that we are in danger of neglecting the weightier matters of the law: our dealings with our bodies and our immediate neighbours. Irenaeus argued that the gnostic despising of the body led to two contradictory ethical stances: that because their bodies were not thought really to be their own, his opponents recommended an ethic either of licence – because if their bodies are not really themselves, it does not matter what they do with them; or of extreme asceticism –

---

19. Stephen Weinberg, *The First Three Minutes. A Modern View of the Origin of the Universe* (London: Flamingo, 2nd edition 1983), p. 155, cited by Midgley, *Evolution as a Religion* p. 75. She rightly sees that this attitude represents highly unscientific melodrama.

because one way to demonstrate the irrelevance of the body is to do without it. Things are not so different now. As Geoffrey Wainwright has recently written in this very connection:

> We live in a very sensate and sensualist society. We are in some ways absorbed in our senses, a people defined by materialism and sexuality. Yet in other ways we are curiously detached from our bodies, as though we were not really affected by what happens to us in our bodies or what we do in them.

He proceeds to draw the conclusion that this is essentially gnostic:

> If our bodies are not us, then we are not responsible in and for them; and that irresponsibility may assume the character of either license or, indeed, of withdrawal. The same phenomenon occurred in the gnosticism of the second century.[20]

In our day, we meet additional forms of gnosticism, particularly in those science-related ethics which either suggest that we may do with the material universe – and that includes our bodies – what we like, because we are not really continuous with the material world; or that it is in effect the deity, so that human action is irrelevant to the way things really are because our genes (or whatever) call the tune. If therefore we think that our bodies are in a deep sense not really ourselves, either because we have absolute control of them or because they have absolute control of us, we shall be indifferent to the implications of sexual behaviour and the status of the foetus in the womb. Gnosticism is not only an ancient heresy but remains the alternative to the Christian doctrine of creation in all eras.

Christian eschatology, by contrast, has the grace of an expectant orientation on the present, where, through Jesus Christ and the Spirit, the coming God's perfecting of things is from time to time anticipated. Eschatology is a way of speaking about the future, but also of the way in which that future is not restricted to the future but breaks into the present, renewing human life for redemptive living in the world. Salvation is indeed nearer to us now than when we first believed. As we have seen, unlike the universe God is not restricted to the past or present or future, but, as Barth has said, is characterised by pre-temporality, supra-temporality and post-temporality,[21] a perichoresis, interanimation of the

---

20. Geoffrey Wainwright, *For Our Salvation: Two Approaches to the Work of Christ* (Grand Rapids: Eerdmans, 1997), p. 18.
21. Karl Barth, *Church Dogmatics*, translation edited by G. W. Bromiley and T. F. Torrance (Edinburgh: T. & T. Clark, 1957–75), 2/1, pp. 620–31.

tenses to which we by virtue of our finitude are restricted. An eschatological ethic of creation will then be dedicated neither to a forcible
bringing in of the future nor of a hopeless fight against death, but to a
response to the gracious action of God in establishing our being and
that of the world, in upholding it and guiding it day by day, and by his
Spirit enabling a faithful response to the inbreaking of his rule.

V TOWARDS AN ETHIC OF CREATEDNESS

From our use of the body we move to our use of the world about us.
Readers who have travelled the whole journey so far will have gathered
enough hints on what kind of environmental ethic is implied in these
pages: one that will be called anthropocentric on one wing of the
current debate, but is yet highly critical of the technocratic attitudes of
much of modernity. What has been attempted is a theological basis for
a right use of the inescapable human dominion, one implying a measure
of human responsibility for the way things are, but also falling far short
of the ecologically oriented theology of creation of Moltmann, which
for all its richness seems to me to be far too dominated by an *a priori*
interpretation of the ecological crisis. The crisis is serious, and yet we
must attend to Christoph Schwöbel's warning:

> Many of the reactions of theologians to the environmental crisis
> focus, quite correctly, on an ethical response to the situation. Since
> we are responsible for threatening far-reaching destruction to
> creation it is argued that it is now our responsibility to preserve
> creation from destruction . . . However, with this line of reasoning
> a number of important theological distinctions are in danger of
> being blurred. Inflicting destructive effects upon creation falls indeed
> within the realm of human responsibility and has therefore from
> the earliest times onwards been interpreted as sin: bringing destruc-
> tion to creation means offending its creator. Yet, the preservation
> or restoration of creation cannot be a human task if this creation
> is continuously created and preserved by God who brought it into
> being in the first place. Theologically, creation, including the sus-
> taining and preserving of creation, is a divine and not a human
> work. Therefore, creation is not in the same sense a field of human
> action as, for instance, politics, science or business. While it is proper,
> and indeed necessary, to speak of the ethics of politics, of science or
> of business ethics, the term ethics of creation contains a dangerous
> ambiguity. It seems that the same absolutism of human action
> which has characterized the human exploitation of creation is now

returning in the guise of rescuing it. The search for relevance, so it appears, comes into conflict with fundamental dogmatic tenets of a Christian theology of creation. What seems to be needed is not an ethics of creation, but an *ethic of createdness* which is informed by a *theology of creation*.[22]

The burden of this book is that modern domination by images of the universe as a mechanism must be replaced by a theology encompassing a range of categories, in the light of which an appropriate ethic will take shape. It is not enough to generalise, for example, the category of life, as Moltmann tends to do. There is human life, animal life and plant life, and forms of created being which are not properly described as living. It is a purpose of a theology of the diversity of the created order to indicate that different forms of createdness may require different forms of human response. To attempt to breed pigs for eating in such a way that they are condemned to painful arthritis is morally objectionable in a way that shaping a tree by major pruning is not, or not necessarily. Similarly, it does not follow necessarily that, simply because animals are alive and feel pain, we should never eat them.

In the eschatological perspective developed in this chapter, one broad criterion can be offered, although the outworking of that in different cases will be by no means obvious. The created order comes from the gracious hands of God; it is good, but participates in different ways in the structures of fallenness. As God's project, it is upheld and directed by him, while those made in his image are placed in such a relationship to the world that they are called to play some part in its perfecting. What constitutes the proper perfecting of any particular created being is not clear, and subject to much argument. It can be argued that to eat a chicken is not necessarily to deprive it of its proper being, while to keep it in batteries, deprived of light, air and space, is. Similarly, the culture of the motor car, with its individualistic and aristocratic associations, may not appear, certainly as it is at present practised, to cohere well with the character of the creation, with its cost to resources of fuel and space, as well as its moral distortion of human relationships.

The matter of time must here recur yet again. Moltmann has suggested that at the heart of the matter of an ecological ethic is our theology of time, while Robert Banks showed some time ago that the

22. Christoph Schwöbel, 'God, Creation and the Christian Community: The Dogmatic Basis of a Christian Ethic of Createdness', in *The Doctrine of Creation. Essays in Dogmatics, History and Philosophy*, edited Colin E. Gunton (Edinburgh: T. & T. Clark, 1997), pp. 149–76 (p. 150).

mechanisation – or spatialising – of time is indeed at the heart of the modern slavery to the clock.[23] Time, as the concept in terms of which we focus one central aspect of what is real, has, if the argument of this book is right, both a reality – albeit a relational reality that takes its being from those things that have their being in it – and a determinate end. That end, indeed, is not simply and narrowly 'temporal' because it is an end that in both senses of the word, of aim and completion, is determined by God. In what happened with and to Jesus the end has, in one sense happened already – that is why 'salvation is nearer to us now than when we first believed' (Romans 13:11) – and yet still has to work out that end under promise. This feature, of an end that has happened and has to happen, is a feature of all biblical eschatology, which is why it is difficult to make sense of what the prophets mean by 'the day of the Lord' and the various eschatological prophecies of the New Testament, Jesus', Paul's and the author of the Apocalypse alike. This 'eschatological tension' should be contrasted with the empty and jejune modern incantation of 'the future' which is only a part of what eschatology means.

That we shall die, and that this is not in every way to be regarded as a disaster – 'blessed are the dead who die in the Lord' (Revelation 14:13) – provides a model for an eschatological ethic of the created world. An over-anxious obsession with ecology, animal rights, and the rest parallels the modern human refusal to face the fact of death. Perfection does not come from ourselves lasting for ever or from attempting to make the earth eternal. How should one bear oneself in a world that, like human being, receives its perfection only on the other side of death? There is one criterion which is universal, and it is that right behaviour to the material world is that which offers those particular events and beings with which we have to do as a sacrifice of praise to God. This has a number of advantages. It prevents us offering the present as a sacrifice to the future, after the manner of modernity's obsession with itself bringing in the kingdom. It thus enables us to treat particulars as particulars, each in its own reality and with its own proper time. When we do that, it is the gift of the Spirit, and we recall that the Spirit operates in both routine and transformative modes. A proper routine is a form of perfection, if it enhances life, for example, as is the miraculous healing of a disease – and everything in between that is right. Because, however, these things are the gift of God the Spirit, who blows where he wills, it is not a rule that can be easily applied. Rather, it gives us a

---

23. Robert Banks, *The Tyranny of Time* (Exeter: Paternoster Press, 1983); Moltmann, *The Coming of God*, pp. 137–9.

question that can be asked of any act or kind of act: Does this offer to God the creator the sacrifice of praise of the perfected creation? The difficulty of application of such a criterion is easily illustrated. The eating of animals might be seen to be justified in the light of the biblical history of their killing in sacrificial worship; or unjustified in the light of the one perfect sacrifice which has made all of that unnecessary, even wrong. My concern here is not to provide answers, but to suggest that a theology of the eschatology of creation does provide essential material for thought about the way we treat our world.

The eschatology of creation can be illustrated at greater length, riskily and apparently frivolously, by appeal to human artistic activity. By art is here meant not just 'high art' but everything from the making of pots for household use to the rarefied activities often thought to be the only activity worthy of the name. It is risky and apparently frivolous, because it may appear that there are more important questions facing the human race than art. But it has been chosen for a number of reasons. One of them is that the topic of ecological ethics is much discussed elsewhere;[24] another is that we need to remember that the ethic of creation is concerned with more than this, and, indeed, if we are to do it justice, must encompass it within a broader framework which will enable a measure of distance to be achieved. Insofar as art is that range of activities in which human agents interact with the material world – with the world we call the creation – to produce things of beauty and use, it is an appropriate place in which to consider what can broadly be called an ethic of creation as that is related to eschatology or the perfecting of the created order. In sum, aesthetics will throw a clearer light on our theme because it encompasses aspects of the human relation to the creation ranging well beyond the problems of modern mechanistic technocracy, and showing that the problem of an ethic of creation, including that of ecology, has historical roots reaching far further back than the modern world.

To the Greeks is owed, as is owed so much of our culture, one of the two streams feeding Western artistic activity. But the chief influence on Christian theology of beauty came, paradoxically, through Plato, who, though a consummate artist himself, was deeply suspicious of art, thinking it socially damaging because it represented human engagement with inferior levels of reality. Here we reach once again the continuing theme in the theology of creation: the tendency of Greece to bequeath to the

---

24. In addition to Moltmann, *God in Creation. An Ecological Doctrine of Creation*, translated by Margaret Kohl (London: SCM Press, 1985), see especially Lawrence Osborn, *Guardians of Creation. Nature and Theology in the Christian Life* (Leicester: Apollos, 1993).

West a low estimation of the value of the material world. As we have seen, Augustine is one of the channels by which the Greek suspicion of matter came into the tradition. O'Connell cites Augustine's *Retractations* I. vi, to the effect that material beauty is 'to lead the reader's mind upward, "through the corporeal to the incorporeal".'[25] Crudely put, for Augustine, material – we might say, secular – beauty is not to be valued except insofar as it lifts the soul above it to the immaterial beauty in the heavens. Heavenly music is superior to any played on material instruments. We meet again the creation's Babylonian captivity, this time in the depreciation of material art.

There has, ever since, been a suspicion of the arts in the Christian West, though it has by no means been universal, and there has also been a tendency to except 'religious' art. One interesting episode which brings out the theological questions involved is the iconoclastic controversy in the eighth century. It involved the question of whether or not 'images' (icons) were legitimate. There was a long tradition, derived from the Old Testament prohibition of images, forbidding the pictorial representation of God in particular, and with good reason when we think of the tradition of portraying God as an old man with a beard accompanied by a young man, with a dove representing the Spirit. In the tradition of the Old Testament, the iconoclasts saw icons as idolatry. But the defenders of icons, who denied that they were worshipped, but rather, as they claimed, the means by which the worshipper could approach God with their assistance, used, among other arguments, a christological one. If Christ became flesh, does not this imply a capacity for matter to represent God? That has remained the position of the Eastern church ever since. Their great theologian John of Damascus argued in the eighth century in *On the Divine Images* that the iconoclasts were Manichaean, in that they had a pessimistic view of matter.[26] At least twice he asserts that the Godhead cannot be imaged (2:5; 2:11). But:

> now when God is seen in the flesh conversing with men, I make an image of the God whom I see. I do not worship matter; I worship the Creator of matter who became matter for my sake, who wills to take His abode in matter; who worked out my salvation through matter. (1:16)

25. R. J. O'Connell, *Art and the Christian Intelligence in St. Augustine* (Oxford: Blackwell, 1978), p. 65.
26. St John of Damascus, *On the Divine Images. Three Apologies against those who Attack the divine Images*, translated by David Anderson (New York: St Vladimir's Seminary Press, 1980), 2. 13.

Whether that argument justifies the attempted portrayal of God must remain doubtful. But the allusion to Manichaeism enables us to make the point so far as the secular arts are concerned. If God created the world, and created the whole world good, should not art, as human engagement with the material world in the production of beautiful and useful things, be among the activities blessed by the doctrine? Certainly, there is in scripture much celebration of craftsmanship, music and architecture as ways of praising God and as good in themselves. The value of the doctrine of creation in this regard is that it enables some clarification of matters about which there is much disagreement in the modern world. Insofar as the modern world has lost a belief in the goodness of the created order, thus far has it come to believe not that the depiction and representation of evil has some part in art – that would never seriously be denied – but that it is in some way the centre. To put it another way, we can say that loss of belief in God has led to loss of belief in the redemptive or at least positive value of human artistic activity. As George Steiner has claimed, until late in the nineteenth century some kind of belief in God underwrote all human artistic activity.[27] The reason is that for there to be art and literature, we need a measure of confidence that there is some kind of concordance or harmony between the meaning of the material world and the meaning of our use of the world. Here there is a considerable contrast between the arts and the sciences, as if the sciences have in some ways displaced the arts as vehicles of human interaction with the material world. Aesthetic criteria are sometimes employed in the choice between one scientific theory and another. If one set of mathematics is more beautiful than another, there is a presumption in favour of its mediation of scientific truth. That was one reason why Einstein believed that Clerk Maxwell's equations were correct. Beauty has deserted the artist, and migrated to science.

Here it may be that what is crucial is the shift that took place in artistic sensibility during the nineteenth century from art as the expression of the world to art as the self-expression of the artist. Science is not concerned with self-expression, but about the truth of the world. What might the doctrine of creation have to say about art? Here we can do no better than what Barth says in his exposition of Genesis 1 in *Church Dogmatics* 3/1 about creation as justification. Because creation 'is affirmed and not denied, elected and not rejected, it is the object of God's good pleasure' (p. 366). This affirmation of the goodness of creation has a christological

---

27. George Steiner, *Real Presences. Is There Anything in What We Say?* (London: Faber and Faber, 1989), p. 93.

dimension, because the goodness of creation springs from the work of God's own Son (p. 370). Accordingly, beauty is part of the order of things; 'an order, beauty and purposefulness which speak for themselves ...' (p. 371). This, however, is not to deny sin and evil, but rather to see them as expressions of the creature's need of God rather than its essential evil. Finally, Manichaeism can be defeated only in Christ. The affirmation of the world depends on the fact that God involves himself in the world to overcome the evil. Therefore, 'Christian faith naturally says Yes to the created world – a secure, definitive and absolute Yes' (p. 385).

Here we reach the eschatological aspect of the doctrine. In so far as art aims at perfection – producing something as good as possible – it aims to anticipate the redemption of things brought about through Christ by God the Holy Spirit. Here we should remember that 'inspiration' is a theological category, but one that finds major purchase in the arts. Inspiration refers to that side of art which is gift, that apparent givenness from beyond that gives artists a starting point and direction for their labours. All true art, and certainly not just religious or 'Christian' art, is therefore the gift of the creator Spirit as he enables in the present antic-ipations of the perfection that is to come at the end of the age. Art is thus one of the human ways of participating in God's project of creation. It is redemptive in the sense that it is an activity which enables the cre-ation to reach towards the perfection that is its destiny.[28] And it enables us to articulate the criterion for an ethic of creation: action for the glory of God. As Christoph Schwöbel has argued, such a theocentrism is cru-cial for the establishing of an ethic of createdness which is to avoid a merely instrumental approach to the created world.[29]

VI FROM ESCHATOLOGY TO WORSHIP

The crucial and definitive illustration of the eschatology of creation comes from Christian worship. In speaking of this, I do not wish to stress the sacraments at the expense of the centrality of the Word. Sacraments are what they are only because they are appended to a word of promise. In any case, our words, too, are part of the material creation. But in terms of the preoccupation of this book with the material world, the sacraments of Baptism and the Lord's Supper are highly relevant in that both employ the material creation as a constitutive feature of worship. In view of the additional fact that they would not be what they are except

28. Jeremy S. Begbie, *Voicing Creation's Praise. Towards a Theology of the Arts* (Edinburgh: T. & T. Clark, 1991).

29. Schwöbel, 'God, Creation and the Christian Community', pp. 168–70.

by virtue of the action of God the Spirit, the mediator of divine perfecting action, we clearly have here a matter in close relation to the
dogmatics of creation. That the non-personal, material creation is used
in various ways to represent the death, resurrection, reign and return of
Christ in glory indicates at the least that the destiny of the whole creation
is bound up first with the incarnate Lord and second with those created
in the image of God, represented as they are by those who worship the
Father through Christ and in the Spirit.

But liturgical worship, while an end in itself as the focus of the
human relation to God, is both the matrix for and model of the more
broadly construed worship that is the proper service of the creature to
the creator. Romans 12, especially the first two verses, sets the scene
with a reference to the *body*: 'present your bodies as a living sacrifice . . .'
The body is that sample of the material creation by which the human
being indwells and so is related to the created world as a whole: the part
both representing and being the means of relating to that part of the
whole in which each particular person is placed. It is through our bodies
that we interact with other human beings, tell the truth or lie to them,
love them or hate them, and the rest; it is through them that we tend
the earth or pollute it. In the broad sense, to present them as a sacrifice
is so to engage with the whole of reality as to enable – or not – that part
of the creation with which we interact to be offered perfected to God
the Father through the Son. Every human act, routine or not, is either
a response to the action of the perfecting Spirit, or it is not. Every act is
either offered to the Father through the Son, or it is not.

The relation between creation and redemption appears in the second
verse. 'Do not be conformed to this world' – that is to say, to this fallen
world – 'but be transformed by the renewal of your mind, that you may
prove what is the will of God . . .'. Once again, there is no rule by which
every case of right and wrong use of the creation can be decided in
advance or infallibly. But there is a criterion, and that is the criterion of
sacrifice, again in the broad sense suggested by our verses. The link with
the preceding discussion of art is to be found in the notion of sacrifice,
which is central to an understanding of the doctrine of creation, although
its centrality requires some explanation. In our language, the word tends
to have a rather negative ring: it is to do with giving up, renouncing
something that we would prefer to hold on to. It often involves that,
paradigmatically in the case of Jesus Christ's 'supreme sacrifice', as a death
for others is often described, on the cross. That sacrifice is the source of
others, in ways suggested by the brief account of sacramental worship,
and shows that 'giving up' is not the only, perhaps not even the chief,

meaning to be given to sacrifice. Crucial for us, at least most obviously, is the sacrifice of praise that is the human response to this supreme act of divine and human love. Romans 12:1–2 can here again be taken as a brief and pregnant exposition of what follows from Christian confession.

But if sacrifice is the central way of expressing human response to God's goodness as creator and redeemer, it is also the case that it is crucial to divine action also. We reach the heart of our question: in what sense is the act of creating the world a kind of sacrifice? As has already been argued, it should not be so described in the fashionable notions of kenosis or self-emptying, as if in creating God can be supposed in some way to depotentiate himself or in any way to do that which is foreign to his nature. The biblical expressions of creation invariably have a note of freedom and joy. They see the act of creation as sheer unnecessitated gift, but in no way a painful one: 'when the morning stars sang together, and all the sons of God shouted for joy' (Job 38:7). The pain comes with the rejection of what we might call the terms of the gift by the creation: its refusal to be God's creation, and its quest to assert its 'rights' against its maker. In that setting, the sacrifice of Jesus' life on the cross is the means by which the true end of creation is attained. The character and time of that end is not ours to know or decide: it is known only by the Father (Mark 13:32). As we have seen, we have a kind of criterion for action this side of the end. But all action takes place under promise, and this is the last thing that should be said in a doctrine of creation. The new heaven and the new earth of Revelation 21:1, signalling its freedom from the evil which delays its coming ('and the sea was no more') is realised first by the incarnation (v. 2), second by relation to God through Christ (v. 7) and thirdly by the pure sacrifice that is enabled by that once for all sacrifice on the cross (vv. 8, 27).

Those written into the Lamb's book of life are those who eschew 'abomination and falsehood', the wrong use of their persons both in themselves and in their relation to others. A similar point is made by Paul's eschatology of creation in 1 Corinthians 15. The defeat of death – Paul's equivalent for the 'sea' of Revelation – comes about by the reign of the crucified, risen and ascended incarnate Lord. The end of the creation, in both senses of aim and completion, whatever time it comes and whatever form it takes, comes when it is finally perfected in God's everlasting kingdom. All human 'ethics', all right use of the creation, all offering of the creation to God the Father, perfected through Christ and in the Spirit; in sum, all right habitation of the world God has made and redeemed on the cross of Christ, takes form under that promise, whether it knows it or not.

BIBLIOGRAPHY

——◦——

Atkins, P.W., *The Creation* (London and San Francisco: W. H. Freeman, 1981).

Barth, Karl, *Church Dogmatics*, translation edited by G. W. Bromiley and T. F. Torrance (Edinburgh: T. & T. Clark, 1957–75).

Bayer, Oswald, *Schöpfung als Anrede* (Tübingen: J. C. B. Mohr, Paul Siebeck, 1990; 1st edition, 1986).

Begbie, Jeremy S., *Voicing Creation's Praise. Towards a Theology of the Arts* (Edinburgh: T. & T. Clark, 1991).

Berkson, William, *Fields of Force. The Development of a World View from Faraday to Einstein* (London: Routledge, 1974).

Bettoni, Efrem, *Duns Scotus: the Basic Principles of his Philosophy*, translated by B. Bonansea (Westport, Connecticut: Greenwood Press, 1978).

Blumenberg, Hans, *The Legitimacy of the Modern Age*, translated by R. M. Wallace (Cambridge MA, and London: MIT Press, 1983).

Bonhoeffer, Dietrich, *Creation and Fall. A Theological Interpretation of Genesis 1–3*, translated by J. C. Fletcher (London: SCM Press, 1959).

Bouwsma, William J., *John Calvin. A Sixteenth Century Portrait* (Oxford: Oxford University Press, 1988).

British Council of Churches, *The Forgotten Trinity, Volume 1, The Report of the BCC Study Commission on Trinitarian Doctrine Today* (London: British Council of Churches, 1989).

Broadie, Alexander, *The Shadow of Scotus. Philosophy and Faith in Pre-Reformation Scotland* (Edinburgh: T. & T. Clark, 1995).

Brooke, John Hedley, *Science and Religion. Some Historical Perspectives* (Cambridge: Cambridge University Press, 1991).

Brown, Robert, 'On the Necessary Imperfection of Creation', *Scottish Journal of Theology* 28 (1975), pp. 17–25.

Buckley, Michael, *At the Origins of Modern Atheism* (New Haven and London: Yale University Press, 1987).

Cantor, Geoffrey, *Michael Faraday: Sandemanian and Scientist. A Study of Science and Religion in the Nineteenth Century* (London: Macmillan, 1991).

237

Cochrane, C. N., *Christianity and Classical Culture* (Oxford: Oxford University Press, second edition, 1944)

Coleridge, Samuel Taylor, 'On the Prometheus of Aeschylus', *Complete Works*, edited by W. G. T. Shedd (New York: Harper and Brothers, 1853), 4, pp. 344–65.

Collingwood, R. G., *The Idea of Nature* (Oxford: Clarendon Press, 1945)

Copleston, F. C., *A History of Philosophy* 1 (London: Burns Oates and Washbourne, 1946).

Crehan, F. J., 'The Bible in the Roman Catholic Church from Trent to the Present Day', *The Cambridge History of the Bible* 3, edited by S. L. Greenslade (Cambridge: Cambridge University Press, 1963), pp. 225–7.

Crombie, A. C., *From Augustine to Galileo. I Science in the Middle Ages. II Science in the Later Middle Ages and Early Modern Times* (London: Heinemann, 1959).

Crouzel, Henri, *Origen*, translated by A. S. Worrall (Edinburgh: T. & T. Clark, 1989).

Dales, Richard, 'The de-animation of the Heavens in the Middle Ages', *Journal of the History of Ideas* 41 (1980), pp. 531–50.

Darwin, Charles, *The Origin of Species*, edited with an Introduction by Gillian Beer (Oxford: Oxford University Press, 1996).

Dillenberger, John, *Protestant Thought and Natural Science* (London: Collins, 1961).

Edwards, Jonathan, *Scientific and Philosophical Writings, The Works of Jonathan Edwards*, 6, edited by Wallace E. Anderson (New Haven and London: Yale University Press, 1980).

Einstein, Albert, *The World as I See It*, translated by Alan Harris (London: John Lane the Bodley Head, 1935).

Farrow, Douglas, 'St Irenaeus of Lyons. The Church and the World', *Pro Ecclesia* 4 (1995), pp. 333–55.

Filoramo, Giovanni, *A History of Gnosticism*, translated by Anthony Alcock (Oxford: Blackwell, 1990).

Foster, Michael B., 'The Christian Doctrine of Creation and the Rise of Modern Natural Science', *Mind* 43 (1934), pp. 446–68, reprinted in C. A. Russell, ed., *Science and Religious Belief. A Selection of Recent Historical Studies* (London: Open University, 1973), pp. 294–315.

Funkenstein, Amos, *Theology and the Scientific Imagination from the Middle Ages to the Seventeenth Century* (Princeton: Princeton University Press, 1986).

Galileo Galilei, *Dialogue Concerning Two Chief World Systems – Ptolemaic and Copernican*, translated by Stillman Drake (Berkeley and Los Angeles: University of California Press, 1962).

Gay, J. H., 'Four Medieval Views of Creation', *Harvard Theological Review* 66 (1963), 243–73.

Gibbs, J. G., *Creation and Redemption. A Study in Pauline Theology* (Leiden: Brill, 1971).

Gilkey, Langdon, *Maker of Heaven and Earth. The Christian Doctrine of Creation in the Light of Modern Knowledge* (Lanham: University Press of America, 1985; first edition, 1959).

Gilson, Etienne, *History of Christian Philosophy in the Middle Ages* (London: Sheed and Ward, 1955).

Gingerich, O., *The Great Copernicus Chase, and other adventures in astronomical history* (Cambridge MA: Sky, 1992).

Greer, Rowan, *The Captain of our Salvation. A Study of the Patristic Exegesis of Hebrews* (Tübingen: J. C. B. Mohr (Paul Siebeck), 1973).

Grosseteste, Robert, *On the Six Days of Creation*, translated by C. F. J. Martin (Oxford: Oxford University Press for The British Academy, 1996).

Gunton, Colin E., *Christ and Creation. The 1991 Didsbury Lectures*, (Carlisle: Paternoster Press and Grand Rapids: Eerdmans, 1992).

Gunton, Colin E., *The One, the Three and the Many: God, Creation and the Culture of Modernity; The 1992 Bampton Lectures* (Cambridge: Cambridge University Press, 1993).

Gunton, Colin E., *A Brief Theology of Revelation. The 1993 Warfield Lectures* (Edinburgh: T. & T. Clark, 1995).

Gunton, Colin E., 'The Doctrine of Creation', *The Cambridge Companion to Christian Doctrine*, edited by Colin E. Gunton (Cambridge: Cambridge University Press, 1997), pp. 141–57.

Gunton, Colin E., 'Relation and Relativity. The Trinity and the Created World', *The Promise of Trinitarian Theology* (Edinburgh: T. & T. Clark, second edition, 1997), pp. 137–57.

Gunton, Colin E., 'Introduction', 'Between Allegory and Myth. The Legacy of the Spiritualising of Genesis', 'The end of Causality? The Reformers and their Predecessors', all in *The Doctrine of Creation. Essays in Dogmatics, History and Philosophy*, edited by Colin E. Gunton (Edinburgh: T. & T. Clark, 1997), pp. 1–15, 47–62, 63–82.

Guthrie, W. K. C., *A History of Greek Philosophy* 1 and 2 (Cambridge: Cambridge University Press, 1962, 1965).

Haffner, Paul, *Mystery of Creation* (Leominster: Gracewing, 1995).

Hawking, Stephen, *A Brief History of Time* (London: Bantam Press, 1988).

Helm, Paul, 'Eternal Creation. The first Tyndale Philosophy of Religion Lecture, 28 June, 1994', *Tyndale Bulletin* 45 (1994), pp. 321–38.

Helm, Paul, 'Eternal Creation. The Doctrine of the Two Standpoints', in *The Doctrine of Creation. Essays in Dogmatics, History and Philosophy*, edited by Colin E. Gunton (Edinburgh: T. & T. Clark, 1997), pp. 29–46.

Hick, John, *Evil and the God of Love* (London: Collins, 1968; 1st edition 1966).

Hill, Stephen R., *Concordia. The Roots of European Thought* (Duckworth, 1992).

Hooykaas, R., *Religion and the Rise of Modern Science* (Edinburgh: Scottish Academic Press, 1972).

Horne, Brian, 'Creation and Creativity', in *The Doctrine of Creation. Essays in Dogmatics, History and Philosophy*, edited by Colin E. Gunton (Edinburgh: T. & T. Clark, 1997), pp. 135–47.

Huff, Toby E., *The Rise of Early Modern Science. Islam, China and the West* (Cambridge: Cambridge University Press, 1993).

Inwagen, Peter van, 'Genesis and Evolution', *God, Knowledge and Mystery. Essays in Philosophical Theology* (Ithaca and London: Cornell University Press, 1995), pp. 128–62.

Jaki, Stanley, *Cosmos and Creator* (Edinburgh: Scottish Academic Press, 1980).

Jaki, Stanley, *The Road of Science and the Ways of God* (Edinburgh: University of Chicago Press, 1978).

Jenson, Robert W., 'Aspects of a Doctrine of Creation', in *The Doctrine of Creation. Essays in Dogmatics, History and Philosophy*, edited by Colin E. Gunton (Edinburgh: T. & T. Clark, 1997), pp. 17–28.

Jenson, Robert W., *Essays in Theology of Culture* (Grand Rapids: Eerdmans, 1995).

Jinkins, Michael, '"The Being of Beings". Jonathan Edwards' Understanding of God as Reflected in his final Treatises', *Scottish Journal of Theology* 46 (1993) pp. 161–90.

Jonas, Hans, 'Origen's Metaphysics of Free-will, Fall and Salvation. A "Divine Comedy" of the Universe', *Philosophical Essays: From Ancient Creed to Technological Man* (Englewood Cliffs: Prentice-Hall, 1974), pp. 305–23.

Kirby, W. J. Torrance, 'Praise as the Soul's Overcoming of Time in the Confessions of St. Augustine,' *Pro Ecclesia* 6 (1997), pp. 333–50.

Klaaren, Eugene M., *The Religious Origins of Modern Science. Belief in Creation in Seventeenth Century Thought* (Grand Rapids: Eerdmans, 1977).

Kuhn, Thomas S., *The Copernican Revolution. Planetary Astronomy in the Development of Western Thought* (Cambridge, MA and London: Harvard University Press, 1957).

Lampe, G. W. H. 'The New Testament Doctrine of KTISIS', *Scottish Journal of Theology* 17 (1964), pp. 449–62.

Lapidge, Michael, 'Stoic Cosmology', *The Stoics*, edited by J. M. Rist (London: University of California Press, 1978), pp. 161–85.

Lewontin, R. C., 'The Dream of the Human Genome', *New York Review of Books* 39 (28 May 1992).

Lewontin, R. C., *The Doctrine of DNA. Biology as Ideology* (London: Penguin Books, 1993).

Livingstone, David N., 'The Idea of Design: The Vicissitudes of a Key Response in the Princeton Response to Darwin', *Scottish Journal of Theology* 37 (1984), pp. 329–57.

Luther, Martin, *Lectures on Genesis chapters 1–5, Luther's Works*, 1, edited by J. Pelikan (St Louis: Concordia, 1958).

Mascall, E. L. *Christian Theology and Natural Science. Some Questions on their Relation* (London: Longmans, Green and Co., 1956).

May, Gerhard, *Creatio ex Nihilo. The Doctrine of 'Creation out of Nothing' in Early Christian Thought*, translated by A. S. Worrall (Edinburgh: T. & T. Clark, 1994).

McFarland, Thomas, *Coleridge and the Pantheist Tradition* (Oxford: Clarendon Press, 1969).

McFadyen, Alistair I., *The Call to Personhood. A Christian Theory of the Individual in Social Relationships* (Cambridge: Cambridge University Press, 1990).

Middleton, J. R. and Walsh, B. J., *Truth is Stranger than it Used to Be. Biblical Faith in a Postmodern Age* (London: SPCK, 1995).

Midgley, Mary, *Evolution as a Religion. Strange Hopes and Stranger Fears* (London: Methuen, 1985).

Midgley, Mary, *Science as Salvation* (London: Routledge, 1992).

Moltmann, Jürgen, *God in Creation. An Ecological Doctrine of Creation*, translated by Margaret Kohl (London: SCM Press, 1985).

Moltmann, Jürgen, *Spirit of Life*, translated by Margaret Kohl (London: SCM Press, 1992).

Moltmann, Jürgen, *The Coming of God*, translated by Margaret Kohl, (London: SCM Press, 1996).

Moore, James R., 'Evangelicals and Evolution. Henry Drummond, Herbert Spencer and the Naturalisation of the Spiritual World', *Scottish Journal of Theology* 38 (1985), pp. 383–417.

Moore, James R., *The Post-Darwinian Controversies. A Study of the Protestant struggle to come to terms with Darwin in Great Britain and America 1870–1900* (Cambridge: Cambridge University Press, 1979).

Nebelsick, Harold, *The Renaissance, the Reformation and the Rise of Science* (Edinburgh: T. & T. Clark, 1992).

Nebelsick, Harold, *Theology and Science in Mutual Modification* (Belfast: Christian Journals, 1981).

Norris, Richard A., *God and World in Early Christian Theology. A Study in Justin Martyr, Irenaeus, Tertullian and Origen* (London: A. & C. Black, 1966).

Oberman, Heiko, *The Harvest of Medieval Theology* (Cambridge, MA: Harvard University Press, 1963).

O'Donovan, Oliver, *Resurrection and Moral Order. An Outline for Evangelical Ethics* (Leicester: IVP, 1986).

Osborn, Lawrence, *Guardians of Creation. Nature and Theology in the Christian Life* (Leicester: Apollos, 1993).

Pannenberg, Wolfhart, *Theology and the Kingdom of God*, edited by R. J. Neuhaus (Philadelphia: Westminster Press, 1969).

Pannenberg, Wolfhart, 'The God of Hope', *Basic Questions in Theology 2*, translated by G. H. Kehm (London: SCM Press, 1971), pp. 234–49.

Pannenberg, Wolfhart, *Metaphysics and the Idea of God*, translated by Philip Clayton (Edinburgh: T. & T. Clark, 1990).

Pannenberg, Wolfhart, *Systematic Theology* volume 2, translated by G. W. Bromiley (Edinburgh: T. & T. Clark, 1994).

Pannenberg, Wolfhart, *Toward a Theology of Nature. Essays on Science and Faith*, edited by Ted Peters (Louisville, Kentucky: Westminster/John Knox Press, 1993).

Peacocke, A. R., *Creation and the World of Science* (Oxford: Clarendon Press, 1979).

Polanyi, Michael, *Personal Knowledge. Towards a Post-Critical Philosophy* (London: Routledge, 2nd edition 1962).

Prenter, Regin, *Spiritus Creator. Luther's Concept of the Holy Spirit* (Philadelphia: Muhlenberg, 1953).

Rad, Gerhard von, *Genesis. A Commentary*, translated by J. S. Marks (London: SCM Press, 1963).

Ratzinger, Joseph, *In the Beginning. A Catholic Understanding of the Story of Creation and Fall*, translated by Boniface Ramsey, O. P. (Edinburgh: T. & T. Clark, 1995).

Reumann, John, *Creation and New Creation. The Past, Present and Future of God's Creative Activity* (Minneapolis: Augsburg Publishing House, 1973).

Rist, J. M., *Plotinus: The Road to Reality* (Cambridge: Cambridge University Press, 1967).

Santmire, Paul, *The Travail of Nature. The Ambiguous Ecological Promise of Christian Theology* (Philadelphia: Fortress Press, 1985).

Schleiermacher, Friedrich, *The Christian Faith*, translated by H. R. Mackintosh and J. S. Stewart (Edinburgh: T. & T. Clark, 1928).

Schmid, H. H., 'Creation, Righteousness and Salvation: "Creation Theology" as the Broad Horizon of Biblical Theology', in *Creation in the Old Testament*, edited by B. W. Anderson (Philadelphia: Fortress Press, 1984), pp. 102–17.

Schwöbel, Christoph, 'Theologie der Schöpfung im Dialog zwischen Naturwissenschaft und Dogmatik', *Unsere Welt: Gottes Schöpfung. Festschrift für E. Wölfel* (Marburg: N. G. Elwert Verlag, 1992), pp. 199–21.

Schwöbel, Christoph, 'God, Creation and the Christian Community: The Dogmatic Basis of a Christian Ethic of Createdness', in *The Doctrine of Creation. Essays in Dogmatics, History and Philosophy*, edited by Colin E. Gunton (Edinburgh: T. & T. Clark, 1997), pp. 149–76.

Scott, Alan, *Origen and the Life of the Stars. A History of an Idea* (Oxford: Clarendon Press, 1991).

Sorabji, Richard, 'John Philoponos', *Philoponos and the Rejection of Aristotelian Science*, edited by Richard Sorabji (London: Duckworth, 1987), pp. 1–40.

Sorabji, Richard, *Time, Creation and the Continuum* (London: Duckworth, 1983).

Swinburne, Richard, *The Coherence of Theism* (Oxford: Clarendon Press, 1977).

Tanner, Kathryn, *God and Creation in Christian Theology: Tyranny or Empowerment?* (Oxford: Blackwell, 1988).

Teske, Roland J., 'Introduction', *St Augustine on Genesis, The Fathers of the Church. A New Translation* 84 (Washington: Catholic University of America Press, 1991).

Thayer, H. S. editor, *Newton's Philosophy of Nature. Selections from his Writings* (London: Collier-Macmillan, 1953).

Tipler, Frank J., *The Physics of Immortality. Modern Cosmology, God and the Resurrection of the Dead* (London: Macmillan, 1995).

Torrance, Alan J., 'Creatio ex nihilo and the Spatio-Temporal dimension, with special reference to Jürgen Moltmann and D. C. Williams', in *The Doctrine of Creation. Essays in Dogmatics, History and Philosophy*, edited by Colin E. Gunton (Edinburgh: T. & T. Clark, 1997), pp. 83–103.

Torrance, T. F., *Divine and Contingent Order* (Oxford: Oxford University Press, 1981).

Torrance, T. F., *The Hermeneutics of John Calvin* (Edinburgh: Scottish Academic Press, 1988).

Torrance, T. F., *Transformation and Convergence within the Frame of Knowledge. Explorations in the Interrelations of Scientific and Theological Enterprise* (Belfast: Christian Journals, 1984).

Trigg, J. W. , *Origen. The Bible and Philosophy in the Third-century Church* (Atlanta: John Knox, 1983).

Vanhoozer, Kevin, 'Human Being, Individual and Social', *The Cambridge Companion to Christian Doctrine*, edited by Colin E. Gunton (Cambridge: Cambridge University Press, 1997), pp. 158–88.

Ward, Keith, *God, Chance and Necessity* (Oxford: Oneworld, 1996).

Ward, Keith, *Religion and Creation* (Oxford: Clarendon Press, 1996).

Watson, Francis, *Text, Church and World. Biblical Interpretation in Theological Perspective* (Edinburgh: T. & T. Clark, 1994).

Watson, Francis, *Text and Truth. Redefining Biblical Theology* (Edinburgh: T. & T. Clark, 1997).

Weinberg, Stephen, *The First Three Minutes. A Modern View of the Origin of the Universe* (London: Flamingo, 2nd edition 1983).

Westermann, Claus, *Genesis 1–11. A Commentary*, translated by J. J. Scullion (London: SPCK, 1984).

Wilkinson, D., *God, the Big Bang and Stephen Hawking* (Tunbridge Wells: Monarch, 1993).

Wolff, Hans Walter, *Anthropology of the Old Testament*, translated by Margaret Kohl (London: SCM Press, 1974).

Young, Francis M., 'Creatio ex nihilo', *Scottish Journal of Theology* 44 (1991), pp. 139–51.

Young, Norman, *Creator, Creation and Faith* (London: Collins, 1976).

Zizioulas, John D. 'Preserving God's Creation. Three Lectures on Theology and Ecology. I, II and III', *King's Theological Review* 12 (1989), pp. 1–5, 41–5; and 13 (1990), pp. 1–5.

Zizioulas, John D., 'On Being a Person. Towards an Ontology of Personhood', *Persons, Divine and Human. King's College Essays in Theological Anthropology*, edited by Christoph Schwöbel and Colin E. Gunton (Edinburgh: T. & T. Clark, 1992), pp. 33–46.

INDEX

‒‒‒‒‒‒ⅉⅉⅉⅉⅉ◉ⅉⅉⅉⅉⅉ‒

243